"The most heartening love story [...]
FRANK COTTRELL-BOYCE

"A fable for our time."
SARA WHEELER

"This is such an inspiring and beautifully written story of brotherly love."
MARTHA KEARNEY

"You close the book feeling deeply moved by the depth of their brotherly love."
Daily Mail

"What Manni and Reuben have created is not just a memoir, or a stunning story, but a manifesto for how life should be lived. Their almost biblical journey of brotherhood shows us that when driven by love, in pure, prosaic form, we will overcome. I will never forget this book."
SOPHIE PAVELLE

"Reuben and Manni's story resonated with me more than anything I've ever read. The love between siblings where one has a learning disability is ferocious but also has complexities which are so brilliantly articulated in *brother. do. you. love. me.* This is a story of our times, so beautifully told and illustrated by Reubs and Manni. Deeply touching and a joy to read."
JO WHILEY

"Truthful, affecting, funny, colourful and profound, Manni and Reuben's great escape memoir deeply resonated with me. Instead of easy answers to questions of dependence and independence, this celebratory tale of mutual rescue took me into their special sibling relationship and gave me the treasure that is the family 'Friday Night Musical'. Freeing and fabulous. I loved it."
SALLY PHILIPPS

"Profoundly moving and hugely uplifting."
MARK HADDON

Poem   <u>Brother</u>

emotional

I just want let you
    know you mean the World
    to me

    And to have you as
    a brother

        I still feel very
emotional close to you

        You always be my
        brother ~~Peace~~

        Brother are so special
love you sleep well tonight

Aslan

My heart belongs
to you

Sleep well

brother

You Raise

Me up

Brother

emotional for

you

love
you

brother

This paperback edition published in 2024
by Canongate Books Ltd, 14 High Street, Edinburgh, EH1 1TE

First published by Little Toller Books in 2022

Text copyright © Emmanuel Coe, 2022
Illustrations copyright © Reuben Coe, 2022

canongate.co.uk

I

The right of Emmanuel Coe to be identified as the author
of this work has been asserted by him in accordance
with the Copyright, Design and Patents Act 1988

British Library Cataloguing-in-Publication Data
A catalogue record for this book is available on request from
the British Library

ISBN 978 1 80530 306 0

Typeset by Little Toller Books

Printed and bound by CPI Group (UK) Ltd, Croydon CR0 4YY.

brother.
do. you.
love. me.

MANNI COE

REUBEN COE

CANONGATE

*Manni dedicates this book to
anyone who has ever lost their way*

*Reuben dedicates this book to his family
and his friend Tommy Boy*

THE CORNER
Archidona, Andalusia
August 2018

There is an unusual depth to the silence. Nature anticipates. The birds stopped singing long before darkness fell. There have been other warnings, rumours too, but out here in the valley, on the other side of the river, news doesn't always reach us.

It starts at dusk. A single, distant rumble that makes the stone walls of the house tremble. A low boom. A timpani roll. The Levante wind that has been blowing for days, pushing warm air inland into the mountains, is damp and heavy, full of evaporated sea. When it meets a huge pocket of polar air, separated 10,000 metres up from the jet stream, the heavier, colder air quickly plummets, forming storm clouds above the Iberian Peninsula.

Growls of thunder follow the lightning, and in the house the young man is standing in his bedroom, looking out of the open window, watching the first drops of rain. During warm summer days and nights the windows and shutters are never closed. Wrought iron bars frame his view of the olive grove as a fork of lightning illuminates the trees. More forks and sheets come, thunder shakes the valley. A bitter wind blasts along the river and up towards the house, searching for ways in, ripping along the corridors as doors free themselves from latches and shutters wrestle with bolts. Usually, rain has individual parts. Rain has spaces between. But these are columns of water, falling vertically from the darkest heights of the night, covering all the surfaces of the farm. Watching the wet cascade from the roof, the young man wonders if this is what it's like to live behind a waterfall.

For centuries, The Corner has stood through similar storms. A cousin of this one raged six years earlier, bringing destruction to the gorge below. A bridge collapsed. The road was swept away. For days afterwards, there were two metres of water inside the house – the stained watermark reminds us, every day, that we are neighbours with the wild. But the house itself – its walls, its roof, its floors – endured.

The young man stands perfectly still, petrified, his form silhouetted against more and more flashes. He will keep standing like this, disappearing into himself, as the storm rages for three more hours. There is nothing he can do. There is nothing more he can say. Perhaps it is during this night that he makes his pact with silence. *If I stand still, if I say nothing, I will survive.* For somewhere in the days and months and years that follow, a part of him disappears. In stepping away from that bedroom window, he will soon step away from himself. The deer probably sheltered in the cave behind the house. The badger was well below the roots of the fig tree. The otter had its holt in Rio Guadalhorce.

What did the young man have? A roof, walls. But that night, if he did cry out, he wasn't heard. There was no one listening. Not even his brother. He had no real shelter, and so he gave himself up to the storm.

I busied myself to find a sure
    Snug hermitage
That should preserve my Love secure
    From the world's rage . . .

Thomas Hardy, 'Misconception'

Boots

1

It can't be morning. I've barely closed my eyes.

Slowly, the winter light brings order to my thoughts. I recall my footsteps late last night, crunching the gravel before I turned the key in the front door and dumped my bags. It took me over three hours from the airport, driving motorway lanes and dual carriageways before the narrow country tracks. It was like driving inside a tree – the trunk becomes boughs, becomes branches and twigs. Even in the dark, I know every twist and rise of these lanes. Something always lifts in me when I arrive in this quiet valley.

I pour boiling water on a tea bag to brew. I carry my two suitcases upstairs and leave them on the floor of our bedroom, under the window with the low sill that looks east over Jess's field. There are her thirty-two sheep.

It's not even 6 a.m. and I need to fill the hours. I pace the length of the living room in socks that pull up dust from the floors. I should clean. I should mop. I empty the fridge of food past its sell-by-date and throw away fruit mouldering in the bowl. I need to hoover up the dead cluster flies.

It's been three months since Jack and I were last here. It's been three months since I saw Reuben.

Before the rain sets in, I go for a walk. Pathways through familiar fields lead me to the village. I buy a coffee from the petrol station and head back with the Sunday papers poking out from under my grey cagoule that I bought in Rome when I took Mum for her seventy-fifth birthday. Turning off Annings Lane, back at the cottage, I check my watch.

It's almost time.

Do I have everything with me?

I don't need anything with me.

All I need is hope, but right now that's hard to find.

The town doesn't look like itself. Everything is veiled with strangeness. Street lamps cast peaks of light downwards through the fog, shops on East Street look like a chain of extinct volcanoes. I carry on along West Street and turn off at the traffic lights.

Once I've parked the hire car outside the house, I stare up at the white walls and fixate on his bedroom window, facing out onto the street. Does he know I'm here? Can he see me waiting? I notice that the white paint below his sill has peeled and chipped, exposing the concrete render below.

At the front door, I press the bell and wait. I can hear the shush of feet against the carpet inside and take a step back. The brass door handle turns and he appears, ushered forward by one of the carers who works in the house. He pauses before crossing the threshold, making sure I'm not a stranger.

There is no embrace. Only raindrops on white PPE.

He shuffles forward, as faint as a shadow.

On the pavement, I manoeuvre him into the passenger seat and load his 'holiday' bags into the car. I shut the boot but before I can get into the driver's side, the carer calls me back to the house: I have to sign for his bank card and something else in a bag. The carer avoids my eyes, and I avoid his. The whole process is a cold transaction. This really doesn't feel like a rescue. There's adrenalin and my jangling nerves, but it's all so awkward. There are absolutely no farewells. Being here feels as if I'm performing some sort of betrayal. Yet, at the same time, the staff are resigned to what's going on, the strange fact of Reuben leaving the house.

I'm gambling, of course. I'm taking a chance. They are still under the impression that he's having a break, a few days away, some well-earned time out. And maybe he is. Perhaps that's all I can do right now, give him an escape from this place, or from himself. This notion of a holiday is something we're all comfortable with, for now. An agreed fiction in which we can continue playing our parts. But I've been here before, breaking my brother out, and that's why I know this is all or nothing. I know that freeing him frees me, temporarily, of the guilt of being apart.

His eyes betray the disquiet. I'm sure he's nervous. He must be. The carers did tell me that he'd sent texts to Mum saying he didn't want me to come: *my home dont want go mummy*

Six layers cover his body. His shoulders are like a flimsy coat hanger supporting too many clothes. There are two polo shirts, a double collar of pink and grey. There's a lumberjack shirt next, the one that Mum bought him from Peacocks. A royal blue Superdry hoodie, a Christmas present from Jack and me. A navy blue puffer jacket from Tesco. And on top of it all, the hand-me-down black raincoat that Tommy Boy gave him years ago. A scarf of dull blues and greens coils around his neck. His black woolly hat is pulled down so low it's almost covering his eyes, trapping his fringe like a net curtain to keep the world out. His beard shows weeks of growth, clumps of grey mottle the dark brown. He's definitely aged. He wears a mask over his mouth, and as we drive away I tell him as gently as I can, 'You can take it off.'

We are not going to live in hiding.

We are going to breathe each other's air.

The wheels of our getaway car spin a little as I turn into West Street. Neither of us speak. I allow the silence in as we gather speed on the dual carriageway – the sign says 60 but I'm at 75, driving as if we're being pursued. *Got to get to the cottage.* That's our safehouse. That's where we can hide. As I indicate and turn into the lanes, the reality of what I've done hits me. Our time together could be weeks, months. I begin to panic but remind myself that this is the point. Being together. Bringing him back from silence.

I have a song prepared, one that he knows and loves, and as we approach the village I press play so Josh Groban can burst 'You raise me up' out of the speakers over and over again. I turn up the volume. Reuben stretches forward to turn it down.

As we rise and fall along past the village, I pretend to blow my nose with a hanky to disguise wiping my tears. I change down a gear, crawling along Annings Lane. His small, pale hand clasps mine. It is a light touch, like a spacecraft landing on the moon. We have contact. His long, dirty nails are at rest.

I gather up his Darth Vader suitcase and his Union Jack holdall from the boot – cow shit has already splattered the car's paintwork. I stand and wait for him to get out. He takes an age to readjust his hat and put his Tommy Hilfiger day bag and his *Joseph and the Amazing Technicolour Dreamcoat* tote bag over his shoulder – there was such fire in his eyes when we bought it after the show, spilling out into the crowds on Argyll Street.

He turns and I lean forward to help him out of the car, but he pauses to check that he has his paintbrush (in his right pocket) and his broken glasses (left pocket) before he puts his feet on the gravel drive. He knows this place – an old agricultural worker's cottage, semi-detached, that used to be part of the farm. I don't hurry him. He walks to the door as if he never wants to get there.

'Welcome back to The Shire, Frodo,' I say before we get to the threshold. 'Shoes off please.'

Inside, I help him shed layers – raincoat, puffer – and as I reach to uncoil his scarf there's a faint resistance, then a fight in his eyes, a look of something wild that makes me feel uncomfortable. It's not that warm in the house. I only turned the heating on for a couple of hours before crashing last night. But that's not why he wants to keep the scarf on. It protects him. All the layers do.

He looks around, panning the room until he settles his sights on the restored pew from St Mary's, where we had the funeral for Jack's mum, Angela. Will he notice anything else? Perhaps the old haberdashery unit (the first thing Jack ever bought for the cottage, long before meeting us). Does he notice the tired house plants? The low dining table? The yellow sofas, faded by the sunlight that streams through the roof skylights? I watch as he searches the garden, looking out to the pond. Surely he remembers the din of male marsh frogs in the spring.

Then Reuben looks at me, really stares inside. I look back and see him properly for the first time. It's still him, I think. He's still standing there, a full head and shoulders shorter than most men his age, with his soft edges and thick brown hair flat against his scalp (I will say nothing to him about the grey hairs). His dark eyes might appear distant – I've been fooled into thinking this before. But hopefully he'll be noticing all the things that are important to him, reminding me how sharp his powers of observation are.

Before he lost his voice, it was impossible to guess what he was about to say next. If there are words inside, they won't come out today. But I'm determined to hold his gaze. I want him to see love and safety in my eyes. 'Everything's going to be OK,' I say. He will talk and smile again, I tell myself. He will laugh, he will dance. But I have to accept that this is where we are. This is who we are. And at least we're both safe and warm and can spend the rest of the day at peace.

Reuben leans in and I take him in my arms. That's when I hear it, or I think I do, just one word, whispered and muffled by layers of scarf. Three syllables separated and staccatoed.

'Fa mi ly.'

We hold the embrace until I can feel him leaning away.

'Do you want to get settled?' I ask. 'Into your bedroom?'

He shrugs, slowly.

'Do you want a cup of tea?'

He shrugs, more slowly still.

'Do you want me to help you get settled into your bedroom?'

His eyes lock on mine.

*

I carry his bags upstairs and start unpacking his things. His clothes are so carefully folded and packed. Did he do this? There are three of everything – three pairs of socks, three pairs of pants, three pairs of trousers, three shirts, three T-shirts. He must think he's here for three nights. I turn, expecting to see him in the doorway but he's not there. He's not on the stairs either. I make my way down and see that he hasn't moved from the living room. He hasn't even turned to face the other way. He's still looking out towards the pond.

I go to him and swivel his body, offering my arm.

His face is ever so pale.

'Why don't you take your hat off,' I suggest.

He refuses.

We climb the three steps from the living room to the hall. Both feet need to be planted on each step, to pause for breath before we continue. At the bottom of the main stairs he looks up – he may as well be looking up at Everest from base camp. It dawns on me that his bedroom and common room at Portland Place are downstairs, so he hasn't gone upstairs for nearly a year.

I count as we climb. One. Two. Three.

He stops to look through the gaps to the wooden floor below.
Four. Five. Six.

He adjusts his hat as it has sunk over his eyes.
Seven. Eight. Nine.

Ten. Eleven.

On the landing, just one more step up to his bedroom door.
Twelve.

At the doorway, he's struggling to recognise his room.

Exhausted from the climb, he wants to sit down on the bed and plants his hand on the stark, white duvet cover, leaving the faintest trace of his palm imprinted. I sit with him as it all begins to sink in: this room, this house. Me.

As we sit, I follow the lines of the dormer window up into the slopes of the eaves and notice how dirty the glass is. I can't hear any tractors on the lane today, no ramblers or horse riders. I feel diminished in the valley.

I turn to him and ask, 'Shall I put your clothes away?'

Socks and pants go into the top drawer. T-shirts and shirts follow in the deeper middle drawer. Trousers and jumpers at the bottom. The chest of drawers is barely big enough for three days of Reuben's clothes. Out comes his Technicolour Dreamcoat, which I put on a hanger and hook to the curtain rail. I put the Darth Vader suitcase in the corner of the room, facing out. I drop his empty holdall alongside and hear a rattle as it hits the floor. His pills. Along with his debit card, that's what I had been asked to sign for when we left.

'Where would you like your Simba?'

I take out the cuddly Lion King and pop it on his pillow. Next to it, on the bedside table, I put the framed photo of Tommy Boy and the photo of the *EastEnders* actor John Partridge. His eyes are elsewhere most of the time, as if it hurts him to look at me.

'You'll be fine here, babes. You're safe now. Just you and me.'

I sit down on the bed and hug him tight. He's so thin. He used to take me down in a wrestling match, but his body is all stringy, his skin dull and saggy. I must weigh him when he has a bath.

'Hey, I bought food last night, on the way down. Let's have a late lunch, then we can chill on the sofa. Watch a film.'

As I leave the room, I tell him I love him and ask if he packed any DVDs. He doesn't reply. 'We've got some downstairs, I think. You stay up here. Settle in. Come down when you're ready. Oh, and Samwise Gamgee sends his love.'

Hearing this, a flicker moves in his eyes and vanishes.

Once the chicken is in the oven, I start to declutter the surfaces. I clean, I wipe. I try to make surfaces sparkle. I find a rhythm for my broom strokes and follow the same pattern with the mop. As the citrus smell of the floor cleaner wears off, I root through the cupboards to see if there are any candles left over from the summer.

Jack always orders a box of rosemary and eucalyptus; I need some of that now, and at the back of a shelf I find one, tucked behind some cans of fizzy drink. I light the wick and that familiar scent of home begins to fill the space. Our Alhambra. This cottage is part palace, part fortress.

I go back upstairs to see how Reubs is getting on in his room. He's standing now, at an odd angle to the bed. He's in a dither.

'Do you need anything?'

He lifts and drops his shoulders.

'Did you bring your felt-tips and paper?'

He looks towards his holdall.

'Do you want to come downstairs and draw?'

He shakes his head.

I leave him to it and busy myself in the kitchen again, turning the chicken over and preparing vegetables. Outside, the garden is muted except for a faint glow that pushes through the grey. It's far too cold to open the patio doors. The pond, emptied of reeds from the winter cut, is a mirror that reflects the sky and my mood.

My thoughts drift. I picture myself back in Granada on that outcrop high above the city, walking around the Alhambra, where grace spills from the gurgling Nasrid-dynasty fountains and the heat of Andalusian sun is cooled by the palace of mosaics and marble in my mind.

How many trips have Reuben and I taken together?

With him, rushing through an airport doesn't get you on the plane any faster. We walk at one-third of everybody else's pace: I go ahead, Reuben follows. One time, when we got to security, I realised that I hadn't checked Reuben's suitcase through, and while he was chatting to the woman queuing behind us, telling her that we were brothers and that we were going to Marrakech, his bag was pulled off for inspection. Noticing, he started doing his thing: nervously, knowingly, rotating his tongue out and back through his lips. I chew the insides of my mouth for the same reasons. When the security guard put her gloved hand into his bag and pulled out a bottle of Tommy Hilfiger aftershave, he knew he was in trouble, even though there was a genuine look of apology on the woman's face.

I chastised him, 'You know you can't bring that on board.'

He watched the security guard put the bottle in the bin.

'But it's for evenings,' Reubs said.

He is worried this will break his ritual – every evening, wherever he is, Reuben switches from his day bag to his night bag and then douses his tummy with aftershave. If asked why, his reply is simple, 'I like it'. In an unfamiliar world, habits anchor who we are.

'We'll get another at Duty Free,' I promised as we left check-in.

'Well yeah.'

'Tommy or Dior?'

'Both?'

'Or we could wait and buy one in the souk.'

'*Souk*?' he repeated, enjoying the sound of the word.

He leant into me and smiled, 'My bruvr you do after me.'

Reuben is not impressed when he comes down from his room. He looks at his plate as if it's the first time he's ever laid eyes on a chicken. Some of the potatoes are burnt. I can't bear his attempts to cut his food so take his knife and fork and do it for him. When I give his cutlery back, he uses the fork to push at morsels.

I begin to panic. A shard of fear cuts through.

I'm fine, I tell myself. We'll be fine.

Food used to be such a point of celebration. He loved eating. Once, when I told a friend that Jack and I had taken him to a Michelin-star restaurant, she looked at me in surprise. 'You took Reuben?' She immediately corrected herself, 'Why wouldn't you?' As if you can't enjoy food because you have Down's syndrome. This afternoon, though, watching Reubs chew with such crushing effort, I doubt either of us would enjoy a posh restaurant.

I finish my lunch before he's really begun and gaze over at his plate, which makes him feel uncomfortable. I begin to clear the table instead, then start on the washing-up.

'What do you want to do tonight, Reubs? Shall we go for a little walk? Or shall we have a little dance? Maybe you want to play a game? Sit on the sofa and watch a DVD?'

His eyes meet mine – I read that as a Yes.

'Fine. That's what we'll do. But will you be alright if I go for a little walk first? Get some fresh air. I need to stretch my legs before it gets dark.'

I lean over him and wrap my arms around his bony shoulders and land a squeaky kiss on his cheek. He screws up his face – the noise or the touch annoys him.

As I turn left past our neighbours, I worry about leaving him. Even for ten minutes. But I need this. It feels good to be walking, and I let out a huge sigh, an expulsion of air that propels me up the lane towards the farm. At the junction, I go straight over where the ground underfoot is soggy. I keep to the verges as my eyes cast ahead, seeing in 100m stretches, tracking the distance ahead like I used to do at school with my brothers, where I ran the 100m and 110m hurdles. Head forward, shoulders down, sprinting from the core until I screamed across the finish line.

There were already three of us before Reubs arrived – Matthew, Nathan and me. We grew up in the Stanmores, where you were only truly from Headingley if you could hear the claps from the cricket ground from your house. We could. Sometimes, through a back gate in the ginnel that cut through from the railway bridge up to Kirkstall Lane, a friendly guard let us in during a break between overs.

The front door of our house, with its patch of garden, led onto 'Our Road', while the back door and yard went onto 'Our Street'. There were two floors, an attic and a cellar. In my memory, the place was huge. But back then I was tiny – Rich the Titch, they called me at school. I was the shortest in my class and didn't begin my growth spurt until I was thirteen. My parents bought the house from an old lady who chain-smoked and kept a parrot in the hall. It smelt of bird shit and the walls were stained yellow from the tar and nicotine.

Matt and I slept under the eaves in the loft – his room was blue, mine was green. We were little scrappers, often getting into fights with the neighbours. Bonfire night was a big thing in the Stanmores, and there were two rival events: ours, at the end of the road; the competition, up by Talbot Terrace. From the end of the summer onwards, Matt and I would knock on doors asking for 'any old wood' that we stored in the backyard. One night, Gavin and Kevin from next door nicked our prize burn: a knackered old dining room table with three legs. We cornered them on the Rec and ended up in a fist fight. They were tougher than us and we lost. I remember the bruises.

On our road, doors were always open and our lives as children were fluid, moving in and out of different houses. David and Geraldine's house was stylish and arty because it had a huge yellow wall with paintings all over it. Liz's home smelt of exotic wood and was filled with textiles. Jerry and Pauline's house was filled with laughter. Tidy Pam's house was immaculate, of course. More affluent friends lived on the other side of the train tracks, in The Turnaways. That's where Angie baked her wholemeal bread (I can still remember the smell of toasted grains) and Tony lived with his shiny new Rover.

Back on Our Road, the Palmers' house spilled over with girls and our house spilled over with boys and bikes and conkers and rolls of lino that we took onto the Rec to practise our breakdancing (backspins, windmills, the worm) to the beats of our super-woofer. We had to save pocket money to afford the batteries. Matt had cool friends and a trick bike. I had a burnt orange Playmaster with a rigid, white plastic seat that I always hated. We cycled to school, come rain or shine, through the woods of Beckett Park and would dare each other to ride the dusty tracks of a jump we called the Big Dipper on our way home.

Our lives orbited the church. Mum and Dad were leaders of

a midweek 'house group', and every other Wednesday evening twelve or so adults would meet in our living room to study the Bible, sing and pray. It was the most popular house group at the church, so the whole congregation wanted to be a part of it. Mike Hepper and Liz Pepper and Liz Hopper were all part of this club – how cool they all were, with their cars, their houses, their jobs, their sense of purpose. Us kids were allowed in for the tea and biscuits at the end, but we listened from the stairs. I had a crush on Liz Pepper and once gave her a Double Decker with a little note signed with a kiss.

My memories of Yorkshire brim like this, with milky tea, flowered wallpaper, washing racks and cola cubes, sledging in Burley Park and kicking leaves in the Dales, hopping buses, watching the Intercity 125, red bricks and BMXs, greenhouses, church spires, hymns and Barrs Cream Soda. Imagine the reaction when Reuben was born. When any baby arrives into a tight-knit community, bonds are strengthened. A baby like Reubs made those bonds unbreakable. Almost forty years on, seven house moves later, my parents have never been able to replicate anything close to the life of the Stanmores. Communities like that, friendships like that, do not come along as often as we might wish.

The light in the valley is already dimming. I turn back before I get to the bluebell wood, reluctantly retracing my steps. This always feels wrong to me, coming back along the same track. But I mustn't be out any longer, not on our first day.

Walking back to the cottage, I bump into Jan on Annings Lane. She's walking their rescue greyhound, Honey, and the sight of them cheers me up.

'Hello you,' she grins. 'All alright? How's Reubs?'

'Not so good,' I reply. 'We knew he was bad. And they kept telling us he was fine!'

'Bless him. Just goes to show. Well, at least he's with you now.

Give him our love. I have some Fallen Orange Marmalade for you. Should I leave it by the back door?'

'Amazing, thank you.'

'Jack OK?'

Jan has a soft spot for Jack, and the feeling is mutual.

'He's fine. Sends his love.'

'Send ours back,' she says and turns right off the lane, obviously doing the circuit clockwise today.

Reubs is still sitting at the table when I stomp back through the front door. He has only eaten half his dinner, and barely touched his drink. I start wondering if everything could be down to dehydration. Could it be as simple as that?

'Did you miss me? I had a lovely walk. I saw Jan and Honey. Maybe you can come with me tomorrow? They'd love to see you.'

Leaving his plate exactly where it is, without so much as a gesture towards me, he takes his day bag off the back of the chair, picks his tote bag off the floor and hangs them over his shoulder, moving past me as if I don't exist, as if he doesn't exist. He struggles up the steps, leaning on the walls for support.

Watching him, all I can think about is repainting the walls last time we were here, and start worrying about his mucky hands blemishing the white. I push the thought away, telling myself not to be so silly, to relax. As his feet disappear over the threshold at the top of the stairs, I can't stop the rush of emotion and can feel a scream gushing up from inside me.

I cover my mouth to stifle any noise, rippling with convulsions. Over and over it happens, until the waves slow enough for me to dry my eyes on a piece of kitchen towel. I breathe. I scrape Reuben's dinner into the compost.

The movement of my hands, scrubbing dishes, cleaning cutlery, absorbs me completely. By the time I lift my head, the kitchen is almost dark. I switch the lights on and the far side of the room is drenched with a warm, yellow shimmer.

The view of the garden disappears in the reflection of the room. It feels like a stage, with an audience out beyond the patio doors, staring in at me and my fragility on display. I'd rather the gaze of other animals. The badger, the fox, the farm cat. The jackdaws that perch in the high branches of the willow. How strange we must be to them. I'm gripped by stage fright and don't know what to say.

Reuben is on his bed when I pop up to see him, hiding whatever he's been drawing, holding the paper face down and looking at me as if to say, 'What the hell are you doing in my room?'

Some of the felt-tips fall to the floor as he stands and walks towards me, scowling as he brushes past. I've rarely seen this depth of anger in him, and I'm not sure what he's doing. He stops at the bedroom door, pushes it closed and wraps his knuckles twice against the wood.

'Sorry,' I apologise. 'I'll knock next time. I came to say you should have a bath. It will help you sleep.'

I step out of his room across the landing, throw a handful of bath salts and pour in the bubble bath before running the water. Steam fills the bathroom. I hear him behind me, gingerly making his way, day bag and tote bag crumpled in his arms.

'Do you really need those with you to have a bath, Reubs?'

He ignores me as he begins to strip, taking everything off except his scarf, slippers and the kind of dressing gown that would melt if it got anywhere near a naked flame. Rather than taking the scarf from him this time, I ask if it would be a good idea to hand it to me, so it doesn't get wet. Reluctantly, he pulls it from around his neck as if uncoiling a boa constrictor. This bloody scarf has appeared in every photo, every video, every image of him since February. I'm sick of it. It even smells of Portland Place.

'Well done, Reubs,' I say as he offers it to me, his eyes following it closely from his hands to mine.

He keeps his slippers and turquoise dressing gown on as I weigh him. At 58 kilos, it's still not great. It's better than he was a few months ago, when he went down to 55. Thank goodness one of the carers noticed he was hiding his food. It was a hunger strike, a way of telling us all something was very wrong.

I avert my eyes as he undresses and slides into the bath, his entire body vanishing under the bubbles.

'Let's scrub you properly.'

I take the loofah and drag it across his skin.

He's felt nothing like this for months. All there have been are gestures directing him in and out of rooms, hands passing him pills, hands making him meals and closing doors.

I draw large circles on his back in bubbles.

I wash his hair and he closes his eyes.

His mouth moves and I can't lip read the words.

I wonder if these tiniest of sensations take him back. If, through touch, he might remember where the loofah comes from. How long ago was it? Four years ago?

'All those places we used to go to, Booba, all the fun we used to have! Do you remember?'

I stop scrubbing. The bubbles are vanishing, the bathwater is already getting cold. I run the hot again.

Those memories must be in him somewhere, but it feels like he's retreated even further since I visited last summer. Soon he'll be out of reach.

When he's dried and dressed in his pyjamas and settled on the edge of his bed, he covers himself with a blanket and lets out a compressed sigh. 'What a day, hey Reubs. You must be exhausted.'

He reaches for one of the pieces of paper on his bed and turns it over to show me a drawing.

It's the bed-time drink he's had every night since we were kids. The comfort of routine. This is something I must work with. But it's been so long since we have lived together that I need to get used to his rhythms again. Without them, we'll get lost out here on our own.

I make his drink and bring it up from the kitchen on a new sketchpad, leaving it as a tray on his bedside table. He gets comfy under his duvet and sips his milk as I chat aimlessly. He doesn't seem to be listening. His eyes are focussed at the gap in the curtains.

'What is it Reubs?' I ask. 'Something wrong?'

He points towards the night, and I understand.

'Narnia?'

He nods to confirm that there's no light outside, no lamppost glowing gold and keeping him safe.

I run downstairs and flick on the outside light. The LED spills its whiteness across the driveway and across Annings Lane. It's not Narnia but it will do. When I get back to his bedroom, Reuben is at the window tugging at the curtain to inspect how bright it is, how much of the world he can see. I walk over to join him and his eyes turn, making sure that I am not Jadis, the white witch.

'Everything's OK,' I reassure. 'I've got you now.'

He looks away.

'I know how you feel.'

When I say this his head turns instinctively, in the fastest movement I've seen him make all day, as if to say: Do you? Although there's no sound in his voice, the fact that his mouth is moving, trying to speak, means that he's in there. My brother, with his visions of Aslan and Mufasa that help him sleep at night.

Do you? Do you understand me?

I do. I remember when food tasted like cardboard and I preferred the taste of cigarettes. I remember when sleep evaded me and weight fell from my body. I remember believing that I could never be happy. I remember wanting to disappear.

I switch his bedside lamp off and lie at the bottom of the bed, careful not to mess with the collection of night props by his pillow. I can still see the moonlight, filtered by the beech trees and the outdoor light.

It feels like there's no path for Reuben. He's so diminished, and more exhausted than I thought he would be. He certainly can't do it alone. It will need a huge amount of effort from him, and an effervescent energy from me. It's possible. We've done it before. I become a Catherine wheel that spins and spins and hopes that just one tiny spark might land. But at the moment, it's as if he'd rather stare at the abyss. I will have to be much more than his brother. I will have to be his carer, his parent, his friend, his interpreter in a world that doesn't want to understand him.

I begin dozing and see the earth splitting. A deep chasm has opened up beneath my feet. Reuben is now on one side, and I'm on the other. I have to decide, quickly, which side to be on. I have a split-second to make the decision. Which way to leap?

I watch the rectangle of dawn through a skylight above my bed. Lying here, stewing, will only make it worse. I hear Dad's words, 'Getting up is a momentary act of will', spoken to get all four of us brothers out of bed and ready for school.

I put my tartan dressing gown on, the one Jack's mum gave me for Christmas last year. She passed away in November but had already bought it and written my name on the label. At the time, I felt odd wearing it. But it means the world to me now, perhaps because Angela and I had a frosty beginning. She thought Jack was taking on too much when he met us. She thought Reubs should be with our parents, or in a care home. We grew to love each other by the end. I remember taking her for lunch once, at The Anchor, and she got a little tipsy on rosé. Her voice had been barely a whisper while she was recovering from throat cancer, but that afternoon, after two large glasses of Côtes de Provence, she boomed in the car on the way home.

'Your voice Ang!' I exclaimed. 'I've never heard it.'

'I know!' she replied. We giggled our way back to the cottage.

The door to Reuben's room is open because we've not shut it since my friend Tash got locked in – there's a pair of pliers on the floor next to it, just in case. His head propped up on three pillows, motionless but for his light breathing, he's sleeping soundly in the midst of his night props – a little bean dog which he has had since he was fourteen, a thin paintbrush, some toilet paper (carefully folded), his *Good Sleep* clipboard and pieces of blank paper with a selection of important words:

good sleep   sleep well
cosy   Aslan
dark outside, lamp post   am fine

It's chilly downstairs, which means it must be before seven, when the heating kicks in. I look at my phone: 6.39, more than seventeen hours before bedtime. I make a cup of Yorkshire Tea with semi-skimmed and honey from The Corner, and think of dear Manolo, the beekeeper. He drove down from the village not long after we moved in, to introduce himself and ask if he could put two beehives on the land. Of course we agreed. Beehives! He chose the location very carefully: a flat piece just off the olive grove, south facing, isolated. Jack insists that Manolo moves like a bee, talks like a bee, that maybe he's transitioning into Bee. He now has thirty hives and gives us a share of this liquid gold. This morning, it tastes like Andalusian sunshine.

If Jack were here, I would be taking him up a mug of coffee and his iPad. I'm always mindful not to pour the skin of the milk into his mug, because he hates it. I miss him. We're better together. But we didn't feel as if we had a choice, not since Reuben's text message. In both our minds, it was clearly a cry for help. It couldn't be ignored. We had to get him out of there. One of us had to be at the farm to organise the volunteers, and cover when there weren't any. My work as a tour guide had run dry, so it was easier for me to fly over straight away.

'You do realise it's not going to be an easy fix?' Jack asked.

We both knew it wasn't a real question. It was a statement of fact. Jack hugged me for ages before I left for the airport.

'I will miss you,' he said. 'Give Frodo my love.'

I shouldn't do it but I reach over and grab Reuben's phone. I start checking his browser and find over 250 pages still open. 'Shit Reubs,' I mutter. There's nothing particularly alarming. He always searches for the same things: *whoopi goldberg, love, lion king, dawn french puddle, miranda, gay kiss coronation street*. He uses the internet just as I would, searching for answers and to make him laugh. I smile at the photo of Tommy Boy and Maxine on his screensaver. Such old friends, so devoted to Reubs.

These past months, I've been spying on Reuben through WhatsApp – there's a section under a person's name where you can see when they were last connected. There were nights when Reubs was on his phone until midnight, then one o'clock in the morning, two o'clock. I confronted his care team about it, but they said they couldn't take it from him. In his welfare assessment, his independence is paramount – as it should be – so they were only allowed to 'suggest' Reuben cut down on his screen time.

Decisions like this always involve so many people. For years, Reuben has had a 'best interest' committee, which includes Jack and me as his guardians, my parents, his carers, his social worker. Decisions also require paperwork, lots of paperwork. I couldn't take his phone off him because I wasn't there, and his carers couldn't immediately intervene because it wasn't within the guidelines of Reuben's best interest.

There was so much going on at Portland Place that I didn't know about, and still don't. Without a doubt, though, I know that it is not in Reuben's best interest to be on his phone all night. Although it was one of his lifelines – it's how he communicated with me, Jack, with Mum and Dad, Nathan and Matt, Tommy Boy, all the people who he loves and who love him. But it's time to wean him off it. Now I don't have to ask the committee, I can encourage him to look elsewhere for human connection.

I think it's as light as it's going to get today. In the garden, the leaves are ground cover now and all the shrubs have recoiled for the winter. Jack's Desdemona and Queen Elizabeth roses are completely dormant. The shape of all the plants will be unchanged until spring. I can't see the lane because the yew hedge and the garage shield the view, but I can hear the tractor from the farm, coming along Shipton Lane.

I can see Terry and Jan's bungalow through the bare branches of the hawthorn hedge. Jan always gets up early to make cups of tea, and if the red flag is up on their post box it means she'll soon be collecting the post. We live close enough to watch each other's lives from a distance, without any sense of intrusion. They know Reuben and I are here, and that seems enough for now. If they think we're having a bad time of it, they'll be over to invite us for coffee and sausage rolls. 'The best neighbours in the whole world,' I call them. They watch over the cottage when we're on the farm in Spain, and I am glad to have them near right now.

I walk upstairs as silently as I can, but Reubs must've heard me because he's already looking my way as I reach the doorway, his head tilted, eyes dark and foggy with sleep. He looks annoyed.

'Morning Boobalish. How are you?'

He pinches his thumb and finger, leaving a tiny gap to measure how he's feeling.

'Bit tired are you? Tell you what, let's go for a walk.'

This is one of Jack's tried and tested techniques: not an instruction but a positive suggestion that doesn't leave space for negotiation. Reubs contorts his face into a grimace, which, while it isn't exactly the reaction I was hoping for, is what I was expecting. It's an emotion, at least. That's good enough for me.

I sit down on the bed and he edges his body away.

'Do you want me to give you a hug?'

A hardness leaves his eyes as I draw him close.

'Now, you better get up. We've got lots to do. I'm going to make us a lovely breakfast. Eggs and bacon. And some delicious bread. We can put olive olo on it.'

Olo is what Reuben calls it, and he always loved the harvest with us at The Corner, picking and pressing olives. He was up early with the rest of us, bashing the trees with a long pole. He would pretend it was a sword or a lance and act out scenes from *The Lion the Witch and the Wardrobe* or *Ladyhawke*. 'If you fail,' he would giggle, 'I will follow you for the length of my days. And I will find you.'

*

I eat breakfast alone. I make a fresh pot of coffee. I wash up. I read emails and reply to most of them, and finally he comes down wearing his pyjamas, slippers and that horrible dressing gown. His day bag and his *Joseph* bag are hanging over his right shoulder.

'Well hello sunshine!' I beam. 'Hungry?'

I give him another hug and he lets his body relax into mine.

'Did you wash your hands?'

His shrug tells me he didn't, so he turns around and starts back towards the stairs. I stop him, 'Reubs, use the downstairs bathroom, babes. There's soap on the side. Here, give me your bags.' He flinches. He doesn't want to be without them.

His slippers slide across the wooden floor.

Ten minutes pass before he reappears, and I notice that his paintbrush has moved – it was sticking out of his day bag but now he's holding it inside his dressing gown pocket, lifting it out as he sits down to lightly bristle himself with it, passing it gently over his skin, as if painting himself.

'Take a seat. Orange juice?'

I line up his pill pots in front of him: vitamins C, D and E, calcium, Astaxanthin, folic acid, Fluoxetine (20mg). Most of them have to be held down and twisted, so he's struggling to turn the cap. I open them for him and place a pill from each onto the table in a multicoloured line. He rearranges them, putting the Fluoxetine last.

Swallowing each is another ritual: first he eases a pill gently through his lips, then he pauses to take the tiniest sip of orange juice, closes his eyes tight and swallows, coming up for air after each gulp. The timing and procedure is identical for each pill, and when he gets to the last one he stops and looks at me.

'Do you know what that is for?' I ask.

He presses his palms together and tilts his head towards them, as if they were a pillow.

'Well, not exactly. It's not a sleepy pill. It's a supposed-to-make-you-happier pill.'

'I really don't think you need them any more, Reubs.'

His face contorts to an ugly scowl.

I put a plate of food in front of him: two rashers of bacon, two eggs, a piece of toast. He looks horrified. This is far too much.

'It doesn't matter how long it takes. I don't even mind if you leave some. But you need to eat, Reubs.'

I don't want to pressure him so walk away and busy myself with dishes and cleaning a couple of cupboards. I then sit down in the armchair with my laptop and order enough food for a small army. I start reading a little more of *On the Red Hill*, and reach the part where Mike and Peredur inherit Reg and George's house. I love reading how they feel as if they're stepping into their dreams. I felt like that when we moved into The Corner. Everything aligned. I'd never felt so complete. Every detail of the house gave me a feeling of nostalgia, as if I'd been there for years. Mum and Reuben were in the car with me when I first laid eyes on it: a whitewashed house standing near Rio Guadalhorce, backdropped by olive groves and mountains. I must have fallen deadly quiet because Mum said, 'Don't you start. You'll set me off.' There was too much to take in. Too many dreams. It was a house that had been in my imagination for years.

Reubs, Jack and I lived there for three years with our merry pack of dogs: Beau the Cocker Spaniel, BB the Spanish Water Dog, Archi the mutt and Duna the Mastin Labrador Cross. Beau was Angela's dog and Jack inherited him from his mum when she grew frail. BB was the runt from a litter of nine puppies from a breeder in Velez-Malaga. Archi belonged to a shepherd who had grazing rights to put his 167 sheep on the land, and when the old man moved (along with his 167 sheep) he left Archi behind. We called him Stig of the Dump at first. He lived in the opposite field and we fed him through the fence, until he made a brave move when we left the door open – we'd gone for a walk and arrived back to find Archi on the sofa by the fire.

He never left after that. And little Duna we found as a three-month-old puppy at the bottom of the olives – there's no way something so small could've walked from the village. Someone must have driven her across the river and pushed her through a gap in the gate. They probably thought that the unusual family in the old house by the river would look after her. They were right.

In those early days, The Corner was filled with a steady stream of friends and family who wanted to see the place and help out on the farm. Most of them got it. Some didn't understand why we wanted to be in a place so cut off from the world, a place that burns with the Andalusian sun in the summer and is so bitterly cold in December and January. I was pleased that Dad was one of those who loved it. When he got back from a walk with the dogs to a place we call Land's End, he told me it was 'The closest I've ever been to The Garden of Eden.' Mum loves it, too, but not for long periods. 'I'd go potty out there. Too far from the shops.' Our friend Jane dubbed it Broke*bank* Mountain. But we didn't care. It was a place where we could all fulfil our dreams. Jack got his chickens. Reubs got the largest wardrobe he'd ever seen, the closest he has ever come to Narnia. I had a house that was built in my imagination. It was a sanctuary for all of us. Every visitor got a 'Welcome to The Corner' poster from Reubs, with a scene from the farm drawn in felt-tip pens. Whenever old friends came, they would say they'd never seen Reuben looking so happy and healthy.

Breakfast takes him over an hour. He eats half, leaving one egg, one rasher of bacon, all the crusts of the toast. He pushes the plate away. I sit down opposite to confront him but can't find the words, so we end up staring at each other. Reuben is defiant. I'm hesitant. Neither of us say a thing until he pulls the plastic orange folder out of his tote bag.

It was at The Corner that Reuben started using weekly charts to give his days and weeks structure. It was a visualisation of his life, with each day usually divided into six sections: *Breakfast, Activity, Lunch, Activity, Dinner, Extras.* This orange folder is crammed with felt-tipped pages, one sheet per week for at least the past nine months. They are a complete history of Reuben's time at Portland Place, told in colourful checklists and charts.

He pulls out Week 38, the current week, and delicately moves it towards me across the table. There is something sacred in these scripts. His distinct handwriting in vivid blue and red, with Saturday's boxes filled with *msli, pack, sndwich something, bit sleep, pasta, shower.* He has also filled in all the boxes from Sunday, the day I picked him up: *msli, brother, sunday lunch something, bath, bit TV hot milk hug brother emotional.*

I take out a clean A4 sheet and write WEEK 1 at the top of the page in bright green. Reubs looks on, fascinated, as if I was engraving a piece of glass. He seems staggered that there can be a new beginning. He brings his lips together and turns them inwards, tilting and angling his head, a gesture he makes when something impresses him. I divide the page into seven columns and six rows, marking the days of the week at the top of each column. I give each row its title but leave everything blank for Reuben. The muscles in his face relax as he slides WEEK 1 into his folder. Later, I know he'll sit on his bed and write what he had for breakfast, *eggbacon.* Then he'll add his lunch, maybe a *ham cheese sw.* Perhaps *something curry* for dinner? For now, he pushes down gently until he hears the folder click then eases it back into his tote bag. The folder is never far away from him. He even sleeps with it by his bed. It's his diary, a mix between *Dear Kitty* and a Book of Hours.

His very first sheets were TO DO lists at The Corner, with blank spaces he could tick whenever he completed a chore – fetching firewood, collecting eggs, hanging the washing out. He would play different music on his phone depending on the task – Jack and I would always giggle when we heard 'Shine, Jesus Shine', because we knew he was in the kitchen emptying the dishwasher.

*

'Right. Time to get dressed, Reubs.'

I tell him to head upstairs but he just stares blankly back. Instead of pushing his chair in like I had expected him to, he stretches out his hands towards me and looks at his fingernails, quizzically.

'Blimey, Reubs. What are those?'

During Lockdown, Mum used to open the sash window of his bedroom at Portland Place, just a fraction, so he could slip his hands out. She would quickly snip his nails, before anyone saw, then drive away leaving the clippings on the pavement outside. I still wonder what would have happened if Mum and Dad hadn't gone back to their home in Norwich. I know they had to sort out problems with their house, and that Dad had hospital appointments. But should they have insisted? Taking Reuben out of there could have made all the difference.

'This can't be five months' growth, surely?'

Reuben looks at me and slides his slippers off.

'Bloody hell, Reubs!'

He frowns.

'Sorry, I didn't mean it like that.'

His fingernails are bad, but his toes are astonishing. Perhaps that's why he always wears his slippers, to hide them. I hadn't noticed them when he took a bath.

He holds on to the wall as we head upstairs, both feet firmly on each tread before he attempts the next. He seems to be counting in his head. I realise that the pain of walking is probably why he's been moving so awkwardly, and even more slowly than usual. Poor man. Why didn't someone cut them for him? His toenails have started to curl under his toes. His left foot isn't so bad, but the nails on his right are scaly and yellow with infection.

When I come back from the bathroom with the scissors, he puts his hand on my shoulder, to reassure me or himself, as I start trimming them as best I can. We will need some proper nail clippers, or something even more robust.

'Some tea tree?' I ask.

He nods and his lips fold into his mouth. His frown deepens.

'What?'

He looks as if he was about to say something, but whatever it was doesn't materialise.

I gather up his dirty clothes and lay a clean outfit on his bed. Blue jeans, a grey T-shirt and a grey cashmere jumper with black shoulders and sleeves that Jack bought him last Christmas. Clean socks. Clean pants.

'Nice *flew!*' I say looking out of his bedroom window, pointing towards the sheep. *Flew* is Reuben's word for *view*, and I say it not to mock him but to trigger something, to remind him of all the things he used to say and loved doing.

Looking at him now, it's hard to believe that Reuben used to walk everywhere when he was at The Corner. It started when we bought him a Fitbit – 10,000 steps became a daily routine, with Archi always at his side. 'Come Archi Boy,' Reubs would say as he set off across the river in his wellies towards the village. He would use Anita's house as his halfway mark, resting in her kitchen as she spoke Spanish (none of which he understood) and gave him a glass of freshly squeezed orange juice with a muffin before he began his homeward stretch.

Anita is in her mid-eighties and has lived there to the movement of the sun for at least fifty years, in a house that looks like a museum of traditional Andalusian country life. She was sad when Reuben left The Corner. She would ask after him whenever we stopped for a natter.

'How is my friend? Give him my love, *pobrecito*.'

'I will Anita. I'm going into the village. Do you need anything?'

'Can you make me twenty years younger?'

When the postman pulls up outside the cottage, there are only bills, no letters or parcels. Nobody knows we're here. We're hiding out, on the quiet. 'Cheers,' he says before zooming up Annings Lane to continue his rounds. I head back inside to the warmth.

Reuben isn't dressed in anything I laid out for him. He has chosen his elasticated tracksuit bottoms, two polo shirts and his hoodie with the hood up. He peers out defensively.

'Well done, Booba.' I say sincerely. 'You wear what you want but you shouldn't put your hood up indoors. It's rude. Oh, and you totally have my permission to tell me to piss off if I'm getting on your nerves, OK?'

He looks offended.

'I'm serious. I bet I'm a right pain in the arse. Giving you nah, nah, nah, do, do, do, hurry, hurry, hurry. It would do my head in too.'

His mouth curves into the beginning of a smile and then stops. He won't let himself go.

'Right. I vote we take a walk to the shop. What do you say?'

He looks out of his side bedroom window, in the direction of the village. All he can see is the hill that separates us from the other end of Annings Lane.

'You've done it loads of times. Remember? You used to walk to The Anchor with your Samwise Gamgee to have a pint.'

My reassurance doesn't work. He raises his eyebrows and his forehead furrows with worry.

Layering up against the cold, I swap out his black woolly hat for his old rainbow beanie that I'd found last night in a bottom drawer. Rebecca, Jack's sister, gave Reubs the hat and the matching snood for Christmas last year. He's always loved rainbows.

I step out into the chill, refusing to acknowledge the reluctance in his body. At the garden gate, I make a mental note to make sure my gestures are gentle, and hold out my right forearm so his left hand can hold on. Every few seconds, his fingers begin to flicker, renewing their grip, prompting a strange sensation in me, somewhere between tickle and annoyance. I say nothing. I focus on the fact that we're walking together, towards the village, one step at a time.

He stops on the lane at the gentle uphill to Jane and Neill's house, and already looks defeated. He pulls down his beanie to partly cover his eyes, and roots himself to the ground.

'Booba. We're only going to the village. It's not far.'

He winces. He mouths something, barely a whisper.

'Say that again?'

I put my ear to his mouth and just make out, 'Half', on his warm breath.

'Well, let's see how we go.'

He pulls on me as we start again.

It reminds me of strolling with my 92-year-old granddad, weeks before he passed, his ailing strength mustered for a short wander around the rose garden before he became too tired and too cold. We are walking even more slowly than that today.

It's frightening how diminished the human body can become. Our capacities and abilities shrink so much that we can become unrecognisable to ourselves and those we love. Even before he and Archi the mutt walked their way around The Corner, doing chores and visiting Anita on the way to the village, he hiked 210 miles along Camino de Santiago, the Way of Saint James. With Reuben, much of how he perceives himself is shaped by how others treat him, on country lanes or in the high street, at home with family or while living in care. It has always been that way. Being Reuben is a self-fulfilling prophecy. If you treat him like a child, like Mum and Dad often do, he will act like one. If somebody has Down's syndrome, we label them as somebody who is different from the rest of society, somebody 'other' or 'special'. Once that happens, usually at birth, how can that person grow up to become anything else? How can they occupy anything – jobs, responsibilities, purpose, relationships – if we keep stripping these opportunities away throughout life?

The sun breaks through and takes the edge off the winter chill. It's almost pleasant, and the countryside is an exaggeration of beauty. The valley cups the river like a pair of hands in an El Greco painting, fine and elongated, with long fingers stretching towards the sea. Even in winter, the fields are so much greener than any green I've seen in Spain. The grass invites us into its softness. Herds of Fresians, with puddles of black-and-white markings, have become unfamiliar to me despite my childhood in the Yorkshire Dales and Berkshire. They swish their tails and watch us too. I feel like a tourist here. Although I'm English, my home and work has been in Andalusia for the last nineteen years.

I stop to hug Reubs and rub his back. He looks at me as if to ask what the hug was for. 'No reason,' I say. 'We're alone until Jack comes over for Christmas. We must look after each other'. I'm longing for that day – when Jack arrives my worries will be halved. Already, a backlog of thoughts and anxieties is piling up. I can talk about things with Jack or Mum and Dad on the phone, but it's not the same as being together.

The valley really is ours this morning. We are the only movement. Reubs seems totally unaware of his surroundings. Whether indoors or out here, it's like he's locked inside a soundproof booth. Walking helps because he's forced to look outwards, but does it really matter if we don't reach the village? However slow we go, I hope that whatever is going on inside his head, will quieten along these tracks. 'The destination is not important.' That's what I always say to the people I guide. 'Arrival is not the most important part of the journey.' This doesn't sound all that convincing right now. The destination is vital.

During our trip to Marrakech, Reuben and I would walk every day: once in the morning, once in the afternoon, and again in the evening. We rested from three until six – I read or worked, Reuben did some drawing (he never travels without felt-tip pens). It was bliss. The only two real destinations during that trip were to fulfil Reuben's wishes: first, riding on a camel dressed as Joseph; second, recreating the scene from *Priscilla, Queen of the Desert* (when Felicia mimes from Verdi's *La Traviata* on top of a silver bus as it drives through the desert).

'Singing on the roof, bruvr. Opera.'

Who was I to stand in his way?

While we walked through the Souks, looking for the perfect technicoloured cloths, we started noticing people looking at us. This isn't unusual. Since childhood, we've been very used to being stared at. On this particular day, we carried on ignoring the attention and got on with our shopping. But the interest in Reuben was unlike anything we'd experienced before. As is usual in the Medina, the storeholder escorted us to a tailor, then the tailor's son escorted us to a soap shop, where the neighbour walked us to his friend's restaurant, and so on. Between all this, however, strangers kept coming up and hugging Reuben. Ladies would run out of cafés to give him freshly squeezed fruit juice, stallholders gave him gifts of stone, leather, cloth, and a loofah.

'What's going on, Reubs?'

'I don't know, bruvr,' he beamed. 'Odd.'

One shopkeeper wouldn't let him go. 'Your brother is purity,' he said. '*Zakat*. When I hug him, I feel like the bad pages of my book are being erased.'

Islamic teachings are very clear: physical or mental differences do not dilute worth, and disabled people are one of the eight groups of people who qualify to receive alms, or *Zakat*, which is second only to prayer in the pillars of Islam. On that Friday, as bodies moved more quickly than they'd moved all week to reach the mosques in the ancient Medina, people's spirituality was heightened, which drew even more attention than usual to Reuben's differences. Although we felt uncomfortable at first, once we understood why it was happening, I can't tell you how much fun it was for the both of us. There was a huge grin on Reuben's face all day.

Further down Annings Lane, nearer the village, folk nod at us over hedges as they go about their gardening chores. Some ignore us at first, but smile warmly when they notice Reuben. He changes them, and this makes me very proud to have him on my arm. Without

Reuben, I'm just a man in his late forties with mad hair who doesn't quite belong here. Is it wrong that I feel a better human with Reubs on my arm? With him, I'm stronger. I belong.

As a gay man with no children, I am not often looked at as somebody who nurtures or cares for others. When I'm with Reubs, there is a difference behind a stranger's gaze. It's the same when I spend time with my nephews, Seve and Leo. The world seems to look at me differently when I'm with them. And perhaps I look at the world differently, too. Reubs has always given me that. With him, walking at his pace, my view is altered.

Perhaps this is the best way for us to navigate the labyrinth we're in. We should walk. Be outside. Be seen. More than ever before, I must learn to live his life. To see the world from his height of 5 foot 2 inches, in much slower motion.

Reuben spies the church tower of St Mary's, standing over the thatched and slate roofs. I know what he's thinking.

'Seeing it,' I say, 'is not the same as walking to it.'

'Arf,' he mouths back, his breath foggy around his face.

'If we walk a little further, we might just find a better view.'

I look at his tired expression, long eyelashes flickering out from the dark stains of sleepless nights and that dim lacquer that coats his eyes. I can't insist on continuing, so make a deal with him instead: 'If we turn back now, at the halfway point, tomorrow we will go a little further, OK? And the next day further, until we reach the village. Littew by littew, my bruvr.'

We turn back for the cottage. He readjusts his grip on my forearm every few steps, and I remind him of a medley we brothers made up from all the different words that he struggled to pronounce when he was little, *Richard, play, monopoly, spoon, sweetie night.* I launch into my best young Reuben impression, 'Fruit Juuuuuice, flay polopoly with a phooooom weetsy niiiight.'

I'm amused but he certainly isn't.

Reuben has always had a lovely, self-deprecating sense of humour, but there's none of it today. He's really not enjoying himself. I wonder if showing him photographs of Marrakech might cheer him up, proof of him riding a camel dressed in his Dreamcoat, or standing atop that 4 x 4 parked in the desert with an eight-metre-long silver cape billowing as an aria blared out of his phone.

The walk wasn't even half a mile but it's further than he's walked in months. When we get back, I let him go upstairs and can see him muttering something to himself, shaking his head as he walks upstairs. He's probably issuing complaints about me as he climbs. I'm fine with that. Having been allowed to opt out of everything for so long, it's going to be hard tackling his lethargy. I want him to make some of those 'best interest' decisions for himself. But we are still quite some way from that.

As I prepare burgers and a huge green salad, I notice that Terry and Jan have already lit their log burner – a fine column of smoke moves into the sky, like a graphite line drawn on blue paper. Jess, from Shipton Farm, is in the sloping field opposite the house, driving the perimeter on a red quad bike, her sheepdog leaning into the corners as they turn. Mud clumps flick off the wheels. She must be inspecting the turnips, as every hundred metres or so she stops, jumps off the quad, and checks a few plants for strength and growth. The sheep are getting hungry, and as the coldest months approach, Jess will need this crop for their winter fodder.

During lunch, I decide not to talk. I want Reubs to notice the silence. I'm intrigued to know how it will make him feel. Will he be uncomfortable? Might he try to fill the gap with words? As he eats, I start to make lists in my head of all the people I can call on for help and support. What we need is a plan. I need a plan. I can't do this on my own, and I'll need the advice of professionals and experts.

So much has gone wrong, so much has been undone. Memories of my brother keep surfacing, making it even more difficult to accept the version of Reuben that is with me now. Where has he gone? I miss him and feel empty in his absence. It baffles me. It makes me hopping mad. It crushes me with sadness. None of these emotions are helpful.

I sign the words for 'I love you, brother.'

He stops, mid chew, and does a double take.

I might be struggling, but his bewilderment is far greater than mine. I tell him again: thump my heart with my closed fist (love) and then bring both fists together and rub knuckles (brothers).

He finishes his mouthful, puts down his fork and looks at his hands. He repeats the message back to me, and it's so much more beautiful when he does it.

After lunch, the afternoon feels oddly normal. The two of us just milling about, doing nothing in particular for the rest of the day. When I stop what I'm doing from time to time, glancing up from writing emails, reading, tidying, I detect a vague amusement in Reuben's face. The hard edges of anger and frustration have softened. For now, this is all we need. This is all Reuben needs, to know he is loved, in a language he is able to understand.

It was September 24, 1983, when Matthew (aged 12), Nathan (5) and I (10) were in a waiting room in Leeds Infirmary Hospital. The armchairs were made of grey PVC and cold to the touch. On each wall, painted hospital-blue, hung a framed print of vases of flowers, with no mount, framed in gold coloured plastic. Stacks of last month's glossy magazines were in an untidy pile on a side table. Some pages had been ripped out and some of the covers were missing corners, perhaps to wrap unwanted chewing gum or to scribble phone numbers on.

Reuben had suffered an unstable lie towards the end of the pregnancy, and when his heartbeat dropped they rushed Mum downstairs for an emergency caesarean. As the hours passed, we were ushered out of the waiting room and back to the Stanmores with Jerry and Pauline, who let us spend the night in their attic. 'Everything's alright,' Pauline reassured us. 'Your mum needs to rest, that's all. Dad will be back for you in a little bit.'

We just wanted to meet Reuben, the fourth brother in our quartet, and up in Pauline and Jerry's attic that night, as our confusion gave way to sleep, I think we all sensed that we were living through something important.

After the caesarean, Reuben had been taken down to the Neonatal Intensive Care Unit. Dad was told he was 'floppy' and that he needed oxygen. They were running some routine tests, they had said. Mum was moved across the ward and was given a private room. It was the next day that a doctor came in and gave them the news.

'Mr and Mrs Coe.'

Mum remembers him bending down on one knee by the bed, ensuring they were on the same eye level.

'We're 90 per cent sure your son has Down's syndrome.'

'I told you,' Mum said to Dad.

Reuben's pregnancy had felt different, and in her second term, while she was walking through the allotments around Headingley, she'd passed a lady carrying a child with Down's. Watching the mother and child, she experienced something of a premonition and remembers thinking, 'Am I ready to have a baby like that?'

There and then, she decided the answer was Yes, she was ready. Dad's response was different. The first words he uttered were, 'How interesting.'

Reuben stayed in observation for forty-eight hours, bottle-fed by the hospital nurses. When one of them brought him up she said to Mum, 'You can't breastfeed these babies.' Mum's reply was typical of the resilience she didn't know she had until Reuben was born. 'Oh give him here,' she had said. 'This one will be just fine.' She cradled Reuben and brought him to her breast, where he began suckling – and didn't stop for fourteen months.

Perhaps it was this moment that allowed us all to breathe a sigh of relief. We could go and see our brother now, Pauline told us, and we careered out of the Stanmores to the hospital in Jerry and Pauline's Vauxhall, anxiously zig-zagging the city streets. When we arrived he was docile, always hungry, with searching eyes and a face as cute as a button. There he was, my little brother, Reuben. I was asked if I wanted to hold him, and remember the feeling of him folding into my arms, a squidgy bundle that never cried. He made me happy.

There was a constant stream of visitors, and Mum's room already overflowed with flowers from the Stanmores and beyond. I remember the hospital ran out of vases. Dad explained that Reuben had something called Down's syndrome, which was a learning difficulty. 'We'll have to learn with him,' he told us. We didn't know another family with a Down's syndrome child. Did it mean we were special? Had we been chosen?

My sense of responsibility for Reuben grew in those early days, and has never waned. Everything was new. Everything was different. But we also wondered if it was a bad thing, and how it would change our lives.

Mum and Reuben came home ten days after his birth. Our house had never been so quiet. Dad explained that Mum was very sore. I think we were all bruised, and as a family we laid low for a few weeks. Pauline, Geraldine and Mrs Palmer popped over with casseroles, stews and a huge shepherd's pie. Angie brought some of her delicious bread. Between the coming and going of neighbours, I imagine my parents tried to make sense of their new reality, together, but also as individuals, wondering what this would mean to the lives they'd shaped for themselves and their children. When Reuben's godfather, Mike Hepper, came to visit, he would play his guitar. In those quiet moments, by Reuben's cot, Mike wrote a song which he later sang at the christening – whenever Mum tells the story, she always ends with: 'There wasn't a dry eye in the church!'

What was apparent from the very beginning of Reuben's life, was that whatever challenges his condition might bring to us as a family, we were never going to have to face them alone. We were surrounded by the Stanmores community, and any question we had always had an answer. Us boys eavesdropped on those adult conversations whenever we could, sitting on the stairs after bedtime or sneaking around the kitchen, to glean what we could from that strange and intriguing grown-up world. We needed to do our own speculating in secret. But it wasn't easy understanding the things we heard. Birth Defect. Trisomy. Chromosomes. Handicapped. Special Needs. Disabled. Retarded. Occupational Therapy. Life Expectancy. Mongol.

We didn't know what to do with all these new words. We had nowhere to put it all. Mostly, we were happy and feeling good about the new addition to the family. Reuben emanated light and we showered him with tickles and kisses and he quickly became the centre of our universe. We huddled around his warmth. He assured us all, with his doe-eyed chortles and chuckles, that everything was going to be OK. But I also remember the sadness in those early days, hushed and unspoken.

Other people started to visit our house too, who were strangers at first, like Reuben's occupational therapist – a kindly lady named Joyce, who smelled of Johnson's baby shampoo and tea. During each visit she'd bring more information – more articles, more books, more pamphlets. Fairly early on, she gave Mum a booklet published by Mencap with a glossy cover, showing a little boy with Down's syndrome wearing a straw hat, sitting between his parents. It looked like they were on the beach. Mum put this booklet and most of the others she was given to one side. I don't think she looked at anything like this for months. She wasn't ready. She wanted to learn *from* him before learning *about* him.

Not everything Joyce left was ignored. She was the one who first told us how to rub E45 cream into Reuben's blotchy skin each evening – she left us two giant white tubs of the stuff that seemed to last our entire childhood. The smell of it (canned milk with cotton) still takes me right back to that house, to Reuben's room on the first floor. Over the coming months, Mum diligently massaged and pummelled his limbs with it, each time she changed his nappy. She sewed tiny bells onto his socks and on the cuffs of his little jumpers, to make him more aware of his limbs. She used to wrap him in tissue paper, and when he moved it would crinkle. Stimulation seemed to be the word on everyone's lips. Keep him stimulated. Don't let him just sit there. I'm pretty sure Reuben's three elder brothers gave him as much stimulation as he'd ever need.

It was much harder for Mum than for any of us. She was the one pushing the pram into town to shop at the Arndale Centre. She was the one dropping us off and collecting us from Headingley Primary School. Inevitably, people stared or stole a second glance, those we knew on the street and even my parents' work colleagues just as much as strangers outside in the street. *Is he or isn't he?* They wanted to know. Mum clocked their reticence and sometimes filled in the gap: 'Yes! Yes he is,' telling them with a certain pride. 'He has Down's syndrome.' She was continually having to step into their silence. One mother approached her in the school playground to get a better look.

'Oh dear, Love. Didn't you get the test?'

Mum fled all the way down Bennet Road, hurtled the pram along North Lane, trying to suppress a rising sob as she waited for the lights at the end of Cardigan Road. She barely kept it under control as she clipped along Kirkstall Lane and burst into the ginnel by the cricket ground, where she bellowed her pain all the way down the alley.

More often than not, people would apologise. 'Sorry. I'm so sorry.' Incredibly, I still hear that today. I heard it last year. I will probably hear it tomorrow or the next day. Why be sorry? What is there to be sorry about? This misplaced pity throws me off balance. I have replied before and I will reply again: 'Don't be sorry.' Reubs is a gift and he enjoys his life perhaps more than you and me. Actually, he helps us enjoy our lives more too. Over the years, it has become a tired rebuff. But all I know is that on those days when I question my own purpose, I always circle back to Reuben because he makes me feel more defined.

At some point growing up, I remember being shown or seeing a graph of development in children plotted against a timeline. *Normal* children, it showed, develop on a clear tangent. Reuben's development potential, plotted alongside this, was shown as a sagging curve that was always some way from the *normal* line. The focus always seemed set on his disability rather than his ability. The tone was always negative, yet somehow Reuben has managed, mostly, not to live in the negative. You'd never hear him say he didn't like something or someone. Being made aware of his learning difficulty, Mum and Dad did what they could to bridge the gap. It didn't make any difference to his three elder brothers, though. We took Reuben everywhere. We became known around the Stanmores as the boys with the Down's syndrome brother, which was a source of pride for us. I for one felt bound to him, like a twin. I still do.

Perhaps we all have emptiness. Mine isn't the God-shaped hole that perhaps my Dad would diagnose – I'm no longer Christian, now I've had the chance to draw my own conclusions. I used to think loneliness was connected to my sexuality. A sense that was heightened when I came out as gay to my family and friends. Because it didn't fit their worldview, I was ostracised for being different, and ended up being alone. 'Oh, you silly billy,' a friend's mother said when I told her. 'You must fight it,' were the words of another. 'I'll pray for you,' they said.

With Reuben, I didn't get all that crap. And with him now, I never feel lonely. His presence completes me. His little hand fills the hollow in my palm. This is not why I love him. I have loved him much longer than I have needed his love. That is the symmetry of our brotherhood.

Even though those early days were hard, people's reactions brought us closer together as a family. We found strength. A solidarity. The peculiar sadness that deepened when people made passing comments, gradually started to dissipate. We were hardening. It also made less and less sense to be sad, because it was completely at odds with the joy that burst from Reuben's tiny being. He defused our anger and our angst. It did often feel, however, that we were the only ones who could feel this joy.

It wasn't until we joined the Down's Syndrome Association in Leeds, that we found other people who felt the same. There was no more 'I'm sorry'. I remember sitting shoeless on the padded floor mats of the main room, watching the other children, and listening to their parents' pride. We had found a tribe. It marked the end of any feelings of alienation. And Reubs even got some new boots, orthopaedic ones, made in red leather and brown rigid soles, stitched like brogues with little silver link holes for the laces.

I still find it odd how much the word 'normal' is bandied around

Reuben. So much of his care and health support growing up was *corrective*, trying to move him away from who he was towards something that was a 'better' fit for the world. And there were endless tools and tricks to help him align more with this idea of normal. Shoes to help him walk more normally, creams for more normal skin, Makaton sign language, and the biggest question of them all: should he go to a normal school?

Why are we always striving to make Reuben more normal? Shouldn't we be encouraging him to be himself? There has always been a tension between who Reuben is and what people believe is best for him, and I'm as guilty as anyone.

Turning the conversation around to focus on Reuben's abilities would have been so easy, yet the opposite became the norm. I remember being told (or did I overhear it?) that he would probably never be able to do a whole host of things. From day one, those comments instilled in our family a determination that we'd do everything we could to prove them all wrong.

I run downstairs from the shower just in time to pick up the phone. It's Reuben's social worker, Sam. I carry on drying my hair while chatting.

'How did it all go? Any problems?'

'None at all.' I reply. 'Emma and the care provider emailed me last Friday, saying I could take him out. I jumped on the first plane I could get. They made me sign for his meds and his bank card, then handed me his bags and that was that. No fanfare.'

'And what's your feeling? How is he?'

I lower my voice, 'Not good, Sam. I'm shocked at how bad he is. They kept telling me he was fine.'

'You're here now. That's the important thing. We'll work out the next move together. You just let me know how I can help.'

When we first met, Sam was sitting with her legs crossed and her right leg wrapped twice around her left like the ribbon on a maypole. She wears glasses and often pushes them up her nose just before she says something important. I admire her dedication to Reuben. Her diligence has been a harbour for all my doubts.

I stop drying my hair and sit down, reassured by her voice and glad of having somebody else to talk to.

'We're both very quiet,' I tell her. 'We're getting used to being together again. I'm giving him lots of cuddles.'

'Good. I bet he was so happy to see you.'

'I think so. He's been putting up a fight. He looks at me as if I'm a difficult path. He's resisting, but something happened yesterday.'

'Did he say something?'

'No. We walked, almost to the village.'

'That's great.'

'There was something else. A little breakthrough, I think.'

I am about to tell Sam about my 'conversation' with Reuben, how we signed each other last night, but her tone is shifting, becoming more formal as she tells me there's a different care home in town we could try, or there's a new supported living facility a couple of hours away. I'm taken aback. Listening to her ties me in knots. I don't feel ready to talk about it.

'Do I have to think about getting him back into care already?'

'I know. Sorry. But these things take time. I'm just trying to get the ball rolling, as soon as possible.'

'I've only just got him out.'

I promise Sam that I'll always listen to what she has to say and will start mulling over the options soon. I also emphasise how grateful I am for her support. I don't tell her how blunt my mind feels, and that I can't think beyond today. This isn't the first time I've had to take Reuben out of care, and talking to Sam stirs those memories.

I say goodbye and put the phone down.

'That was Sam, Reubs. She sends her love.'

Needing to get that conversation off my chest, I want to tell him that he's definitely not going back to Portland Place, and that she is talking about other houses he could go to, better places. But I can't do that to him. We've barely begun. I will have to plan ahead for his future, as we always have done before, but he is far too fragile for fresh starts. At the moment, I have him here and I can safeguard his feelings.

I walk through into the kitchen and throw the towel in the washing basket. I make myself a coffee and join Reubs at the table as he eats his porridge, each mouthful moving like a tiny arc on the tip of his teaspoon. I need some music to settle my thoughts, so I reach for my phone and play Dmitry Myachin through the speaker. I look over at Reuben to see if he's listening too, but he doesn't seem interested. I play one particular track, again and again, letting the melody fall on both of us, drip-feeding music where words fail. Reuben looks at me. I put my hand on the table half between us, palm upwards, fingers open.

He looks at my hand and I wonder if it seems too far away.

He looks back down and studies his porridge, then my hand again, and allows his arm to move across the table. Gently, I interlock fingers. He lifts his eyes and whispers, 'ingya'.

It's one of the first words he ever spoke, when he was about three years old. It became part of our family's vocabulary in an instant, but none of us ever knew what it meant. Years later, we asked Reuben if he knew what it meant. He replied, 'ingya', and smiled. It refers back to itself and means everything he struggles to express and much more.

ingya

It is the first time I've heard it for years, and here it is, an unearthed relic. This one word is a portal to everything, a tiny opening to a series of underworld tunnels and caves. For the moment, we have come far enough. The music still plays and I could sit like this all day. There is no sense of urgency. We have our starting line.

When I do leave, heading upstairs to finish off getting dressed, I'm so afraid that this connection will be snuffed out by the time I come back, that as I leave the only thing I can think of saying is, 'When you've finished breakfast, take your plate to the sink.'

Reuben David Coe turned our lives downside up.

Dad's first words at his birth, 'how interesting', could have gone anywhere. Thankfully, because my father's naturally inquisitive, all the reading and research he was doing for Reuben made him deeply aware that there were whole segments of society that needed help, and he wanted to give them his attention. His job as an Educational Welfare Officer for the city council no longer motivated him, and at the same time Mum wanted to be nearer her own father, who had lived alone in Surrey since our grandmother passed away. Little by little, both of my parents were getting ready to leave the Stanmores and Leeds altogether. They were gravitating south. And the letter arrived when Reuben was eighteen months old, after two sets of interviews with a Christian charity in Berkshire called Oakfield Court. They had decided that our dad was an answer to their prayers – he was committed, hard-working, had a son with Down's syndrome, and had a religious calling.

Oakfield Court was a residential home for twenty adults with varying degrees of need. They offered Dad the job of running it, and at first he had to commute between Reading and Leeds, returning home exhausted every ten days to take three days off. Up until then, the only car my parents had ever owned was a royal blue Opel Chrysler that my maternal Grandfather gave to us. But ever since the bottom of it had fallen out as we drove through a field to a car boot sale, they hadn't had a new one. My dad's parents stepped up, though: Granddad gave us his pride and joy, a bright red VW Beetle that didn't have a scratch on it. The beige interior was spotless, and it had a looped handhold on the passenger side that my elegant Nanna's hand used to clutch on bends in the road. This is what Dad chugged up and down England's motorways in, until both his stamina and his marriage started showing strain.

Mum was at home with four boys under thirteen. It was also 1985, which meant all dads were still meant to be the breadwinners and that it was definitely the wrong year to sell a house in the north of England. Their four-bedroom terrace in Headingley would only fetch enough for them to buy a two-bedroom house or a maisonette off the M4 around Reading. Being my parents, they started praying. Their church in Leeds was praying too. The community at Oakfield Court was praying.

But nothing changed. The months stretched on and Mum became evermore exhausted and frustrated, so the trustees at Oakfield Court offered us the staff flat in the attic until Mum and Dad could find a house they could afford. This is how it came to pass, after many years, that we left the Stanmores. Half of Our Street stepped out to wave goodbye to us boys in the back of Grandad's VW Beetle, with the distinctive purr of the engine under our bums as we sat, nervous and excited by the prospect of a new life down south.

We descended on Oakfield Court like a blizzard from the north. Mum, Dad, Nathan and Reuben moved into the two-bedroom attic flat while Matt and I slept in one of the empty residents' rooms on the first floor with its thick pile carpet, hollow fire doors and a radiator that belted out so much heat that we lived with the windows open. We loved it. Oakfield Court was an adventure. School, on the other hand, was a total shock. We were completely unprepared for the hostile welcome us northern boys got in a southern school. We talked weirdly, none of us really made friends, and the end-of-school bell was always a massive relief.

As fast as we could, it was back to Oakfield Court to hang out in the kitchen, muck around in the halls, join the arts and crafts workshops in the garden, or help one of the residents with their chores. Setting the tables with Annie would become a song. Sweeping the floor with Rachel turned into a musical. Sitting in the living room with Mark and Ian would morph into *Star Wars*. Oakfield Court was a treasure trove of fun and unforgettable people like David (whose only word was 'strawberries') or Maureen (who used to take her teeth out and tell Mum she wanted to sleep in her bath). Then there was Brian, who could scald himself with hot water because he had no nerve endings in his hands, or the lovely Pam who just smiled all the time. And while Esther spent her afternoons brushing her hair and staring out of the window, Jim would be marching the corridors on the first floor dressed in his military uniform shouting, 'Heil Hitler!' Occasionally, Sarah would make an appearance with a tea cosy on her head, clapping and telling herself not to be so silly.

Every day at Oakfield was completely unpredictable. Everyone who lived there was completely original, a one-off, yet a vital part of the whole. Differences were celebrated and loved. A pursuit of happiness and fun was encouraged. The antics of the residents, along with the sense of community, became part of our family's DNA. Living like that showed me that Reuben could always be a part of a whole, and he lapped up all the love he could get.

As a twelve-year-old who was anxious at school, worried about being northern and being the smallest in his class, I discovered that society isn't very good at embracing differences and finds it much easier, for some reason, to rely on definitions for different kinds of people. I remember wondering why, at school, these differences weren't celebrated in the same way they were at Oakfield Court. Why did they want to teach us to be the same? To survive school, I spent breaktime and lunch trying to look busy, doing loops of the school grounds with a purpose in my stride, all in an attempt to hide my differences.

In contrast to Mum's joy at her new home life, Dad found those months really tough. He was never off duty, could barely rest, and was desperate to find our new home. A year after moving south, they decided to really stretch themselves financially and we all squeezed into an end-of-terrace in Tilehurst, on a road that never felt like home. We muddled through and tried our utmost to keep ourselves out of the neighbours' lives. Nathan found golf. I found athletics and drums. Matt missed Leeds terribly (and is now living back in the north, happily married to Liz with their two boys Jacob and Isaac). Mum and Dad found a new church. Reuben always found everything he ever wanted.

Just as I'm beginning to plan how we can fill the day, I hear the tap of raindrops on the skylight windows. They begin slowly enough for me to identify individual beats, but the tempo quickens as the sky darkens. I walk up to the terrace and watch the rain as it begins to lash the pond, unsettling the tightness of its surface. At the far corner, I can just make out Jack's stone Buddha, facing east, the bulk of him barely visible. He is part ornament, part water-level marker. If his body is out of the pond water, the level is low and we have to refill it from the brook. No need for that now. Buddha seems to be battling back the tide, half of his face submerged.

If we were isolated before, we are now marooned. I can't take Reubs out in this. I run through a mental list of indoor activities. I remember his colouring book and pop upstairs to discover it's not in his tote bag – I did ask the carers to pack it for him, but either the message never got through or he asserted his right to leave it where it has been since I bought it, at the bottom of the chest of drawers.

Reubs is in his room, taking an age to get dressed. Every fifteen minutes or so, whenever I return to check on him, he's freeze-framed into another tableau of powerful slowness. It's like turning the pages of an enormous comic to find each page is the same. Pants. One sock. Two socks. Fifteen minutes on, trousers. 'No, Reubs,' I suggest calmly. 'You had those socks and pants on yesterday. Remember. Clean underwear and T-shirts every day.'

Saying this is a mistake. It takes him right back to the beginning of the process. Pants. One sock. Two. Fifteen minutes, trousers, and it's a full hour before he's dressed with slippers on. Everything in him then resists the idea of coming downstairs. But I have an idea, and I don't care that it's early or give two hoots that Reubs looks at me as if I've finally lost the plot.

While he's fiddling with his day bag, I teeter on the top step of the stepladder, my head and shoulders poking into the loft above the bedroom. There are two boxes of Christmas decorations and a Santa Sack filled with stockings, along with Reuben's Father Christmas outfit and rolls of wrapping paper sticking out of the top. Bingo. Just where we left it all last year, carefully put away. I am so impressed by our organisation but admit that it's Jack who insisted on putting it away properly.

'Right, Reubs. I don't want you to get wet but I need you to help me. Stand by the back door, open it when I carry the trees in.'

I find the boot towels by the boiler, still stained from last winter, and lay them on the floor. I open the door and run into the rain. The noise on the hood of my jacket is deafening, and already the wet is finding a way to trickle across my skin. Tree number one is in a pot over by the logs, number two is on the lawn beyond the terrace. Getting wetter by the second, stumbling the first tree towards the house I yell, 'Open the bloody door!' There's a tiny slit of Reuben visible and I almost topple him barging through.

In the house, I can see just how much the trees have grown. They drip dry on the towels while I make myself a cup of tea. Reubs disappears back upstairs. He's been trapped in a bedroom for nine months, apart from meals alone in the dining room and an occasional swing on the garden seat. An ever diminishing, lonely world. I may have broken him out of those four walls but he hasn't left yet. He's still locked away inside, not necessarily because he wants to be. It's what he's used to.

A WhatsApp message pings into my phone from Reuben.

Is not Christmas yet Not fuss me brother.

I type my reply, grinning, *It's an early Christmas. To get ready. Keep nice and cosy and safe. Luffly.*

He types back, *Give me new DVD. Something Whoopi Goldberg. Love you. Mini row.*

I let out a huge belly laugh.

A mini row. Have we had our first fight? Our first family *flewd.*

And then it dawns on me, what he means is Cadbury's Mini Rolls. He's having a sweet-tooth craving. The food I ordered is due tomorrow, but I don't think I ordered any mini rows.

While the Christmas trees dry, I spend an hour or so uncoiling the lights and finding the extension cables. I put a box of decorations next to each tree and go back upstairs, where Reuben is sitting cross-legged on his unmade bed, staring at an envelope with a red felt-tip pen in his hand.

'You be careful with that,' I say. 'Don't get any on the sheets. Why are you writing on an envelope?'

He looks at the exposed nib then lifts the sketchpad and opens the cover to show me it's empty.

'Oh, dear. Why don't you come down to help instead? You decorate one tree, I'll do the other.'

He curls his lips, biting them inwards as he nods, defeated by the lack of paper or my persistence. We head down together and start unpacking and choosing our decorations. Some are from our first Christmas with Jack at The Corner, not long after we moved in. It was so cold we nicknamed it 'the fridge' – despite being in the mountains, there's no heating other than an open fire. But the three of us were happy falling under its spell. I had been guiding an American family right up until Christmas Eve, and was excitedly driving home with the radio blaring *villancicos*. I tried in vain to find a tree but everything was closed and ended up practically forcing a bemused man in a petrol station to sell me the poinsettia by the till.

We took lots of walks down by the river that winter, and one afternoon Jack and Reuben found a prong of wood that looked like Saruman's staff from *Lord of the Rings*. From then on, Reubs decided that The Corner must be Middle Earth, that he and Jack were Frodo Baggins and Samwise Gamgee, and of course I became Gandalf the Grey, much to Jack's amusement. That's when their adventures began in earnest, the happiest hobbits you will ever meet.

More and more I'm tending to slip into the past. Nostalgia gives me comfort. But because those days were so filled with laughter and love, it makes the present much harder to bear. There is such a chasm between then and now. That was that life. This is this one. I can't figure out which is the dream. I just hope we haven't lost our Frodo Baggins.

In the living room, bags of tinsel and baubles are spilling across the floor. All that remains for me to do is add the star, crowning the top of the tree. Reuben has tucked himself away from me, around the corner, almost out of sight. I catch him in mid-decision, frozen to the spot with a furry owl dangling from the forefinger of his right hand. There are three other decorations on his tree so far: an angel, a wooden heart, a little boy wearing a blue scarf and woolly hat.

'Well done, Reubs. That looks great.'

I hug him, careful not to crush the owl.

He expels something as I gently squeeze – is it disappointment? I stand by the tree so he can hand me decorations, but he finds it hard to choose so we swap positions. I choose the decorations and he finds a place for them on the tree. A snowman, a gold star, a wooden plaque with the words *Love You* scorched into it. A tiny home with snow on the roof, a stocking, a Christmas pudding, a cracker, a reindeer and a golden pomegranate. We manage to finish half of the tree before Reuben stops. He looks at me, his eyes are pleading. He's not ready to decorate a *whole* tree. Littew by littew. He tries his best and I can't ask for more.

The shape of him glides upstairs.

I finish the tree and enjoy a lighting ceremony all by my silly self. I hope he felt something. Sometimes, I can sense that he knows where he wants to be but doesn't know how to get there. He can see the old Reubs but doesn't know how to find him.

'All you have to do is survive.' That's what a friend of mine said, after experiencing a complete breakdown. 'By surviving, you are buying yourself time.'

Perhaps the hope of getting better is enough, or all we ever have. Right now, Reubs is happy to exist and not leave his mark. And that should be OK. He doesn't want to leave footprints at the moment, in the same way he doesn't want his voice to resonate in a room. His clothes have become a forcefield, a protective layer upon layer built up so he can hide away. Each day they appear in the same order. Undershirt, shirt, hoodie, scarf, hat. And whenever he thinks I'm not looking, he wears his face mask indoors. He must have a secret stash somewhere, because when I confiscated it earlier another appeared. His pockets are always filled with toilet paper, too. Reams and reams of it stuffed into every pocket of everything he wears. I've no idea why. It's like Reubs is trying to bury himself in all this stuff, protecting himself in the only way he knows how.

Although I don't completely understand why he's doing all this, it does make me think that taking him out of Portland Place was the right thing to do. I know this is a tightrope, and that every step we take must be measured and gentle. But when I have my doubts, I don't need to look very far or think too deeply to be reminded. I dread to think what might have become of him, so alone in that room. He may well have been allowed to disappear completely. And then all I'd have left of him would be in the past.

It was in 1995, after years of dedicated service, that Dad was made redundant from Oakfield Court. They could no longer afford to pay him. To face redundancy at any age is tough, but becoming unemployed at fifty was complicated by the fact that Dad was still supporting a family whose own lives were shaped by where he worked. He tried temping for two years, and on days off he drove from interview to interview and opened one rejection letter after another. It's only now that I fully understand how testing those months must have been. Occupied as I was with my own journey into adulthood, I didn't notice his general mood worsen. But Mum did, and she reacted quickly by walking into a local travel agent and telling them that she wanted to send her husband away.

'I can't watch him moping about the house any more. Where can I send him for a week in the sun?'

He ended up alone in Torremolinos, near Malaga, in a four-star hotel. His room had a balcony overlooking the sea. Dining by himself on the first night, a group of other guests assumed he was a widower and invited him to join them. 'No, I have a wife,' he told them. 'She sent me here to get some sun.' Although none of the other guests could wrap their head around the idea, those seven days away were just what he needed. He swam in the sea, read on his balcony, took the bus to Gibraltar. We were all proud of him because he came back with a spring in his step and was offered a job at the very next interview. This time, we didn't need to move far – near Newbury, which was the same county at least – but again found ourselves in temporary, rented accommodation in Upper Bucklebury, just along from the petrol station in the village. Because the house had three bedrooms, I lived in a caravan in the garden and went to the local school with Matt to finish our A-Levels. Matt went to university after that, and I went travelling.

Which meant that Nathan and Reuben spent their adolescence together – Mum has always said that Nathan brought Reuben up.

It wasn't long after Reuben had turned nineteen that the local authority pulled the plug on his education. At the time, I remember not understanding why they did that. Now, looking back, I'm dumbfounded and angry. They had only just given Mum and Dad the results of his assessment, telling them his mental age was between seven and nine years old. Although my parents had expected that, it must have still been a blow to have your child defined quite so bluntly. Again, this compares Reuben to the idea of what a 'normal' nineteen-year-old would be, or a normal seven- to-nine-year-old. What a terribly cruel way of understanding what the best support might be. Labelling first, then the blow of not even offering any options for education. Even if we accepted the assessment of his mental age, how then does it make sense to stop teaching him?

We took the matter into our own hands, and through a dear family friend, Hugh, we found Reuben a place at the L'Arche Community home in Bognor. The funding available from our local authority in West Berkshire wasn't going to cover all the costs, so to help Reuben raise the extra money, Nathan and I decided to take him on a pilgrimage along Camino de Santiago. Three brothers and a dog (a miniature schnauzer called Monty) – the story caught the attention of the local press and we quickly raised enough to secure his place at L'Arche. But then our local authority came back and refused to fund Reuben, unless he stayed in the county. We had no choice. Mum and Dad couldn't afford L'Arche, so Reuben had to go into a home in West Berkshire.

The disappointment was difficult to bear, and although we all felt as if Reuben's future was being compromised, things actually started well when he moved in, mainly because he had a really good key worker who kept him occupied and healthy. For the first four years, with Mum and Dad down the road and friends of my parents in town, he was well shielded and supported in the community.

*

When Mum and Dad neared retirement, they decided to move to Norwich where Dad was born, enticed back by a role for him in an inner-city church. They had read somewhere that the grieving process for people with Down's syndrome could be more drawn out and complex, so they hoped that establishing Reuben's independence might help make it a little more bearable after they were gone. Reuben also wanted to stay in Newbury, where he did drama with Zippy and put on musical productions with Pat in the front room of her house every Saturday morning. We all agreed it would be better for him to stay put where he was settled and less reliant on his family. There was also the thriving church community that Mum and Dad had been part of in Berkshire, who would surely look after him too.

Before they moved, Mum and Dad had started a trust for Reuben. The money we'd raised on our Camino de Santiago pilgrimage hadn't been spent, and when Aunty Eva (my grandfather's sister) passed away, she left Reuben £8,000. A family friend, Bertrum, became the trustee and everything was in place to cover Reuben's primary needs and education. Mum and Dad could retire to Norwich without worrying, and we three brothers could make a start with our own lives. I, for one, assumed that Reubs was being looked after and cared for. But we were all lulling ourselves into a false reality.

What we forget is that things are always changing. In the care system, the quality of care is only as good as the people who are working in any particular home or organisation. People retire, quit or get ill, which is what happened to Reuben's lovely friend, Pat, whose departure put an end to their musical productions. That's when the management at the house started filling it with temporary agency staff, who neither knew Reubs nor cared about him. One of them even bought a £800 plasma TV using Reuben's bank card. And while this was going on, not a single person from Mum and Dad's church took Reubs under their wing or made sure he was alright.

At around the same time, Reuben began to drink and developed a hoarding disorder. Because the carers were not officially allowed into his bedroom, unless he invited them, nobody saw the piles of junk that were accumulating behind his door – on one visit, Mum and Dad cleared eight black bin bags and threw away his sheets because they were so filthy. I flew to the UK to confront his carers, but they defended themselves rigorously, reciting carer terms and policies as they sat with coffee and cakes on the picnic table in the garden. They were all doing the 'best they could within the guidelines'.

In the time I spent with Reubs, however, he seemed placid and happy. He had even found a new friendship with another tenant and this seemed to bolster his confidence. He has never really had friends of his own, so hearing this made me happy. Maybe it wasn't all that bad, I thought. Perhaps I was overreacting. So we let this tick along for a little while longer, until one Sunday afternoon when I called him and things unravelled.

Reuber Booba sat on a wall
Reuber Booba had a great fall
All Booba's ladies and all Booba's men
Helped to put Booba together again.

Reuben rarely lies. He might not answer straight away or at all, shrugging and averting his eyes. But he eventually gets to the truth, and it was no exception when he picked up the phone that day.

'Hello, bruvr,' he said chirpily.

'Hello my Booba. Alright? Are you having a good Sunday?'

I was probably imagining that a family from Mum and Dad's church had invited him to theirs for Sunday lunch, but Reuben didn't reply.

I asked again, 'You alright, babes? Where are you?'

After another pause he admitted, 'In Sainsbury's, bruvr.'

'What are you doing there?'

'Buying Vodka Pops.'

Enough was enough. I arranged for Reubs to fly out to Spain. At the airport, I waited and waited until finally a member of the ground staff brought him through arrivals. He ran to me and we hugged like we hadn't seen each other for years. He was huge, the heaviest I've ever seen him, dressed in his pyjamas with a hoodie thrown over the top. His hair was long and unkempt (I'll spare you the detail of his nails). When I asked the carers at the home for an explanation, they said he wouldn't get up and when the taxi came to take him to Heathrow, their only option was to wrap him in a hoodie and throw him in the cab. There was so much wrong with that explanation.

He never went back to Newbury. I pulled him out of the home and he came to live with me and one of my best friends, Debs. It was 2013, Reuben was about to turn thirty. We all lived together in a duplex in San Pedro de Alcántara. It took a little while to settle in, and I wouldn't have been able to do it without her – people like Debs are few and far between. But his life became radically different to what it had been. Importantly, he began to understand how unhappy he had been. While he was at the care home, in the day to day of living, he had nothing to compare his life to. I don't think he could comprehend or express what he was going through.

Late sunshine illuminates the pond and the garden. It has stopped raining and the willow glistens by the bend in the brook, branches glowing a soft golden-yellow. Earlier, Ali from next door dropped a chocolate cake off at the back door, with a message in bold letters of encouragement and coloured kisses. When I tell Reuben about it, he comes downstairs in record time. We have a slice together at the kitchen table, then he moves off and settles into the blue armchair by the front window with his sketchpad. He sits there, quite still, half lit by the lamp on the side table. He looks like a Vermeer painting, a study of concentration as he sketches lines to label the animals he's drawn. He colours the sheep in a vibrant pink, the cow in yellow and the rabbit and the robin in brown. After dinner, we watch a bit of TV before hot milk and honey, and just before he goes up to bed, he hands me a white envelope. I wait for him to leave, then turn it over.

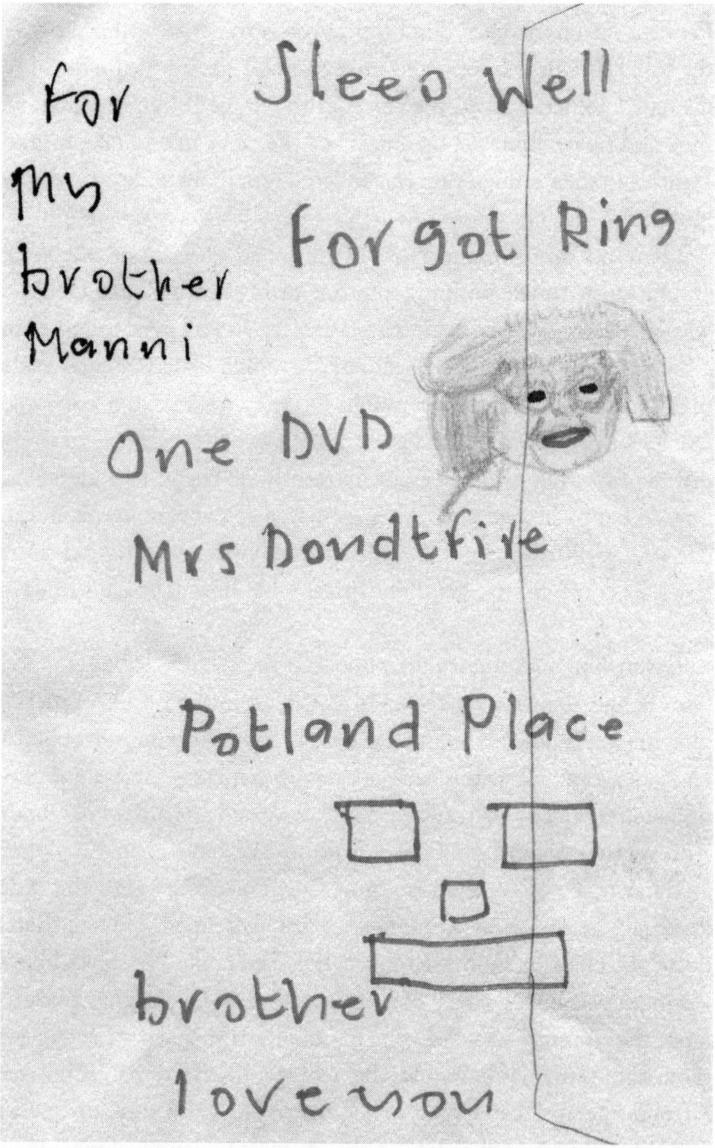

for
my
brother
Manni

Sleeo Well

Forgot Ring

One DVD

Mrs Doudtfire

Potland Place

brother

love you

The soundtrack of these last few days has been cutlery scraping, jaws chewing, breakfast and lunch and dinner dishes being washed up or loaded straight into the dishwasher. Then nothing again, until the absence of sound creates its own noise. Usually, I rise at dawn and make tea until I'm sufficiently awake to make coffee, then wrap myself up and walk the lanes before Reubs wakes up. Each morning I plan for two walks: this first one for me, then another later on for Reuben.

It's been helpful to claim these first hours of the day as my own. I follow paths and cast ideas ahead then reel them back in. If unresolved, I cast off again and again. I never pass anybody, but the repetition and growing familiarity of what I see in the dawn means that I don't feel alone. A couple of times, I've even managed the six-mile circuit to the beach and back. No matter how far I go, whenever I get back to the cottage, Reuben is still asleep, not yet ready to face the first challenge of opening his eyes.

This morning, I woke him gently at 8 a.m. Not early, not late. I perched my bum half on the bed and waited for him to stir. I put my hand lightly on his arm. There was no reaction. A tractor rushed by on the lane, off to feed the cows no doubt, but still no movement, no change in his resting face.

I am still sitting here, waiting, looking around his room at the clothes strewn around the floor: yesterday's outfit in one clump, the day before in another, dressing gown and night bag below the window. There is a sort of order to the chaos, like a jumble sale organised into seasons. I wait a while longer, hoping he can sense me with him. His finger twitches, I change my position to hold his hand. What else can I do to help him *want* to wake up? How can I reassure him into another day? I draw a blank on words so lightly brush the back of his hand with my thumb. *I am here.*

I will sit here for as many minutes and mornings as it takes.

Soon, longer days and more light will break this monotony of darkness. The primroses will colour the banks, the wild garlic and bluebells will start pushing. The swallows will return, then the swifts. I can hear the tractor turning back into the end of the lane. The cows are fed. With these sounds of the day, Reubs must be able to sense the waking of the world, the valley coming to life.

The hawthorn hedge down on the lane is backlit by the rising sun, bare branches outlined with faint rays. The passage of light reveals splits I'd never noticed in the trunk of an ash tree growing from the hedge. The branches are more defined, too, the shadows hardening the edges. My gaze lands back on Reuben and fixes on him as the muscles in his face begin to tense. Peace is leaking out. The contours are hardening, his brow furrows. How difficult it is to start another day. What strength, what will, to haul his mind into another reckoning. It would be so much easier to keep sleeping.

It takes a while for his eyes to open, as if prising open the letterbox of an abandoned house. He focuses and finds me, then quickly snaps his eyes shut again. Not quite ready. He puts an arm up to partially cover his face, but the light still seeps through his lashes, and slowly, slowly, he submits to the fact and his lids rise and fall, and then there they are, the whites and deep browns of his eyes. I hope he knows I'm not going anywhere.

Once he's ready to lift himself from bed, I scurry off to give him space, coming back to check every so often to gauge his progress. Sheets back. Roll over. Sit up. Feet on the ground. Stand. Dressing gown on, day bag in hand. It's past 9 a.m. when he reaches the bathroom and starts combing his hair with flicks and strokes of the black comb, over and over again, lost in the rhythm and sensation of the gentle pull against his scalp.

I head back downstairs and holler up as I lay the table for breakfast. Any words will do. Words of encouragement, words of emotional blackmail, promises I can't keep. Words of doubt that I don't really mean, words of hope, words that are completely pointless. I'm on my second cup of coffee and ready for my third when I hear him cross the landing. I jog up to tell him breakfast is ready. But he needs the loo so breakfast will go cold. I pour and finish that third cup of coffee, then read the day's news on my laptop and wish that I hadn't. Finally, I hear the toilet flush and climb the stairs to resume coaxing. I see Reubs standing in front of the mirror. He doesn't notice me. He is too focussed on putting toothpaste on his brush, careful not to look at the mirror. He knows his reflection is there, staring back at him, but he doesn't want to look. I can't bear to watch.

All of us, at different times of life, obsess over something not quite right about ourselves. I wish I was taller. I wish I wasn't so tall. How can I cut my hair to make my face not look so podgy? I wish I had a flat tummy like that man in the magazine. I wish I was more outgoing. I've never liked my ears, I can't stand my stumpy legs. I've given up worrying about the hair on my back. Whatever it is that doesn't quite conform to the idea of ourselves, causes us varying degrees of anxiety, pain and – at worst – sickness. What must it be like for Reuben?

The last time I pondered this in any depth, it completely floored me. We were still living at The Corner together, and a reluctant Reubs had agreed to go out on a sea kayak – he was so worried that he looked like the figurehead of a Spanish galleon, his body gripped by a sculptural tension as I paddled through the breaking waves. When we got further out it was a mill pond, not a wisp of wind. It was high summer. All was well with the world. Reuben started to relax and really enjoy himself.

'This is life, bruvr,' he said smiling. 'Lookin' at us.'

'It's perfect, isn't it!' I replied.

'Well…'

'Well what?' I asked. 'How could anything be better than this? What would you change?'

He didn't reply at sea. He waited for me to paddle back to shore.

He waited until people were beginning to pack up umbrellas and towels, getting ready to leave the beach. He waited until we had walked back to the car park, loaded up and were sat with the engine idling. He looked deep into my eyes and said, 'My face.'

Sam hasn't wasted any time arranging an appointment with a speech therapist called Alice, who is young and pleasant and has a calmness that reaches out of the laptop screen. We watch her sitting in her office with a large mug of coffee, she chats and watches Reuben eating his breakfast.

'The last part of his communication to return will be his speech.' She is explaining how Reuben's cognitive speech is processed. 'You or I can formulate a sentence without thinking through every word. We dominate the structure of language subconsciously. Reuben, on the other hand, has to process each word as if it was in a box that first needs to be opened before the meaning can be released. Each word takes a huge conscious effort.'

Alice is right, Reuben has never really communicated in full sentences. Words are indicators, clues to meaning. Gestures are part of his grammar. His grasp of tenses has always been pretty fluid. Like any language, his takes time to learn. But once you get the hang of it, communicating becomes playful and imaginative. Catchphrases and movie quotes are the towers of his wit.

I sit and watch him eat half of his cereal, one nibble at a time. He gathers a tiny amount onto his teaspoon and then, rather than putting the whole spoon in his mouth, he lifts individual oats with his lips. I remember when he was known for never leaving anything on his plate, raiding larders and returning for third and fourth servings. Now, like everything else, food is something he's wary of. It takes him almost an hour to finish half a small bowl of *msli*, and when he's done, routine dictates that he must get the smallest glass in the cupboard and half-fill it with water. If I suggest that he should finish the water, he turns his back so I can't see him.

I don't want just this half of my brother, I want all of him back. I know the other half is in there somewhere. Perhaps this is a kind of hibernation, a survival mechanism. If he can no longer draw up the sap of himself, he must shut down to live through the winter in his head. How did my jubilant, happy-go-lucky, daring young brother get lost in silence? Now he walks as if he's made of paper, and sits down as if his body is made of delicate crystal. There are so many unanswered questions around depression, if that's what has locked his voice away. The doctors and psychologists certainly think so. Or did he need that label so they could prescribe him that green and yellow pill that I hate so much. I'm sure they've caused his lethargy. It's always the last one to be swallowed, pinched between forefinger and thumb every morning, kept until the end and sinking him into a fog. He's been taking them for eleven months now. He clings to them as if they're part of him, and swallows in a ritual of peculiar celebration. It's very troubling to watch.

How am I going to help my brother? He needs to rediscover that intricate web of himself. Who is Reuben? What are his dreams? What does he believe? How can I help him overcome the fear and reclaim himself?

If he whispers at all, his voice is as thin as cobweb. I can barely discern a word. It's hard enough to witness how far Reuben has slipped away. I'm finding it hard to connect with him. It's like learning to love a stranger. Alice explained that I must find new ways to reach him. When I told her about the messages and drawings in his sketchbook, and on the envelope, she was enthusiastic. 'He *will* talk again, when he's ready.'

He will talk again. I cling to those words.

I snatch another look at my brother, and all the glance does is confirm what I already know: that he's sitting, eating breakfast, still bolted away behind vaulted doors. If his mind were more awake, perhaps life would just be too overwhelming, like it was on the day in Antequera. On the day of his breakdown. A visceral overload. Is this a sort of coma? A prolonged slowing down in order to heal. A numbing down of existential doubts.

When we've said goodbye to Alice, Reubs finishes his breakfast and goes upstairs to loiter in his room. Of course, he'd prefer to stay there all day, doing nothing, saying nothing, as he's used to. Should I leave him to it? I can't. Something in me just won't let that happen. I head up and suggest he joins me downstairs with his *Joseph* tote bag filled with his sketchpad and box of felt-tips. Most of the old pens are dry, but he won't use the new ones I bought him and leaves them like a rainbow on his bedside table.

He comes downstairs but decides he'd rather not sit with me in the kitchen. Instead, he chooses the high-backed armchair by the front window and sets himself up. He starts to draw, then stops again to pull the footstool closer to use as a table. He pushes the felt-tips slowly against the paper, tongue out, head cocked and moving side to side occasionally to gauge his progress.

He chooses his colours with great care, each tiny movement, every single individual mark scratches the page with precision. Watching him, my smile becomes overwhelmed with feeling, a rush of warmth that moves me to tears. This is the kind of silence I can love. *This.* I back away quietly, not wanting my presence to distract him, and get on with a few chores around the house.

Throughout the morning, whenever I'm passing, I catch a peek of him still drawing. He has become his own sternest critic, ripping up anything that doesn't finish as it ought to. If the words are not correct, if an image does not quite do what he wants it to, they are

The Lion

Aslan

the Witch

nd the Wardrobe

evil
White
Witch

The
Lion King

Ready bed 9   Sleep

10   Sleep Well

~~my~~ David   lie in for me

Hot Milk Honey

The Lion King
Ending

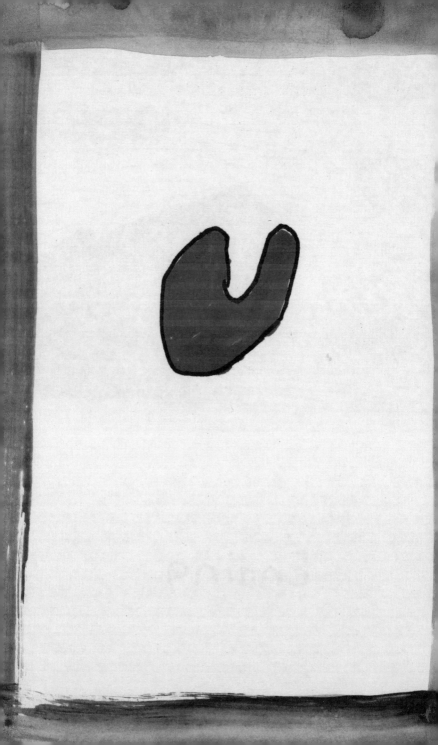

scribbled out and done again and again. He draws like this after lunch, into the afternoon and evening, pictures of his lions: Aslan, Mufasa, Simba. He relies on memory to recreate the scenes from the books or movies, those moments that they first strode into his imagination and came to embody everything that was safe and strong. He then shifts the focus of his drawings to the relationships that these lions have with others, Aslan with Lucy, Simba with his father Mufasa. More than any other image, he draws a single heart with a split down the middle. Over and over, a broken heart.

By the end of the day there is a small stack of A4 paper, inked with Reuben's inner world. What a beautiful, astonishing thing to have witnessed. I feel blessed. Although most of the images seem sad to my eyes, a huge weight has lifted because at least he is expressing himself. Reuben has been drawing who he is, all day. What precious things these pieces of paper are.

When he's finished, I collect them carefully from where they've spilled over from the footstool onto the floor, holding them as if they were rare manuscripts, felt-tipped hieroglyphics carrying deep secrets and distant truths. After all that, after all those pages and pages, there is only one A4 sheet that he hands me before he heads upstairs to bed. It's upside down again, but rather than wait for him to leave, this time I turn it over while he's still manoeuvring around the kitchen, making himself a mug of hot milk and honey. There are no words on this one. Just a single red heart in an ocean of yellow.

I'm in a hurry to call Portland Place before Anna arrives. I don't recognise the voice but ask if I can pop round later in the week. I give her a list of things that Reubs is asking for.

'Sure, I'll have a rummage in his room,' she says.

When she calls back thirty minutes later, the penny drops. I realise that it's Emma who's telling me there'll be a small box in his room with the bits she could find.

'I found the ring,' she says triumphantly. 'Everything else is in there, apart from his *Mrs Doubtfire* DVD. Can't find that anywhere. I've put a whole handful of other ones in there instead. And there's a box of his Christmas cards.'

'That's great, Emma. Thank you.'

'How is he?' she asks.

I'm surprised by her question. Although I don't know her very well, she is one of the good ones and I want to give her an answer. But I panic, I don't want to talk about our plans because I don't know what they are. What if she asks when he might be back?

'He's in a terrible state,' I reply. 'It's going to be a long road.'

She inhales a parcel of air, as if to start speaking but nothing comes out. There's so much more I could say in the space between. I'm not comfortable with the depth of our exchange, though, and am hugely relieved when I spy a van slowing in the lane and pulling in. Our food!

I say my quick goodbyes and rush out to help the man with our legion's supply onto the front step. The amount of boxes and bags looks obscene. I've tried to order as healthily as possible. Turkey fillets, bread, cheese, pastas, noodles, milk, yogurt, and then a whole crate of fruit and vegetables. Reubs is definitely craving sugar: fizzy drinks, biscuits, cakes, things he never really used to eat. But as a special treat, I've got a salted caramel tart and macadamia vanilla custard. Along with this van-load, Amazon drivers have been leaving boxes by the gate. I did try to resist but it's all so easy to order everything we need: Reuben's vitamins, sketchbooks, extra socks, loo roll, toothpaste, light bulbs, yeast and flour for baking bread. Yesterday afternoon, collecting a parcel became a half-hour task for Reubs. I'd much rather he was collecting eggs at The Corner.

I'm still unpacking and organising the fridge when a car pulls up, so I ask Reuben to get the door. As Anna steps into the cottage I can tell she's quietly soaking up the atmosphere, reading the mood of the house. I say my hello from the kitchen, leaving them to it. They greet each other properly in the living room, and the whole process from then seems to me quite sacred.

When I'm done in the kitchen I sit on the sofa watching them, still giving them space but able to witness Anna's exquisite gentleness as she sets the exercise mats on the floor. They both lie down, opposite each other, and she raises her hands and starts by flickering her fingertips, the wing beats of a butterfly. She's looking for a way in and waits until Reuben picks up on her gestures. Slowly, he begins to copy her movements. They shadow dance as the music begins to play – she knows what Reuben will connect with, those gentle or epic pieces from movie soundtracks. *The Fellowship of the Ring, The Shire, Concerning Hobbits*. She's looking for Reuben in all the places he likes to inhabit.

It makes sense to have a good accomplice. Someone who can help us through. Earlier in the week, I thought of calling Angie but the day centre was closed. Sam can't really do visits and is stuck at her home office. We can get Tommy Boy and Maxine on Zoom.

There have always been people, outside of our family, who have fought Reuben's corner over the years. Thinking back to the reasons we took Reuben out of care last time isn't easy, but over the last few days, remembering Pat and Zippy in Newbury, I've found it easier to admit that I can't do this on my own. I am too close to

Reubs. He needs to be able to trust someone other than his brother.

I emailed Anna and explained what had happened to Reuben over the last few months, and what was going on now. Could she help? She wrote back in minutes and we spoke on the phone. I was so relieved that she agreed to try again. She remembered Reuben from last September, when he joined her performing arts group. It was at around the same time that we rented Mum and Dad a place in town so they could help Reubs get settled.

When Reubs and I first met Anna, we liked her instantly. She's tall and striking and has an originality about her, and has this way of pausing just before she speaks, to make sure that the words come from a place of deep understanding. She kept her eye on Reuben after that first session, when he sat at the back with his coat and scarf and hat on, refusing to take part. She wanted to get through to him.

Here in the living room, she and Reuben are back together, converging on the senses – hearing, sight, touch – while I relax into the idea that I am not alone. They make eye contact, which Reubs finds really difficult at first. By holding his gaze, patiently insisting, Anna is able to ignite a flow between them. It's entirely beautiful to witness. It's as if they're both underwater, suspended in their movements. She has devised a sequence for Reuben to follow, putting his fingertips and palms together, then hands on knees and chest and face and head. Once he's completely engaged, she asks him to take the lead, so she can follow him. Such a simple gesture, but quietly radical. Nobody has asked to follow Reuben for years. Hardly anyone has ever asked him to be in charge. My mind casts back to a day we were walking on the Camino together, when Nathan and I went on strike and told Reubs he had to be the guide and we would follow. He was thrown by the whole plan at first. For most of his life, he has followed. Needless to say, we didn't cover much ground that day, travelling in Reuben Time as he deciphered the path.

Before Anna leaves, we share some quiet words and she looks at me with a deep stare of complicity. She *knows* Reuben. She has seen the video of him dressed as a nun performing at a gay bar in Spain – I showed it to her not long after we first met. She's also seen the photos of Reuben giving a speech in St Paul's, during the celebration to launch a map that he'd drawn for people visiting the cathedral. She's heard all about the karaoke performance at a pub in Berkshire. With one foot outside and her hand on the door frame she says, 'I will get him performing again.'

In that moment, I have every reason to believe her.

But after she leaves, as the hours pass, that telephone call with Portland Place starts to loom. Anna's warmth is eclipsed by a big, black cloud. Since being here, he hasn't once mentioned his room or his life there, except in passing to ask for his Frodo ring, *Mrs Doubtfire* DVD and other *stuff n things*.

Does he want to go back? Should I ask if he wants to?

I know he wasn't happy there. Every time I talk it over with Jack, we still both agree that what we're doing here, burning bridges, is best. Because we have pulled him from the house, we have to commit to his care for the foreseeable future. We both know that. But am I really ready? Can you ever be? As a Spanish resident, since Brexit, how long can I legally be in England these days? What about my work in Spain? What will I do here for money?

There are always more questions than answers.

I dig deeper into my convictions and remind myself of those feelings that drove me onto the plane, into the hire car, and along the motorways and country roads to that white house with its chipped white paint. I think about the text that Reuben sent me at The Corner, and I imagine him shut away in his room above the street, one finger desperately prodding out the message, one word at a time: *brother. do. you. love. me.*

I email Sam and ask her to serve notice on Portland Place. She does it straight away, without question or hesitation. She writes back to tell me, *It's done*. It's now official. They know he's gone. It wasn't just a holiday. Reuben has escaped for good. We have raised anchor, and all I have to guide us is a belief in the brotherhood that Reuben and I share. We are alone. We are never alone.

By mid-afternoon, between reading, writing and staring out of the window, I embrace the uncertainty of the day. I look over to Reuben, sitting opposite me at the table, wondering if the silent pulse of the cottage is affecting him as it is me. He's motionless, stoically gazing. During one of my glances, he starts working in his new sketchpad, using his old felt-tips. I put my book down so I can watch. When he's finished writing, he slides the pad across the table. Written in bright red, I read it twice before looking up.

What we do tonight brother

I'm about to speak but reach out towards him. He reads the gesture and passes me a green felt-tip. Below his question, I write another.

What do you want to do tonight, Reubs?

I twist the pad around and push it back at him. He scans the page, picks up his pen and starts to write back. I watch each letter emerge, blooming out of the white page, reading his reply before he turns it back to me. *Don't know something*

He passes the pad to me, I scribble quickly, not wanting him to lose the momentum.

DVD?

Well yeah we can. No Mrs Doubtfire DVD brother

Oh dear – What film then? Hook? Sister Act?

Surprise brother

How exciting!

Love you brother

Love you too

How much

More than Willy Wonker's chocolate factory

Something similar to a stifled laugh croaks at the back of his throat. That's the first true sound I have heard Reuben make since breaking him out of Portland Place. We both put the lids back on our felt-tips and smile.

Nettax
~~I with Folow Him~~

Film
Jister
~~Teope~~

Whoopi Goldberg
Oh Happy Day

love
you — brother

Robin Willams

Peter Pan

Hook

Mrs Doudtfrie

Mrs Doudtfrie
Ending

We step out into Annings Lane and lift our faces to harvest the warmth of the sun. 'Fresh air, Reubs. Shall we go all the way to Santiago?' He slaps my arm but barely makes a dent in my jacket.

'Grab my arm, Booba and let's find out how far we can walk.'

He stops in his tracks, grabs his ear and looks at me.

'Yes,' I reply. 'We'll play it by ear. Ear by here.'

He walks a little further and stops, repeating the tug of his ear. Did I just see a glint in his eye or was it a reflection of the sun?

'Yes, ear by here. But let's see how far we can go.'

I do everything I can to take his mind off the walk, pointing out things as we go, filling the quiet with whatever chatter I can think of. Before we know it, we're up and over the brow of the hill by the Dairy House and can see past the caravan park, almost to the sea. He stops and gestures towards the village sign, looking pleased with himself.

'I know. That was quick wasn't it. You see, we *can* do it. We can do it! We can do it!'

It's a line he knows from the musical *Kinky Boots*, which we saw together. He shows no reaction right now, but this line is for my benefit as much as his. Can we do it? I still think we can.

I call out the house numbers along Annings Lane as we walk, before taking the short cut through to the old mills on the Grove. This is my favourite part of the village, with its houses built with Forest Marble. When we reach St Mary's church Reuben stops, takes a photo on his phone and sends it straight to Jack.

'Angela, bless her. That was a year ago now. We have to make the most of every day. We only get one life, Reubs.'

He screws his face up, hopefully not because he disagrees but because he doesn't understand what I mean. I clarify, 'We're only here once so we have to live the best life possible.'

He shrugs.

'Oh, OK. So how many lives do you think we get, Reubs?'

He holds his forefinger up in the air.

'Exactly. Time is always getting on.'

Since Sam sent that email, now that it is all out in the open, I'm no longer worried whether I did the right thing by taking Reuben. But care is all about being surrounded by the right people: Anna and the speech therapist, Alice, have reminded me of that. Being able to live with Reuben like this, so closely, is a wonderful thing. But it is also extremely intense and difficult, more so because we're brothers. The emotional depth and personal history that I bring isn't necessarily the best way of caring in the longer term. That I know his routines and daily needs in minute detail, means I can anticipate his moods and read his emotions as they contour his face. I can also probably offer a strong perspective on how to motivate him, how to push and nudge him to expect more of himself. But brotherhood brings a whole layer of attachment and love that can sometimes complicate, not heal. I've tried to be more detached. I've tried to remove myself from him, but usually this comes across as being cold or angry or frustrated, which are truths I'm not so proud of. We're good at being together, most of the time. But we also need to learn to trust others. To help him find his place in this world, means I need to be able to live without being worried about whether he's eating properly or being stimulated enough, or whether it's wrong of me to live so far away.

We carry on to the Post Office, where there's a warm greeting inside from Viv as we enter.

'Hello there, Reuben. Alright?' She points below the counter. 'Look, we've still got loads of your cards. Selling well, they are.'

During my last trip here in the summer, when I probably should have taken him out of Portland Place, Angie and I managed to motivate him enough to design five festive cards, with the idea of raising money for the NHS. Angie helped him package them at the day centre, then distribute them to shops around town and here at the village stores.

'Your card, Reubs,' I remind him. 'They make a difference. People love them.'

His lips move inwards and he tilts his head to look at them, not making eye contact with Viv or me. There's a bit of a pause so I intervene before it gets awkward.

'Do you have any Mini Rolls?' I ask.

'Mini Rolls? No, but we've got Mr Kipling Angel Slices, right there on the round table, look.'

Reubs picks up a packet to inspect them but doesn't look sure – they're not Mini Rolls.

'We might be here for a while,' I explain to Viv. 'Is that alright?'

'Yeah, fine. Just move over there a little.'

We move to the side, leaving enough room in the shop for the next customer to get served. Reubs turns over the packet a few times, but eventually decides that Mr Kipling's will do. He also wants to buy some of his own cards. There's no point explaining that it really doesn't make economic sense, so instead I remind him there are some at the cottage.

'You can use the ones you've got at home?' I suggest.

I feel awful denying him the pleasure, but money is tight and will be getting tighter. His trust allowances are dwindling and my funds are far from buoyant. The bills at the cottage are OK, but Reubs is still having to pay out rent on Portland Place. Even when the three-week notice period passes, he will still be 'occupying the room' because they won't allow us to collect his belongings, not until he moves into another sheltered home or he officially lives with me. Until then, it's against the rules.

Santa Claus
The Movie

But I can't do it to him. He's walked all the way to the village. Of course he can buy a packet of his own Christmas cards. What was I thinking?

It takes an age for him to find his wallet and then tap the machine with his debit card, but this shop is a place of patience and he's so happy with his purchases. He can't fit both his Christmas cards and the cakes in his day bag, however, so I wait for him to work out what to do. Eventually, he hands me the cards and I pop them into the pocket of my raincoat as we walk out and head back towards Annings Lane.

On the way back, I attempt to spin Reubs while humming the theme tune to *Strictly*, but feel my dodgy back about to go so have to swap him from my left arm to my right, mid-spin, to avoid cramping up. The result is rather fumbled, and Reubs isn't impressed.

Up the last hill, past Dairy House, I push him. It's a trick I learnt while we walked the Camino. If I rest my fore and middle fingers very lightly right at the bottom of his spine, on the coccyx, and apply the gentlest pressure, he sails uphill at twice the speed.

When we reach the garden gate, I sing his praises.

'You did it, Booba. You walked the whole way.'

As I hug him, he leans and looks around my shoulder, back up the lane to retrace his steps.

Poem   <u>Brother</u>

emotional

I just Want let you
Know you mean the World
to me

And to have you as
a brother

I still feel very
motional Close to you

You always be my
brother ~~Plase~~

Brother are so Special
love you sleep well tonight

Aslan

My heart belongs
Sleep Well to you
brother
You Raise
Me up
Brother
emotional for
you

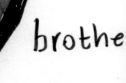

brothe

Boots

for
my
brother
Manni

Sleep Well

For got Ring

One DVD

Mrs Doudtfire

Potland Place

brother
love you

Paill

The Lion

Aslan

the Witch

and the Wardrobe

evil
White
Witch

The
Lion King

Ready bed 9   Sleep

10   Sleep Well

my David   lie in for me

Hot Milk Honey

The Lion King
Ending

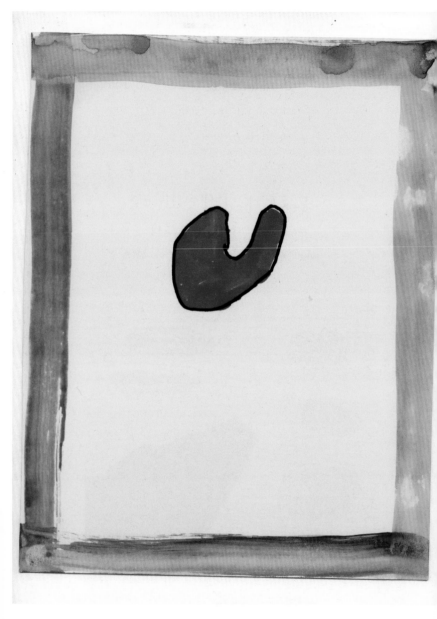

Film
Jister
~~Tape~~

Whoopi Goldberg
Oh Happy Day

love
you
— brother

brother loveyou

Robin Willams

Peter Pan

Hook

Mrs Doudtfrie

Mrs Doudtfrie
Ending

Santa Claus
The Movie

Brother's bench

6 m

8 m

What
a eveing

Sleep
well
family
love you
from

Happy New

Year
2021

Family

He's Dead
He Was My Friend
Fox eat Archi ~~too~~

Just
Celebrate
his life
brother

~~Peom~~

~~no one understands~~

Don't Worry
You got me

~~Poem~~
Peom

Spain

love you
Sleep wel
tonight

Love Will Find A Way

brother

am Sorry

Brother card

love you

When Sam shared the news that Reuben wouldn't be going back to Portland Place, the care provider got in touch to 'raise a concern' that I was moving Reuben against his will. One of the carers had reported the text message he sent to Mum, *my home dont want go mummy*. Finding out about this, Sam could tell me, the care provider had informed social services. They also mentioned that Reuben didn't always want to take my calls, and that they don't know why this was. There's now a question mark hanging over what we've done, and I feel sick. My head spun listening to Sam tell me all this.

Are they saying that I don't have my brother's best intentions at heart? If not, then it must mean my intentions are misguided. I feel in the wrong. Am I guilty of kidnapping my brother?

Sam reassured me that I was not guilty, and reminded me that Reuben was bound to be apprehensive about coming away with me. He's scared of change. He was scared of leaving the room he'd been a recluse in for months. If you mix fear with a generous helping of apathy, sprinkle it with depression and anxiety, ill health, muscle wastage, vitamin and mineral deficiency, any of us would be reluctant to do absolutely anything.

But how was he allowed to get like that in the first place? Isn't that the real question? Is it in his best interests to become a ghost? By raising the alarm, we have now entered a place of conflict, of right and wrong.

There is obviously genuine concern. Sam only sent the email to them a couple of days ago, and already this afternoon we are expecting a visit from Reuben's psychiatrist. Sam assures me that it's just routine, but the timing and the speed feels anything but routine. Maybe they will take Reuben back. Perhaps my plan, quite unintentionally, is doing Reuben harm. Surely it can't be just bureaucratic. Surely they can't just be covering their own backs. They must still care for Reuben too. Don't they?

I find the whole thing degrading to the core. I have tried to explain so many times, the tension between their concept of care and the life I know my brother is capable of living. In phone calls, on Zoom conferences, in person, in emails, in letters. Whatever the means, the point I'm always trying to make is the same: that man, filled with silence and sadness, is not the brother I know. He is not fine. He is not happy. He is not well. He is not living his best life, and to me that means that whatever decisions were being made – daily, hourly, monthly – were definitely not in his best interests. My decisions to fly in and take him away were probably rash and impulsive, and perhaps they were even wrong. But what's even more wrong is who he has been allowed to become. What other real choices did I have? He's my brother for fucksake, and I love him more than any other being. That anyone might suggest otherwise, winds me up. I feel as if I'm standing in the dock, accused of lacking love. What do I have to do to prove myself? Leave my partner? Leave my home? My friends? My life at The Corner? My work? Surely not, but that's what I've done because I think he was being damaged and sinking further and further away. I have the unyielding support of Jack, my parents, my brothers Nathan and Matt, Sam, Angie at the day centre, friends like Tommy Boy. But still there are people who sit on Reuben's committee of best interest who do not support my actions. I should have nothing to feel anxious about, knowing his psychiatrist is coming. Yet I'm shaken. He will be asking Reuben questions, but I am the one on trial.

By the time I hear a car pull up outside, I have had time to sweep, mop, straighten the cushions on the sofa, fold the blankets, wash up, take the recycling out and wipe down all the surfaces. It has to look like I'm on top of things, and completely relaxed. This is the kitchen of someone who is coping. Shit. I really should have shaved

Reubs. I didn't even think. That beard ages him fifteen years. At least he's clean.

I've exchanged emails with Dr Aaberg and seen him on Zoom, but today is our first meeting in person, and the tension I'm trying so hard to conceal winds down a notch because he's such a gentle person, with very polished manners. His car (Toyota Corolla), his clothes (grey dress trousers, white shirt, sleeves crisply folded back to the forearms), stout brown dress shoes (polished), his paperwork (individually filed and labelled RC), are all immaculate. Someone who looks after themselves so well can surely be trusted with Reuben's wellbeing, right?

Greeting him, I'm reminded of the first ever 'best interest' meeting we had. The whole committee was on Zoom. Dr Aaberg introduced himself and then turned his camera off because he didn't want Reuben to be stressed by so many faces on the screen. I was impressed by that gesture. It was considerate, and as we grapple with the gravitas of this moment, I tell myself to be patient with him, be calm. He's not here for me, he's here for Reuben.

In the living room, he turns to Reubs but before he can say anything more I interject, 'You might need to do this as written questions and answers. We've been communicating on paper.'

Dr Aaberg starts digging in his bag but I fish a sketchpad from the cabinet and put it down on the kitchen table for them. Reuben walks over to the sofa, sits down and pulls a blanket over his knees, ready to do things on his own terms. Dr Aaberg follows him and sits opposite, leaving just about the right amount of distance between them. He doesn't ask me to leave but I feel it is expected, so I retreat, trusting that Reubs will be able to express enough of his own truth.

Upstairs in my bedroom I try to read, but spend the time straining to hear anything but murmurs from downstairs. I start to get fidgety. It's an unnatural place to spend the afternoon. I leave it another ten minutes, check my phone, then can bear it no longer and head back down, moving through the kitchen quietly without making eye contact, busying myself with putting a coloured load in the washing machine, and then it finally comes, I hear Dr Aaberg say, 'We'll leave it there. Thank you for your time, Reuben.'

I come into the room as Reubs shuffles off. His work is done, and he looks tired from the strain. There are two sheets of questions and answers on the coffee table. I glance at them out of the corner of my eye.

Do you love your brother?
Do you like living with your brother?
Did you like living at Portland Place?
Do you miss Portland Place?

They are all fair questions but I can't stop my panic, hoping Reubs hasn't just derailed everything, and that despite the stress of it all, I have read correctly my brother's feelings and needs. Dr Aaberg starts talking to me as I glance at the answers.

'Yes'
'Yes'
'A bit'
He misses some staff.

What happens next is unexpected.

I'm asked to sit down on the opposite sofa, distanced but still close enough for proper eye contact. Dr Aaberg talks and I listen. He explains that Reuben seems happy to be here but that he also misses some elements of Portland Place, some of the staff and his room, his Aslan mural especially. He goes on to say that he knows Reuben has felt isolated before, and that he wonders if Reuben accepts that he has Down's syndrome, a question that completely baffles me. Then come two things that shatter the earth beneath my feet. First, he tells me that I shouldn't be over ambitious for Reuben's recovery, then continues by saying he thinks Reuben should go back to Portland Place.

I'm spinning as I try to grasp the wheel of his words, and am thrown back to that ginnel near Burley Park in Headingley, when four kids chased me and wanted to beat me up. The utter terror. I also feel the flames of anger rising, and glance over at Reuben's answers to make sure Dr Aaberg knows that I've read them and to see if they give any further clues as to how he has reached this conclusion.

I stutter, 'We need time. But are finding a way.'

Dr Aaberg is nodding and starts to shuffle his papers back into his bag, readying himself for an exit, pleased that we're so obviously in agreement. Nothing about what I've said or what I think is remotely close to an agreement.

'On the idea of his going back to Portland Place, Doctor. I'm sorry, but I left you and Reubs alone because I wanted you to hear Reuben's own ideas. Did he actually tell you he wanted to go back?'

'Not exactly. But he is not against it.'

'Right.' I pause inside the storm clouds in my head. I take a deep breath. I am not angry at Dr Aaberg, on the contrary, his approach to care is exemplary. I'm not necessarily angry with the carers at Portland Place. I am angry at *all* of it. I am furious with the care provider that runs the house, livid with their mismanagement. Dare I use the word neglect? It seems strong when it's written down or spoken, but my brother lived lacking: lacking in routine and responsibility, he lacked exercise and fresh air and sunlight. The care provider told me they were struggling to get enough staff, with three on-duty carers doing their very best for seven tenants. But their management of that particular supported living facility held my brother submerged and forgotten for months.

I remember one Saturday evening, only a few weeks ago, when Reubs sent me a WhatsApp saying, *Am Wish watch Strictly my TV.brother.love you brother.* I knew from experience that when Reuben eventually communicates a need, even if it is the need to watch TV, it means that he really is at the end of his tether. Confused, I wrote an email to the care home. *Is Reubs' TV not working?* The reply came back: *We encouraged him to watch and he said he couldn't. I spoke to D— yesterday, who I think tried to tune his TV.*

I was dismayed. How many months has he been there? Ten months? I didn't even think to ask. I just assumed somebody would have sorted it for him, so if he didn't feel like being in the communal lounge (which was often) he could at least watch his favourite shows. I wrote another email in rage and their reply came back with, *Had he asked us to connect his TV, we would have.*

That evening, they did have a word with Reuben and found out that, funnily enough, he did want his TV plugged in, and explained that if he needed anything else, that he should just ask. Nobody in the house could fix it, so in the end they called a technician to come out and take a look, but by the time the guy came, I had arrived on the scene and taken Reuben away. To rub it in, the other day I got a bill through the post, *Check for fault on television system – £45.60.* We had no choice but to pay it. I've been quietly compiling a whole host of similar complaints that I might need for a moment like this.

'Would you mind if we go outside to talk?' I ask Dr Aaberg.

Out on Annings Lane, in the cold of this early-December morning, I launch into an impassioned explanation. I have to set the record straight. As I speak, the words pour out of me. I don't need to concentrate because the dates, the facts, are unstoppable as they flow. I can sense Dr Aaberg's dismay. He came here upholding a process and a system, and was sent with a narrative that suggests the carers of Portland Place and the care provider know, more than I do, how to protect my brother and how to provide for him.

I glance up at Reuben's bedroom window and lower my voice, hoping he's not listening. I don't want him to hear how our family left him there, reassured and hopeful, with the promise of regular updates and assurances that the staff would uphold his diet, take him on regular walks, that the house was sociable and (when the group car eventually arrived) they would all go on regular excursions. They also said they'd spend time completing Reuben's activity books with him, and make sure he was washing properly. They would even take him for haircuts in town, make sure his nails were treated regularly; they would support him to live a happy, engaged and varied life; they were sure he'd love it there and stick to his routine and not spend too much time on his phone. It all sounded so promising.

As Dr Aaberg listens, I know that I have to say something about how it started positively and that I understand that, just five weeks after Reuben moved in, the world changed and how it was difficult for everybody, living through a pandemic. But as I start saying this, I realise that I'm not entirely convinced. Even under the circumstances, I am not sure that a failure of management and collapse of communication is in anybody's best interest.

'Do you agree with this?' I ask, turning the question back to Dr Aaberg. But only rhetorically because I can back this up by describing how my emails to Reuben's carers were often not even replied to. I was shielding like the rest of the world, desperate to be in touch, but try as I might, days would pass when every call, every email went unreplied.

'I'm sure the carers were too busy or too stressed,' I add. 'But all I wanted was assurance. At the very least, I needed to know that they were continuing to provide care for my brother.'

In the end I gave up trying to get hold of them. I still had limited direct contact with Reuben, and when the odd phone call to the house did get answered, the voices I heard on the telephone were stressed and anxious, and always had something else to do.

Of course, Reuben is just one person. His story is just an indicator – there are hundreds of thousands of similar experiences, where vulnerable people in care were left confused and alone. But what baffles me and bothers me is why people in different kinds of care homes and supported living facilities, throughout the UK, were left like this. It is supposed to be a profession of care. Why weren't the carers able to care?

I know from experience that the pandemic is not to blame – this isn't the first home I've taken Reuben out of. The cracks in the system were there long before, and they are going to get worse. I feel so let down, but it's Reuben who has suffered neglect. It's Reuben who was left in his room for up to ten hours a day, for how many months?

I tell Dr Aaberg about the one image that has come to define

Reuben's life in those last few months, taken by a local photographer who was documenting Lockdown. Mum and Dad had gone back to Norwich by then. I still couldn't leave Spain, so when I heard about Eddy's project I thought that some sort of connection, even from a stranger, would be better than nothing. I arranged for him to visit Reubs. At the time, there was strictly no contact allowed with anybody in residential care. Reuben was waiting by the window when Eddy arrived, and as he clicked away, skilfully and respectfully recording this quiet tragedy, Reuben raised his arm and pressed his hand against the glass.

Describing the image to Dr Aaberg, it begins to represent everything that can go wrong about the way we care. I start with the sash window, with its chipped white paint, divided into eight panes. The upper four reflect only the sky and a single power cable. Through the lower four, Reuben's torso inert behind glass, dressed in a pink T-shirt, black sweatshirt and scarf. His face is central in the panels as he peers into the middle distance. There is no focus to his gaze, his mouth hangs low. An upturned crescent moon. The lines in his hands are flattened, his fingerprints obscured by the glass. That hand tries to connect with a stranger. There is also a determination to his pose, and in the end there is a flow of respect in the image. Nothing robbed, nothing captured or taken away.

In the bottom half of the image, there are more telephone and electricity cables, criss-crossing the street, the untouchable spaces that Reuben and so many like him were severed from. He was kept inside for his own safety, but the toll it took on his mental health is incalculable. When Eddy emailed the picture, I instinctively right-clicked the mouse to search for similar images on Google. A whole host came back, all of them prisoners peering out from their cells.

When I stop talking, I can see that the light in Dr Aaberg's eyes has gone. He looks down at his shoes, thanks me and gets in his car. I am left on the lane with the echoes of my words blending with the birdsong as the noise of his engine fades.

I glance again up at Reuben's bedroom window and his face is peering back at me through the glass. Bless his little heart. Bloody hell. How must he feel? Being passed around like this, from pillar to post, from a brother to parents to carers, from a family home to supported living and back again. What does home even mean to him?

I have felt terribly guilty ever since the storm, since the panic attack, since that day when Reuben thought he might die. And although we have made many sacrifices to try and patch Reuben's wounds, I can't heap all the blame on Portland Place. It's so much more complicated than that. When I care for him, or when Jack took on his care single-handedly for an astonishing nine months, Reuben gets better. But he also regresses, quickly, whether he's with carers or when he lives with my parents – he adapts to their tendency to over-protect him, as any parent would, by doing less and less for himself.

But even with an army of support and love, Reuben still doesn't have a life of his own. He still doesn't have *his* home. For four years, our home was his. I thought he would stay with us all his life. Jack and I were certainly planning on it, but not being able to learn Spanish and our rural location were not ideal for a young man who needed to be out and about in the world, to feel the warmth of human connectivity. That isolation, the lack of professional care, the storm, his diagnosed thyrotoxicosis, his painful case of gout, the heat, the heart palpitations from drinking real coffee that morning – looking back they all contributed, I'm sure of it. He has been so incredibly brave.

I blow him a kiss at the window and wait until it lands in his understanding, and for him to react. Slowly, he blows one back and I catch it with a clenched fist. He raises his right hand to the glass and pushes his palm against it. I raise my hand to align with his, in a gesture we both understand.

*

Back inside the house, I stop myself from launching into a full blown analysis with Reuben. But as Dr Aaberg vanishes from our day, leaving us alone, there is one thing I know with absolute certainty: how Reuben sees himself in the world is just as important for him as it is for anybody else.

I ask Reuben to come downstairs and help me unroll a huge length of printer's card that our neighbour Terry gave us back in the summer. It's been sitting on the church pew in the kitchen for months, but now it has a purpose. On it, I draw circles overlapping with different coloured felt-tips. Reuben likes seeing me use his old pens as I label each circle with obvious opposites: tall or short, old or young, happy or sad. We start on the simple ones. I ask Reubs to write his name wherever he sees himself.

'Be honest, Reubs. Don't worry about what I might think. Speak from the heart.'

'Heart,' he repeats by placing his hand on his chest.

Life has displaced Reuben. The system, be it what it may, has failed him. His family is part of that system, whether I like it or not. He has fallen through the gaps. Does Reuben have a learning disability or do we have an understanding difficulty? We pathologise the condition but are too busy to listen. We fail to put ourselves in Reuben's shoes because we lack the imagination to empathise. The problem is not his, it is ours.

As he gets the gist of the exercise, I make the options a little more obtuse, and leave him to go through them sitting by himself on the rug in front of the log burner – I don't want him to be guided by the way my facial expressions respond to what he's writing.

He calls me back when he's finished.

'Well done,' I say glancing across the paper.

The revelations are mainly positive. He's not sad. He's only a little bit lonely. He isn't worried. But some answers are more complicated, like he doesn't want a relationship with a girl or a boy. 'Just need my family,' he writes in the circles. Then there is this: 'Don't have Down's syndrome.' That's the last thing he writes.

Dr Aaberg was spot on. Despite our different viewpoints, it was very sharp of him to ask if Reuben's sense of isolation comes from him not accepting his condition. And here it is, written in bold, red felt-tip.

In the 'Portland Place' circle, he hasn't written his name. Instead, he's put 'My bed there.'

'Look,' I tell him. 'We don't have to think about it for now. Let's just play it by ear. We're here for a holiday, and then let's see what the New Year brings, eh?'

He looks baffled at what I've just said. He should look baffled. I haven't talked to him about the next steps. I was trying to coax it out of him, objectively.

I smile, trying to make my face as reassuring as possible.

'Bruvr,' he asks. 'Walking will make me good sleep?'

'It will, my darling. You will have an amazing sleep.'

I am half-way into the kitchen before I realise that he has just spoken for the first time, with full voice.

2

Growing up with Reuben has taught me not to take life too seriously. From an early age, he learned to be teased by three older brothers with giggles and grace as we layered nicknames on him: Reubs, Booba, Boobs, Boobalicious, The Reubenator, Reuber Booba, Bond Reuben Bond, 0021, the list goes on. But we have never, ever crossed the line. We've always laughed with Reuben. And I believe we have a licence to be that way, because anything else feels contrived. Do you know brothers that don't tease each other? Why behave differently unless you want someone to feel different?

As boys, we even took advantage of Reuben being a 'special' member of society. Because he and his primary carer enjoyed free public transport, it meant we could drag Reubs into Reading town centre every Saturday without paying the bus fare. We called this 'playing the Reuben Card', and to this day his misspent youth in shops means he loves browsing any high street.

When we were flying to Marrakech, it was announced over the Tannoy that only the first forty passengers could carry their cases on board. I looked at the queue of at least sixty ahead. 'Right Booba,' I said. 'We're playing the Reuben Card.' He always knows what to do: the tongue comes out and his walk gets extra wobbly, and that day we skipped the queue and boarded with an elderly lady in a wheelchair and a mother with three young children. Another time, en route to see our brother Nathan, who lives with his family in America, Reubs and I stopped in New York for a couple of nights and decided to try for tickets for *Billy Elliot* on Broadway. The box office sold us 'limited-view' seats in the upper circle for $40 each, but when we walked inside it was obvious what we needed to do. We looked at each other and Reuben had a wicked glint in his eyes. Before we got to our seats, I stopped to talk to an usher.

'We've come all the way from London,' I said. '*Billy* is Reuben's favourite… The tickets were a gift… But he's forgotten his glasses…'

I had to swallow a giggle when Reubs decided, impromptu, to make himself cross-eyed. What else could the poor usher do?

'Wait there, just one minute.'

She returned with two tickets, row 13, centre stage.

High five Booba.

We all want to jump the queue or get upgraded seats. We feel special. We've got ahead of the crowd, we've beaten the system. But being special also means you're *special*, that you don't fit in.

This is why Reubs would be the perfect spy. He can walk into museums without a ticket. In airports, as well as being allowed to jump queues, he can also (more worryingly) get through security the wrong way. All spies are invisible, hiding in the shadows. Not Reuben. People notice him, how could you not? They see him – Reuben Bond, 0021 – and yet he's still completely invisible.

What does this say about how society responds – or doesn't know how to respond – to people with Down's syndrome? It can be fun, getting up to mischief with my brother, but I'd rather he was noticed for the right reasons. For being him.

Over time, I've shared these queue-jumping stories and more with siblings of people with Down's, and every time our exchange of anecdotes bring tears of laughter. They all have similar experiences. Not only are their siblings the glue that holds their families together, but they have also opened doors to countless adventures and unexpected, precarious journeys of learning and acceptance. People with Down's have an openness and warmth that most of us conceal, along with an innate sense of fun and truth that breaks through barriers, wherever they go.

Reubs is my best mate. I have always told him my secrets, and he always deposits them away safely inside himself, where nobody else can reach them. He also looked after me when I was in my twenties, during my first heartbreak, and again when one particular relationship took a very dark turn. Reubs never did like him. I got carried away with the excitement of opening a coffee house in Seville, with its classical quartet playing midweek and open mike sessions on a Sunday. I was the only one who didn't realise my partner was a compulsive liar and a cheat. Only when I was in hospital, with a record of cuts and bruises, did my courage outgrow my fears enough so I could walk away. Reubs was there to pick up my pieces, and to make me cups of tea.

'Don't worry, bruvr,' he reassured. 'You got me.'

Try as I might, I cannot accept that Reubs will not get better. Maybe time will prove me wrong, but until then I will fight with everything I have, alongside everyone else who loves him.

Most days in the cottage, it feels like Reuben and I are performing in a silent film. Hours pass with barely a sound, and then the soles of his slippers scratch across the floor, or my fingertips boom as I tap them against my skull. I don't think I could be here on my own, trudging through winter light.

Living remotely at The Corner, I'm convinced that Reubs felt lonely but didn't know how to explain it. He loved his brother and he loved his Samwise Gamgee. He loved his littew room and he loved his walks with Archi Boy to visit Anita. He loved it when the volunteers who worked on the farm invited him next door for lunch and dinner. He never asked for more, although I suspect that he was looking for a different kind of love.

In Andalusia, Jack and I took him along to an annual celebration hosted by a community organisation run by families of people with Down's. As we drove up to the venue, beautifully dressed sons and daughters and proud parents were making their way – all that was missing was the red carpet. In the ballroom, there was an explosion of affection and laughter as they hugged and complimented each other on how *guapa* or *guapo* they looked. I have never seen so much love in one place. Afterwards, we signed Reuben up to be a member of Down's Malaga and took him to more gatherings and events. We thought it would be good for him.

Diego, a dear friend who lives in Seville, has always had a soft spot for Reubs. Once he told me: 'It's not the fact he has Down's. The true barrier is language. We have a tremendous connection, but I can never follow it up by talking.'

A couple of the volunteers at Down's Malaga spoke English, but not one of Reuben's peers did, and he began to dread going. He was the person sitting in the corner, not wanting to take part. Something that should have been fun and inclusive, turned out to be difficult and alienating. Looking back, I realise how uncomfortable Reuben must've felt whenever we had our Spanish friends over for lunch or dinner at The Corner – because deeper levels of connection weren't possible, Reubs must have switched himself off.

There were signs of his unease, physical signs. During the winter, because he wore shoes or trainers, we hadn't thought to look closely at his feet. In the late spring, when he started dressing in sandals, we saw that one of his big toes was completely black. I took him straight into the local medical clinic for blood tests, and he was diagnosed with gout. Although Reueben seemed to welcome the attention his ailment brought – finally, these weird pains had a name – it was terrible that he wasn't able to tell us about it beforehand. How long had he been suffering? And all through that winter and early spring, he was still walking his 10,000 steps to the village and Anita's house and back. It must have been agony.

My mind has wandered all over the place these last few days, looking for someone or something to blame. I try to stop myself, but there is something cathartic in it, and perhaps a little sadistic too. After all, I have blamed myself more than anyone. I could keep pointing the finger at the neglectful care of Portland Place, or that first home in Newbury that Reuben went to as a young man. Wasn't it their job to care? I could blame the system. In the past, I might have blamed God. I have even blamed the heat and the fact that we lived in my idea of paradise, surrounded by olive trees and silence. While I'm at it, I could blame the fact that Reubs loves *gambas pil pil*, the spicy king prawns that became his staple until his gout flared up. Then I could go back to the beginning and round and round, blaming myself, my parents, or Reuben's inability or refusal to learn Spanish that kept him so isolated while the rabble of our friends laughed for hours under the fig tree in the garden.

Blame always looks backwards, I know that. And it never helps me understand how best to support Reuben. Yet here I am, still casting into the past, asking why? From the moment I woke up this morning, I have been walking back into the memory of that unusual late summer heat. *El veranillo del membrillo*, it's called. The little summer of the quince. The poetry of its name conceals how searing and suffocating the heat can be.

Our brother Nathan was visiting with his son, Seve, and we had driven to Antequera. I wanted to get Nathan and Seve up into the fortress, from where they could get a view across the ancient city and glimpse the dozens of towers and façades of convents and chapels and monasteries. Reubs didn't want to go any further. His foot was bothering him, he was waning in the heat. I found him a shady spot underneath a bougainvillea and gave him a bottle of water to sip while we were clambering the ramparts.

He seemed to have cooled off by the time we got back, although he was quieter than usual as we all walked to lunch. Nathan and I giggled and nattered our way to the tapas bar, as brothers do, in high spirits. I hardly noticed when Reuben grabbed my arm, just a little tighter than usual, steadying himself. We had just ordered a first round of food and hurried the drinks out when Reuben collapsed. He fell into my arms and towards the floor, hot, trembling, damp with sweat. It was a seismic panic.

'Don't want to die, bruvr,' he sobbed. 'Don't want to die.'

The other three at the table were up and out of their seats. The owner of the bar, Charo, who knows and loves Reuben, raced to be part of the human safety net. We became a bundle of limbs in a crowded restaurant, tangled in a confusing silence, all searching each other's eyes for answers, reassurance, something. We hadn't stopped Reuben from falling. All I can hope, looking back, is that we softened the landing.

I've no idea how long we stood like that, holding him until the trembling slowed. There were aftershocks, too, tremors that shook through all of us once he was able to stand up and breathe again. We held him tight, wiping away his tears. He was deeply confused about what had happened. He was so vacant. His eyes were like glass. Part of my brother had been lifted away, and whatever had replaced him had already worked into the deepest part of him.

Don't want to die brother. When did these doubts begin?

I haven't really heard my brother speak since that afternoon. Immediately after, he still tried to whisper and was often very lucid. Occasionally, there was even a glint in his eye that suggested Reuben was still there, not far below the surface. But weeks passed and nothing much changed. It became more apparent that we couldn't just leap back into the skin of our lives, with me busy with tourists and Jack needing to travel back to London for work. The stress was monumental. We didn't know what to do.

Jess turned her sheep out into the sloping field across the brook. They are a mixture of North Country Mules, Suffolk and Dorsets – and they are hungry. Rather than being allowed to roam at will, every few days Jess moves the electric fence to reveal a new corridor of turnips. Sheep are fussy eaters. If given the run of the field, they'd eat the parts they want and leave the rest. Instead, they are held in narrow strips of hunger that forces them to eat every last morsel of each plant. They are eating the field back to bare soil, their grey forms like powdery smudges on parchment paper.

I never know whether it's recycling or household rubbish, so Reubs waits to see what bins Jan wheels out before wrapping up against the elements, complete with his rainbow beanie. His movements outside are meticulous. Never have I seen bins so carefully positioned. I want to keep watching, but Sam rings and pulls me away from the window to answer.

'So you've read all of Dr Aaberg's report?' she asks.

'What a relief,' I reply. 'Complete U-turn from when he was here. He said things I didn't want to hear.'

'He only had one side of the story,' Sam reminds me. 'You did really well. You stood your ground. That can't have been easy.'

I don't know how to reply to this. Sam's right, it wasn't easy. And the days after, while I waited for the report to come through, were complete hell. The doubt was terrible. Even now, although Dr Aaberg supports us, being reminded of my depths of uncertainty makes me ill.

I try hard to consciously shift my head space before carrying on the conversation, 'He's got Reuben to a tee, though. He understands his isolation, and what he was saying about Reubs not identifying as Down's.'

'I'm sure getting him into a more mainstream situation will help. There is still a possibility of that other place in town. It's smaller. With people his own age, but with the same care provider.'

'I think we've burnt our bridges, don't you, Sam?'

'No, I don't think you have at all. We'd have to get a swap approved. There is a young lady there who could take Reuben's spot in Portland Place, which would suit her better.'

'I don't want anyone else to have an upheaval. Seriously. If there isn't a natural opening, I think we should just hold out.'

She pauses before adding, 'Remember that other place?'

'Where is it?' I ask her.

'Stourcastle.'

The name means nothing. She might as well have said the moon. 'Reubs won't be able to cope with another change,' I insist. 'He's just not strong enough. Not yet.'

'Then there might be a Shared Lives possibility.'

Shared Lives is a government scheme that connects people like

Reubs, who would benefit from a more mainstream lifestyle, with host families. These are people – single people, couples with kids, without kids, elderly couples – who have room in their houses and a space in their lives and their hearts for an extra person.

'Tell me more,' I urge.

'Her name is Becky. She's in Emminster. She's hosted before and is really switched on. She'd like to meet you both.'

'That's good,' I say, distracted by the back door opening and the appearance of Reuben. He's pleased with himself, I can tell, but he's holding back any real expression. He takes his beanie off.

'Did the bins,' he whispers.

I gesture towards the phone, telling him Sam sends her love. He smiles and I send love back on his behalf. I want to put the phone down so I can trot over and give him a big hug through the layers of his coat and hoodie and polo shirts, but Sam has one more thing to tell me.

'Remember, back in the summer, we applied for an allotment for Reubs? Well, he's been awarded one by the council. It's right by the river, on the new plots.'

'That's amazing.' I say across the room so Reuben can hear, 'Reubs has his own allotment!' But he looks bemused, not excited, so I elaborate, 'It means your own piece of land, brother.'

I thank Sam again for all she's doing, fighting Reuben's corner. I would be lost without her. 'And Jack will be back soon,' I add as a parting comment. 'Everything is better when we're together.'

After putting the phone down, I search through my emails for the number of the person at the council, to see if we can visit. I speak to a helpful woman on reception who promises to get hold of the gent who looks after the allotments, so we can make an appointment. 'He's usually down there on Wednesdays and Thursdays, after lunch,' she explains. Waiting for her to call back, a daydream of Reuben emerges in my thoughts: he's walking around the plot, making plans, harvesting vegetables, the proud custodian of a small piece of land.

If I don't speak, neither does Reuben. In the cottage, we are living in a persistent silence. There are days when I create a conversation, asking for nothing in return but gestures or drawings to chivvy along the chat. But there are days like today, when I don't have the energy. Silence becomes the default setting. It's not uncomfortable. It's just sad. It rips me in half not to hear his voice.

When he heads down the stairs for breakfast, clutching the bannister with his left hand and steadying himself against the wall with his right, I hold my breath for as long as it takes for him to reach me, but run out of air.

He's wearing that same old turquoise dressing gown – the highly flammable one that has come to symbolise his desperation at Portland Place. I wish he wouldn't wear it. Along with the scarf, I want to throw it all away.

'Morning, brother,' I say, wanting to stay chirpy. 'How are you?'

He replies as he usually does, holding thumb and forefinger close together. I could slide a feather through the space between. At least we start the day with a hug.

He turns away to line up all his pills on the breakfast table. He then slides open the cutlery drawer – his hands move so slowly that it looks like he's trying to play knife and fork Jenga, delicately removing two of each without displacing any others. In jest, I move just as slowly while opening the fridge, placing the milk, opening a cupboard, settling the jam on the table. He tuts at me and I can still just about hear his voice, thin and rasping as he speaks, 'Bruvr.'

During the ritual of taking his pills – vitamin E, vitamin C, calcium, multi-Vits, D10, Astaxanthin, folic acid, Fluoxetine – I realise there are only eight pots, not nine.

'Reubs, one's missing. Where's your vitamin D?'

He ignores me, carries on swallowing pills.

'Reubs, where is your vitamin D?'

He's definitely choosing to ignore the question.

'Don't you want to take it?'

He shakes his head.

'Why not, Booba?'

He shakes his head again.

I quiz him and he mouths the letter D.

'D?' I ask, trying to read his eyes.

It takes a little while to dawn on me, and when it does I don't know whether to laugh or cry.

'Are you serious?'

I'm angry at first, confused. But saying it out loud makes me giggle, 'Do you really think the D is for Down's?'

He nods, looks down at the table and whispers without looking up, 'Well, yeah, bruvr.'

His entire body slumps. I realise my laugh was wrong and far too loud. I move around the table and bring him in close to me.

'Reubs, darling, it doesn't have anything to do with Down's. Vitamin D is what we get from sunshine. It makes us happy. And anyway, there's nothing wrong with who you are.'

He rubs his chest above his heart, moving his hand in clockwise circles, before standing to walk across the kitchen. He opens one of the drawers, moving the tea towels out of the way to reveal where he's hidden the tub of vitamin D.

Reuben and I flew back to the UK together a few weeks after his collapse in the restaurant. It was the summer of 2018. We were heading over for Mum and Dad's fiftieth anniversary celebrations, but Reuben was profoundly unhappy. Everyone was shocked by how empty of joy he was. As a family, we decided he should stay with Mum and Dad in Norwich for a while, to give him – and me – a break. But I think we all knew it wasn't just a holiday.

Not long after I left him, a local GP saw Reubs and prescribed 50mg of the antidepressant Sertraline. He assumed Reuben must be depressed, and no doubt he was. Those 50-mg-a-day did the trick alright, pushing him so far into a marsh of tiredness and apathy that he wasn't able to have any existential thoughts at all. It was at around the same time that he started layering his clothes, one garment on top of another. Mum and Dad, like any parents, wanted to protect him. They didn't want to confront these mental shields and didn't see that it was harmful, so long as Reuben was comfortable and felt safe.

When Jack and I went back to see Reuben in the autumn, we were shocked to the core. Being with him every day, my parents witnessed his decline but didn't notice his deterioration. One of Mum's cousins, Ken, had kindly driven Reuben down to London from Norwich, so my parents could have a breather and he could spend some time with us. I had unpacked and arranged some of the things I'd brought with me from his room at The Corner, but forgot all about them when Reuben walked gingerly through the door. He was wearing a coat and woolly hat indoors, with an inflated travel pillow wrapped around his neck. He was supporting himself with Granddad's old walking stick. Always the joker, we thought it was Reuben's act to make us all laugh. The smiles slid from our faces when Ken shot us a look to tell us it wasn't meant to be funny.

We kept Reubs close for the first few days as we tried to peel away his layers. I hid his travel pillow, Jack tucked the stick behind the door. We both worked hard to breathe fresh energy into his days. He had changed so much. Most of it was an uphill battle. Then one morning, unprompted and completely out of the blue, Reubs pushed the Sertraline to one side and refused to take them.

'Make me feel funny,' he whispered.

'What do you mean, they make you feel funny?'

His reply was resolute, 'Don't want them.'

The NHS guidelines tell us that antidepressants should be administered with therapy, yet they so often aren't. Reubs, at this stage, certainly hadn't been offered therapy. None whatsoever. Resources are stretched, I get it. But why are pills a first option rather than a last resort? Surely, we should try non-chemical first? Or at the very least combine pills with therapy, with the emphasis always being on openly talking about the causes. These pills (SSRI, or Selective Serotonin Re-uptake Inhibitors) don't seek out the causes, they muffle the symptoms.

Perhaps caring has become too risky and expensive. It's so much quicker and cheaper to hand out antidepressants. *Here, take these and let's see what happens.* That's the norm, even though all the people I've met who have been involved in Reuben's care know that other avenues should always be explored before pill-popping. Despite how low he was, he independently decided to stop taking them. He wasn't enjoying the drug swamp.

In the weeks we spent back in England with Reuben, it was clear to Jack and me that being with my parents wasn't working. Reubs had vanished even further. Something had to change. What could we do? We talked about him coming back to Spain, we talked about him staying with Mum and Dad, so long as he was actively engaged in building a life of his own. Nothing was quite right. 'What about London?' Jack suggested. 'I'm working there so much.' It sounded completely mad, living apart so Jack could look after my brother, but when we started to break down how it might work – the days and weeks we'd be apart, the to-ing and fro-ing of a long-distance relationship – we started to realise that it wasn't hugely different to how we already lived. Jack was away in London for weeks at a time sometimes, while I was on the farm or busy running tours. If I met them every other month, either in London or at the cottage on Annings Lane, we wouldn't actually be seeing each other any less. But it would make a huge difference to Reuben.

In February 2019, Frodo moved to London to be with his Samwise Gamgee. Gandalf the Grey stayed in Spain, and so it was that my two hobbits began nine months together, organised into tight systems of routine and activity. Twice a week, a carer would come to the house to spend the day with Reuben (one of them looked like a Pied Piper, one of them rarely appeared on time, one of them was lovely, but then got a new job and moved away). Every Wednesday, Jack took Reuben to his workplace, and the atmosphere in the office changed. Somebody would always take him out for lunch if Jack couldn't, and Reubs had his own desk. That's when he was at his brightest. He felt like a cog in a wheel and immediately started to improve. He would spend the day colouring or completing pages from his activity book. Jack told him it was vital work, which was key for Reuben. Creating this purpose is not deceitful. It's love.

There is no greater love, in fact, than shielding somebody from the thing that causes them pain. We dilute the truth. We create an alternative universe, a place where Aslan and Mufasa roam and look out for him. Of course, Reuben shouldn't have to compensate for being himself. But the world isn't like that, and never will be. We have to create these safer places in the imagination. So what if Reuben genuinely believes that Jack is his Samwise? So what if he lives in a borderland between reality and fantasy? The landscape in Reuben's head is one of the best places on Earth.

After nine months, Jack's effort to look after Reuben without me took him to the far edges of resilience. Living for Reuben, not yourself, takes its toll physically and mentally, as I am finding out again now. Jack's relationship with me suffered because he was away, and I was having a difficult time at The Corner, coping with volunteers and the amount of circuit tours I was guiding around Andalusia.

At the time, tourism was booming in Spain, and I was driving hundreds of miles a week to Jerez or Granada or Cordoba, keeping clients happy with boozy lunches before taking them to Marbella. Most days, I was too exhausted to think about Jack and Reubs. All I wanted to do was crawl into bed. One Thursday evening, having been up since six in the morning and driven close to four hundred miles, I fell asleep at the wheel. The hum and thud of tyres woke me up as the car drifted out of the motorway lane. I pulled over, my heart racing. Something had to change.

I am so proud of Jack for those months. He was determined to get his Frodo Baggins back, and he did. But in doing so, Samwise Gamgee wore himself out. Inevitably, reluctantly, Jack had to hold his hand up and say he couldn't do it any more. He was exhausted. We reacted quickly and asked my parents to temporarily move to the cottage on Annings Lane, so Reuben could live with them until we found him a placement in sheltered housing. That's when Portland Place popped up on our radar. Because he was already familiar with the town, staying there made sense.

The gent with the keys is waiting for us at the entrance to the allotments. With a string of appointments to get through, he's in a hurry to show us the plot this morning, and although we were here before him, I don't think he can quite believe how slowly we move through life.

We walk over to the far end and he unlocks the fenced-off area next to the river, just as Sam had described it, a rectangle of land measuring 6 x 8 metres. Clipboard in hand, the gent explains the rules. 'A tool shed is allowed. No other constructions apart from plant and vegetable supports.'

Reubs pulls on my arm and whispers in my ear.

I nod and turn to the man.

'Is he allowed a bench?' I ask.

'I don't see why not,' he replies. 'You'll need to speak to your neighbours to agree on the best spot.'

We look around, half expecting to see a buzz of activity.

'It's winter,' he reminds us. 'You'll not see many of them for months.' He turns and addresses Reuben, 'I hope you enjoy your allotment, young man.'

I'm glad of this distraction at the allotment. We were wet but happy when we arrived in Emminster earlier, hopeful I think. Sam had arranged for Becky from Shared Lives to meet us in the café, and straight away we liked her. She was fun and chatty, and has been a host carer for years. She loved Reuben and had her head screwed on in just the way we like. In a half an hour, we exchanged the stories of our lives. It felt like we were speed dating. We told her so much, and found out so much about her. We even told her we were off to the allotments afterwards, to see Reuben's plot, and she told us about a shed manufacturer on the edge of town.

We hover by the plot as the gent hurries back to his car, taking it all in. 'Reubs!' I cry. 'Check you out!'

He holds his hand out flat and pushes his fingers downwards in a flapping motion – he's telling me to calm down. Quite right, too. This is his place, I have to behave myself. I keep my mouth shut and give him time to explore. He starts to circumnavigate the edges, planting his wellies firmly on the grass, stopping occasionally and tapping his temples, as if he has an idea. He looks taller, as if a sense of ownership is affecting the way he's standing.

I didn't understand why I left Emminster with such a hollow feeling. It had seemed like everything was falling into place – we liked Becky, she liked us, there was space in her home for Reuben. We thanked her and Sam for meeting us, and told them we'd all be in touch again soon. It all seemed so positive. But being here at the allotment, watching my brother dreaming in his own garden, I am no longer sure that being in another person's home is the right thing.

Reuben moulds himself to whoever is looking after him – isn't it what we all do, to fit in? That's what happened at Portland Place and with Mum and Dad. It's what happened in the months of living with Jack – it seems unthinkable now that every Wednesday he was always up and dressed and ready for the office at 7.30 a.m. He was also eating well, exercising regularly, and felt needed.

Mum and Dad's life, on the other hand, has a different pace. When he lives with them, Reuben slows down and becomes the child-son of his parents again. He starts calling them 'Mummy' and 'Daddy'. He also goes to church, praying and following in his father's footsteps. When Reuben moved back with them in

Norwich, his gay flag disappeared.

As his brother, I have tried and often failed to find ways of life for Reuben where he can be himself. A couple of years before we met Jack, when he lived with Debs and I in Marbella, Reubs worked as a volunteer in a restaurant (although our friend who ran the place had to let him go because he was eating his body weight in tapas every shift). Then in Torremolinos, he became a member of a gym and went by himself on Mondays, Wednesdays and Fridays to walk 3km on the treadmill. He also used to go shopping by himself, catch buses on his own. He was out there, living his life independently. But being with Mum and Dad didn't work. And I suppose you could say it didn't work with Jack in London either, not for long enough. While you're at it, you could add that being at The Corner for four years was a failure too.

It all depends on how you judge the 'success' and 'failure' of Reuben's many lives. Perhaps each one is just a means to an end. But that assumes there is an ending, a settled, happy place at the end of the rainbow. At the moment, I don't know what that ending is. I do know it's not with Mum and Dad any more. He's too old for that. And it makes me feel sad to think it, but that life is probably not with Jack or me either. Becky could be the answer – she's very experienced and obviously incredibly caring. But as Jack and I both know, dedicating yourself to Reubs is a complex responsibility, and I just don't think moving into her space is the answer. What Reuben really needs is a place of his own.

On the drive home, we make for the beach and become two among the few who are brave or mad enough to be out there as the rain picks up, hunkering into our jackets as we dip fish and chips into tartar sauce and ketchup.

Reuben pecks at the batter and mutters, 'Arf,' as he folds half his fish and chips back into its paper. We thank Liberty and Nathan at the restaurant by waving to them from the cliffside lawn and begin our saunter down to the beach.

'Did the mushy peas give you a boost?' I ask, preparing Reubs for the walk ahead. 'If we go faster, we'll get back sooner.'

'How?' he asks, more with his eyes than with his voice.

'Because it won't take as long if we walk quickly,' I explain.

He asks faintly, 'Bruvr, did have luffly day?'

'The day's not over yet, Booba.'

We stop on the path before reaching the beach and hug.

I don't care who's watching. I don't care who might be sitting in their car, wondering who we are. Reuben's fingertips stroke my shoulder with the tenderness of a man who understands love. Yet so much love passes him by. He barely has the chance to express it. Perhaps letting him love me is the best medicine of all. We linger in the wind, on a cliff by the sea.

'Emotional,' Reubs says.

I take his half portion of fish and chips so he can link onto my arm. I set an even pace but he drags behind like a bike with its brakes on. I try the other technique and lay my fingers on his coccyx, pushing him gently forwards. When we get to the beach, he wants to take a photograph of the crashing waves.

'For my Samwise Gamgee,' he says, snapping away.

'I miss him too, Booba. A lot. You'll see him soon.'

'I hope.'

Watching the waves, my thoughts turn inwards, wondering how it will be with the three of us when Jack arrives.

Reuben keeps taking photos, hundreds of them before turning his lens on me. I strike a pose which makes him grin.

'By the way', I remind him, 'it's Reuben's turn to make pudding tonight.'

Back at home, settled in the living room, I watch an entire episode of *Ru Paul's Drag Race* while Reubs prepares and then delivers a slice of lemon tart with a heap of ice cream. He's scratched 'love you' on top using the prong of a fork.

I eat up before the letters melt.

'And remember,' I chant to the TV, copying Ru Paul's catchphrase. 'If you don't love yourself, how in the hell you gonna love somebody else? Can I get an A-MEN?!'

I don't get an AMEN back, just a roll of the eyes.

I switch off the TV and we finish our pudding in peace.

Before Reubs makes his hot milk and honey, he gathers his night bag and slides over to me, his slippers crunching on tiny pieces of grit on the floor. He hands me an A4 sheet, face down as usual, and plants a sloppy kiss on my cheek. He moves off more slowly than usual, I suspect because he's overfilled his mug and doesn't want to spill any on the stairs.

When I can no longer see him, I turn over the page and study the secret garden he's dreamt up for his allotment.

6 m

Brother's bench

8 m

'It will make you have an amazing sleep,' Jack tells Reuben, trying to convince him to go for a walk. 'All that fresh air. So good for you. Let's go and find Middle Earth, Frodo.'

We bundle up against the cold and head east along Annings Lane, in the opposite direction of the village. Reuben stops even before we're through the garden gate. I know what he wants to ask: *how far?*

Jack arrived late last night and already I'm starting to feel the weight of worry lift. For the time that he's here, I don't have to carry the full brunt of Reubs's welfare. We can discuss things properly and take it in turns to stay upbeat and positive. Most importantly, I can share my fears and keep checking in with him. I still need to be reassured that I've done the right thing.

They stop in the lane so Jack can bend and tie Reuben's shoelace. From a distance, the scene looks so tender. Seeing them together after all these weeks gives me joy. They could be brothers or a father and son. But that's not who they are. They're friends. They're hobbits. And they care about each other deeply.

From the moment they met, Jack and Reubs hit it off. It was December, 2014. We were on a plane from Malaga – Debs, Reubs and I, heading back to spend Christmas with Mum and Dad in Norwich. I had the seat next to Jack, and clocked his Alexander McQueen boots and his sheepskin jacket. When the three of us clustered around him, Jack remembers thinking, 'Oh no, some dodgy couple and their Down's syndrome son.' But curiosity got the better of him, and two-and-a-half hours later, he knew all about us, starting with the fact that Debs and I were only friends and that Reuben was my brother.

He was drawn to us. Drawn to something he'd never known.

When we landed, Jack stayed behind to accompany Reuben through passport control. I felt bold and gave him my number as we said goodbye. 'Good to meet you, Simon,' I said.

'The name's Jack,' he replied before merging into the Christmas crowds at Arrivals.

Jack and I had both reached that stage in our lives when we knew what we *didn't* want, and it was obvious to us both that we were meant to be together. But before things got serious, I had to tell him that I was scared that he'd walk away, like others had done before him, because they couldn't handle a relationship with three people in it.

'You do realise,' I said. 'If you and I are going to make a go of this, then it's not just me.'

'I've known that from the very beginning,' he replied.

Every few hundred metres, Reuben keeps stopping to mark out the same question: *how far?* Jack motivates him by cutting the walk into intervals, setting a new destination after each short pause. Let's walk to that oak tree. Let's walk to that farm. Let's walk to that gate. After we cross the field, Reuben leans into Jack. He really doesn't want to carry on. I close the gap to help.

'You can't stop here,' I say.

'Am done,' he mouths without sound.

'Come on, Reubs. We're more than halfway,' I lie, pointing into the distance. 'Going forward is the quickest way home.'

I need to be gentle. Anything too pushy or radical or rushed will throw him off kilter. Jack stays neutral, careful not to intervene.

We had a big chat last night, after Reubs had gone to bed. He respects the routines I'm trying to find, the everyday challenges that arise. He has done it, too, so he knows what it's like. We agree that Reuben is locked away behind a series of doors, and that every activity – the walking, the promise of an allotment, even having breakfast and brushing his teeth or asking him to wash the dishes – could be a key.

'It's about making decisions for himself,' I concluded to Jack. 'Because everything was done for him at Portland Place, the layers have been stripped away. Basic skills. Choices. Opportunities. He was disintegrating.'

Not one to gush with praise or approval, it was just too soon for Jack to say whether he thought my thinking was right or wrong, and his trip isn't going to be long enough for him to get too involved. But being able to offload is good for me, and Jack is always quietly encouraging. He doesn't have the answers. Nobody does. It's obvious that I'm feeling delicate and he nourishes me with titbits of positivity. I know he'll worry when he leaves Reubs and me after Christmas. But for now there are these paths to enjoy, this sunshine on our faces.

At the edge of the wood, before our long homeward stretch, I reach a stile and stop. I turn around to see Reuben and Jack dappled with sunlight, and I know they'll be exchanging whispers and gestures about Ents and trees that uproot like Tolkien has them in *Lord of the Rings*. Jack follows me over the stile in one stride, but Reuben stands peering at the insurmountable hurdle in front of him. It's a tricky stile to negotiate, but Jack and I don't need to consult each other to know what to do.

Reubs stands, stares, carefully considering. He shakes his head – the rise and sharp fall of the stile is too much. He stays put and takes off his rainbow beanie, preparing his surrender. He's beginning to panic, to overheat.

Jack and I agree that Reuben needs to rediscover his ability to choose. Shall we go right or left? To the lane or across the fields? Brown toast or white? Elderflower or lime cordial? Shall I go over this stile? Usually, when I ask him these simple things, he just shrugs. He wants to know what *I* think. It's almost as if he doesn't care or doesn't want to care. These gestures are the most frustrating.

Jack approaches the stile calmly and runs through the possible manoeuvres, touching the wood with his mittened hand to show Reuben where to place his feet. Reuben's tongue protrudes and he swallows hard. He knows I'm watching but refuses to make eye contact. I turn my head away, not wanting to put more pressure on by staring, but keep being drawn back. It becomes agonising to watch, yet there is absolutely no reason for Reuben to be afraid. There is no danger here. No doubt the muscle wastage has weakened him, but he can do this, he's more than capable. To help him would be to deny him. This one stile, made out of ash, at the top of Jess's sheep field, stands in front of Reuben like a kingdom of possibilities and failures. He can choose to tackle it, or he can choose to stay separated from us. Home beckons. The log burner is lit. Soon, he'll be able to prop himself up on a big yellow cushion with nibbles and his sketchpad. I could be home by now, with the kettle on.

He rises slowly, meticulously putting both hands and feet on the steps and posts. He begins shifting and hauling his weight, balancing on the highest step. As his feet find the other side, he expels air and tilts his body in a gentle arc downward, then lets gravity do the rest, pulling his feet to solid ground, reconnecting with the grass and his family.

The only way to describe the look in his eyes is to compare it to a rainbow. He did it! He climbed over his fears, and for just a few wonderful minutes he forgets himself. He loops his hand through Jack's arm for the final downhill and doesn't notice that he's walking at our pace. Two hobbits, Frodo and Samwise, followed by Gandalf the Grey. I just about catch Reubs saying, 'We get all warm. Cosy for nipples,' and then Jack's reply, 'That's right, Frodo. All cosy with nibbles.'

When Jack was still the full-time carer for Reubs, just after we had made the decision to move him down to Portland Place, the first job on our list was to contact social services. After several phone calls with administrative departments fielding our requests, we were put in touch with the Adult Learning Centre and assigned a social worker called Eleanor, who chatted through all the paperwork with saintly patience. At this point, Reuben was given a case number and was referred to as 'RC' in paperwork – from then on, the emails became encrypted for privacy and we were sent codes so we could access confidential documents and web portals.

I remember explaining how concerned we were for Reuben's future and the supreme effort it had required from Jack to keep him from becoming completely submerged by his fears. The psychologist who assessed Reuben, along with his GP, suggested we put him back on antidepressants, 20mg of Fluoxetine this time. Jack insisted, 'Frodo is not depressed!' It was almost a year since Reubs had taken himself off Sertraline, and I agreed with Jack but didn't know what else to do. I felt desperate and – stupidly – ignored Jack and listened to the medical advice.

In this language of medical correspondence, RC was already anonymous and was starting to lose any sense of community and place in the world. Reuben loved walking down a street with people saying hello. By agreeing to the pills and the medical intervention, I was complicit in a process that muffled my brother's thoughts and personality, and took him out of that high street, so people could no longer stop and say hello or throw him a wave to acknowledge his existence.

I tried to balance out the medication by plugging him into the local community, and it was heartening to discover all the activities and support groups around the town. Eleanor put us in touch with Angie at the day centre, and from there we found a creative club called Bumblebees that met up regularly around town and out in the surrounding countryside. Then there was the Friendship Club that got together every month at a coffee shop, and another organisation called Speak Up! that helps people build their social confidence. It was thanks to this network that we found our way to the lovely Anna, who ran performing arts sessions.

To discover all these people and different groups, most of them stitched together by volunteers, made me feel more relaxed about settling Reuben into Portland Place. Taking him round, I started to see a way for him to create a social life for himself. In rooms filled with like-minded people, I was seeing his tribe right there, sitting on chairs and huddled around tables. But Reuben wasn't really interested. The Fluoxetine didn't help, I'm sure. Yet it was more than that. Something was holding him back, and it can't have been the language barrier this time.

Reubs must have always struggled with accepting Down's syndrome. It's so obvious. Anybody would. Yet why did it take Dr Aaberg to remind me? He could see it, even if I didn't want to. Thinking back, I do remember Reubs returning from school and locking himself in his bedroom because somebody had said something cruel in the playground. I can't remember how old he was, but obviously old enough for the other children to notice difference. After a while, Reubs opened the door with the most difficult question any son could ask his father.

'Why do I have Down's syndrome, Dad?'

How on earth do you answer that?

Dad thought for a moment.

'I know it's hard for you, Reubs. Your family love you just the way you are. You are a gift. But you won't have Down's syndrome in heaven.'

I still really struggle with what Dad said to Reubs that day. It planted a false hope that for years has bewildered me. In retelling it now, I recognise this myth-making for what it is: a story of evasion. And I'm guilty of the same. Aren't we all? This is what we do, time and again, shape make-believe worlds to avoid the pain. Because the truth can be so painful, we have created myths that cast Reubs as something he might never be. No wonder he would rather live in Narnia than our world. I would, if I was him.

But in trying to protect him, is it wrong to nurture fantasy and escape? In conversations with Dr Aaberg (and in the report that I was so terrified to read), he said that Reuben recognises that he has Down's syndrome but does not see it as something positive, and that his reluctance to accept himself would inhibit recovery.

Over the years, I have heard Reuben say many things that reflect this truth. 'I'm Downs inside, but not outside.' 'Down's people have different faces. I got a normal face, bruvr.'

This rejection of himself is completely understandable. But the self-escape may have also caused him harm, because now he rejects people who could become friends. Even though Reuben went to a school for 'special needs', he always related to his teachers more than his classmates. Having us three older brothers, he was always surrounded by our friends. Then his life with us in Spain unwittingly provided a scaffolding for Reubs to shield himself from his reality. I'm convinced that if he could find one friend, just one, then it would help him hugely on the road to self-acceptance. I am also convinced that being loved – not by me or Jack, not by Mum or Dad – by someone we haven't met yet, he would find it easier to look at himself in the mirror. But when I was taking him to all these wonderful clubs and meeting groups, he just wasn't strong enough to engage and start seeking out friendships. He was too fragile. Too bunged-up with Fluoxetine. So many of life's opportunities are dependent on timing, and this was simply not the right time for Reubs.

I did keep plugging away with him, until one evening I drove him to a tenpin bowling evening organised by a different group he hadn't been to before. I parked the car by the harbour and we walked into the town centre. I realise now how tough it must have been for him, how uncomfortable he must have felt, being somewhere he didn't want to be, with people he didn't know or trust. I introduced myself and gave Claire, one of the carers, a little of the back story. A young guy called Steven recognised Reubs from the day centre and came over to say hello. They fist-bumped.

I left him to it and strolled along the empty beach, peering in at the warmth of the Royal Hotel and admiring the Victorian seat shelters along the promenade. It was too cold to sit outside, so I stepped into The Ship for a pint and a fish finger cobb before heading back to collect Reubs. He seemed pleased to see me.

'Did you have fun?' I asked.

'I did, bruvr,' he whispered in my ear as I hugged him. 'Did get strike, bruvr.'

'Did he?' I asked Claire over his shoulder.

'Yes!' she replied whilst shaking her head.

I thanked her. I thanked them all. I hope they realised how grateful I was. It must have been that night that Ruebs sat down and wrote in felt-tips, *Steven did say hello to me. He is a bit friend.* He didn't tell me that. I doubt he told Steven or Claire. Reuben's way is to write himself down. He's more himself on the page. The only reason I found out is because the piece of paper he wrote it on was crumpled into his trouser pocket. I took it out and unfolded it before the ink and paper went through the wash.

Dawn is winter blue. It feels like a gift, so Jack and I embrace it with a walk into the village, and after the triumph of Reuben clambering over the stile, we've decided not to pressure him into coming with us. It's his turn to decide. If staying at the cottage is what he wants to do, then he's free to make and live in his decision.

Stepping out, the light glistens on the icy grass and our conversation is about loved ones far away. We are enjoying each other's company but skimming over the surface. We both know my emotions are running fast with the river. I feel safer in the shallows with Jack, but I can't suppress my thoughts for long. I start telling Jack about Alice, the speech therapist, who explained how Reuben opens an individual box in his mind when he unfolds a word and builds his sentences. Jack imagines Reuben's thoughts as willow seed drifting on a spring day, always floating out of reach. I then move our conversation on to the recurring question of the antidepressants.

'Do you think they are numbing his mind?' I ask Jack. 'Taking the edge off his ability to react?'

After we circle back to the cottage, all the freshness and hope that this clear, still morning has lent me, vanishes when I find Reuben still in bed. It upsets me seeing him there. I leave Jack downstairs and don't even try to stop the anger rising, 'For goodness' sake, it's Christmas Day!'

I pull the quilt away from him and know immediately that my movements are far too brisk. Reuben's body tenses and his eyes fill with panic. The guilt of what I've done completely dissolves my anger, and I sit on the mattress.

'What, bruvr?' His whisper is scared.

'Don't you want to get up and enjoy Christmas with us?'

'It's hard, bruvr.'

'What's hard?'

He shrugs his reply, so close to expressing himself but pulls back into his shell. I can see the struggle, plain as the day. I will probably never understand how hard it is.

I leave him in bed and turn back downstairs, wondering how many days this has taken us back. I miss my brother. I miss the way he used to walk with pride, wherever he went. It's still there, I'm sure of it. I can just about feel its glow, but only because I know him so well and can read the trail of clues he leaves. Those images of Aslan and a broken heart. 'Fa mi ly,' the first word he almost said when we got back to the cottage. Maybe he thought we'd left him for good. Only his imagination, his drawings, kept him going. When nobody else was there, thank goodness Aslan kept him safe. As pangs of guilt crush me inside, the only redeeming thought is how staggeringly brave my brother is. We should never have put him in Portland Place.

As the sun creeps higher, it turns into one of those winter days when the air is chilly but if you wrap yourself in layers, it's warm enough to sit in the sunshine. I sit outside with Jack, trying to coax Reuben. Unsurprisingly, he didn't join us earlier as we shivered through champagne merriments with Terry and Jan next door. He sat on the sofa instead, with a blanket around his knees. But now it's just the three of us, I'm determined to get him out.

'Reubs, come and get some real vitamin D.'

Resist. Resist. Resist.

'Come on, just five or ten minutes?'

He holds his right hand up, splaying five fingers.

'Five minutes? Deal! Come on then.'

As he comes out I stand up and leg it inside, run upstairs and reappear wearing a Father Christmas outfit, complete with beard, belt and crooked hat. Reuben and Jack are dismayed.

'Well, neither of you are going to wear it, are you?'

Jack and Reuben shake their heads.

'Unthinkable, a Christmas Day without Santa.'

Reubs has had the same outfit for at least twenty years. Same beard. Same belt. It fits me perfectly but is massive on him.

I wander across the garden and get in the pond, in full Santa. They think I'm drunk on Terry's champagne, but I do it to shift my mood or raise a smile from them.

The water bites at my flesh.

I think of absolutely nothing else but the cold.

I stay in as long as I dare and focus inwards as my body screams.

'You nutter,' Jack says, coming over to offer a towel. 'What's he like, Frodo?'

Reuben tuts, raises his eyebrows and shakes his head.

I love it when they are in cahoots, Frodo with his Samwise Gamgee, taking sides against Gandalf.

I dry myself with frantic rubs before running upstairs to stand in a warm shower. As I glance out of our bedroom window, I see Reubs checking his phone. He mutters something under his breath and walks back indoors. Five minutes must be up. The sodden Santa hat and beard are limp and formless, draped over the curved back of one of the metal garden chairs.

Christmas lunch, as always, takes longer to prepare than expected. Reubs and I set the table while Chef Jack busies himself in the kitchen. I keep our glasses topped up.

'Fancy a Buck's Fizz, Reubs?' I ask him.

No. He's fine with the elderflower cordial and he wants to take it back to his room. I remind him that lunch is nearly ready and he shows me his phone to make a point: it's almost 4 p.m., not lunchtime.

'It's Christmas Dunch,' I reply. 'Lunch and dinner into one.'

He doesn't like the idea one bit.

'It's not the end of the world.'

As Jack carves, my phone pings with a message from Reubs,

sitting opposite me: *it is actually*

'It is what?' I ask.

He looks down and starts typing while I start dishing out the potatoes and vegetables. My phone pings again: *end of the world*.

I laugh out loud.

I can't tell, though. Is he genuinely annoyed? Or is he referring back to the first time he responded like that, when we were in Andalusia and decided to cancel a restaurant reservation? Neither Jack or I were in the mood to go out, so dinner became a miserable selection of leftovers. Reubs was not at all happy. Ever-hungry, he scowled at us, miserably. 'Cheer up, Frodo. It's not the end of the world,' Jack said. His reply had been an identical, 'It IS actually.'

We laughed about that one for days – the idea of missing a meal used to tie Reubs up in knots.

'Right boys, I think we're ready.' Jack proceeds with ceremony. 'You first, Frodo.'

'Cheers,' I say and then add 'Salud.'

Reubs rolls his eyes.

'Cheers,' Jack says. 'Merry Christmas.'

There isn't much cheer in Reubs, though. He refuses to pull the cracker, doesn't want to wear the paper hat, ignores all the bad jokes, and only eats half his lunch without uttering a word, barely taking his eyes off his plate before going straight back to his room.

I start to clear the table while Jack sits down under the tree, a grown man cross-legged in an ocean of presents.

'Frodo Baggins,' Jack shouts up. 'Ready for presents?'

No, he's not. There's no reply, nothing stirs.

'Siesta for us then,' I say to Jack.

He agrees and takes up his usual sofa, pulling a blanket up.

I do a bit more washing-up before settling on the opposite sofa and drift asleep thinking of Mum and Dad and the big family gatherings we had at the house in Headingly, all the parents getting tipsy while kids weaved around them, propelled by sugary drinks and plastic toys.

I wake up with Reubs standing over me, stroking my face. He's obviously used the afternoon quiet to think, to reassess. He wasn't sulking upstairs because lunch was so late. Perhaps he was busy looking for the keys to open all the boxes in his head.

'My bruvr,' he says quietly.

'What is it?' I whisper, not wanting to wake Jack up. 'Are you ready for presents now?'

'I am.'

He drops a wet kiss on my cheek.

'You do my head in,' I say.

As he gets up, something cold and wet brushes my face. He's holding the Santa outfit in his hands. 'Is wet, bruvr,' he says.

For a split second I think I'm still dreaming, but the dampness on my fingers is real. He must have been outside to fetch it from the garden. I take the outfit from him, tiptoe to the kitchen and pop it in the tumble drier.

'Shhhh,' I mouth to Reubs, holding my finger to my lips, pointing to Samwise Gamgee. Reuben's eyes sparkle with the energy of an accomplice.

Never before have I willed wet clothes dry with such urgency. I go back to the drier and count the rotations. I want Reubs to have this moment. I want him to realise that if he has an idea or wish like this, even if it comes to him in a quiet moment alone, that he should make it real.

The outfit is so synthetic it dries in no time, and I watch from a distance as he dresses with precision, adjusting his beard and belt. He then glides across the floor, this vision of red and white, to Samwise Gamsee.

'Blimey. It's Father Christmas,' Jack pushes out through a yawn. 'At last! I thought you'd forgotten about us!'

It's the slowest distribution of presents in the history of the world. We average one every five minutes, but we have nowhere to go, no one to see, nothing else to do. Jack and I lull ourselves into the moment and unwrap in slow motion to fill the gaps between each gift. Reubs has had enough joy denied him in his life, especially lately, and we're not about to deny him this.

When Jack and I finish, Santa waves goodbye and disappears upstairs, returning a little while later as Reuben.

'Frodo,' Jack says. 'You missed Santa. Where were you?'

Reubs points upstairs, looking glum, and all his presents, piled high on the sofa, do nothing to alter his expression. The sparkle that was in the room has suddenly gone. Reuben in Reuben's clothes looks as unhappy as I have ever seen him. He gives each gift a quick glance and then puts them all straight back into his tote bag, ready to take up to his room.

'You haven't finished, Reubs,' I say, pointing out the two presents left under the tree.

I bring them down for him and a hush falls. One is a very big box that arrived by post a week ago, sent from friends Josh and Rhea. Reuben unwraps and pulls out a shiny array of plastic *Lord of the Rings* characters. The other present, sent by our brother Nathan and his wife Kate, has a Frodo Baggins dressing-up cloak inside. A smile forms on Reuben's face. It's a real smile. Not the one he forces out for a photo, but the one that springs up by itself from the inside when he thinks the world isn't watching.

I resist telling him how excited he should feel, how lucky he is to have such lovely friends and family who care about him. Instead, I watch from afar as his hands slowly explore the shapes of the characters – he knows them all so well, and I see the connection in his face. The smile doesn't last long, though, a few seconds at most. But just about long enough for Jack and me to witness.

Reuben takes his bounty up to his room and we don't expect to see him until bedtime. But he has other things on his mind. The presents have ignited an old habit, and he reappears on the stairs wearing the Frodo cloak, playing the theme tune to *Lord of the Rings* on his phone. His face is completely illuminated with the closest thing to happiness I've seen in weeks. I don't care that most of it happens half-hidden by the Frodo cloak. The grin is wild proof that Reuben is still very much with us, perhaps much nearer the surface than we realise. Jack and I exchange knowing glances and chink wine glasses to mark the joy that has just appeared in front of us, even if it's partially in disguise.

After the storm, once Reuben was back with Mum and Dad in Norwich, I went to his bedroom at The Corner. I wanted to gather his things before Jack and I travelled to see him for the first time since he'd left Spain. There were odd socks strewn around the room. A glove with no matching pair. Scraps of his handwritten notes and beautiful drawings in bright felt-tip colours. The four walls ached without him. Outside, the flat line of dawn pulled away the dark on the eastern hill, illuminating rows of gnarled olive trees. Below the farm, the river was just audible as it carried spring waters down from its source at Villanueva del Trabuco.

Fear inhabits all of us at some point in our lives. It may be a temporary feeling that washes over us, but it can also enter the very fibre of your being. Nobody ever invites it, fear barges in.

I sat on the bed trying to understand why he was thousands of miles away. I was clinging to the precious four years that he had lived with Jack and me, and desperately needed to make sense of the strange, terrible months that had just passed. Was it the language barrier that isolated him? Was it my fault for being away? Did it start at the restaurant, in the heat of summer? Perhaps there never really is a beginning, a particular moment or a particular place where things become undone. But even now, whenever I look for reasons, I always end up back in that beautiful room at The Corner. A place that had become so full of fear for my brother.

Reuben knew there was a storm coming. We all did. Radios buzzed with speculation, televisions chatted, and all talk in the village and with neighbours was whether it would be as bad as the storm of

2012, the *tsunami* they called it, which is permanently remembered on the village noticeboard with photographs of the damage and destruction. Every time I caught Reubs checking his phone for weather updates, I told him it would be fine. I would be back soon, I reassured him, and Katie would look after him. She was a lovely person, a true friend. But how I wish I'd been there to comfort him.

The storm raged outside and inside. For hours he stood in the room, alone, with so many questions, so many doubts, wondering why he was stuck there. Why me? Will I always be left behind?

At around 3 a.m. he dialled Mum, but she was sound asleep and didn't hear the phone. He called her again and again. Who else could he have called? His brother was far away. Katie was asleep on the other side of the house, and he didn't want to walk to her in the dark. Perhaps Aslan was the only one who helped him that night. Maybe he pushed his hand to the back of the wardrobe to see if he could escape, step through into Narnia. Perhaps that's where he's been ever since. With Aslan, Lucy, Peter, Susan, Edmund, Mr Tumnus and Mr Beaver. Or perhaps he didn't get there. Perhaps there was only this world. Only that storm. Was it the moment he began to disappear? He may have finally collapsed in a restaurant in the heat of *El veranillo del membrillo*, but that seismic event started earlier.

Alone, abandoned, did the dread take hold of him that night?

'Don't want to die, brother.'

And what of Reuben's brother? All the while he was asleep in a nondescript hotel room in Seville, and when he woke up the following morning the damage was done. Fear was part of Reuben. It had forced its way in and was burrowing inside, changing his embrace, making his eyes glaze over, altering his posture. In the same room, sat on his bed looking at the remnants of his life with us at The Corner, I didn't know how to find my way back to him.

I keep dreaming that Reuben and I are at the bottom of a pit. My eyes struggle to adjust to the contrast between the darkness and the bright blue circle of light that crowns the pit like a halo. The walls are too high to climb. We both know there is a world beyond the circle of light, with movement too swift for us to see. I turn to Reuben to ask him what we should do, but I have lost my voice and begin to panic. I hold his hand and the fleshy part of his palm fits perfectly into the hollow of mine.

'It's alright, bruvr. I understand.'

'Will I?' I murmur back.

'I do,' he assures me.

We can hear birdsong but it's too difficult to differentiate from the sound of our breathing. It's like learning to listen all over again. The final sound of the dream is a thought tearing me awake.

The valley is gripped by ice. Most days, it barely thaws before dark. I search the sky for sun spaces, ever hopeful, but all January has offered so far is a blanket of cloud. Up the lane, a mains water pipe must've burst because there's a permanent tentacle of ice reaching downhill towards the cottage.

Having Jack here last week, I was able to let go of the reins. Nothing much happens during the lull between Christmas and New Year. Nothing is supposed to happen. We spent many lazy afternoons on the sofa with the log burner lit, not to take the chill off but to keep us suspended in limbo for as long as possible.

I tried not to think about Jack's imminent return to Spain. Neither of us mentioned it. He spent as much time with Reubs as he could, stepping into the daily routine and helping him wake, shower, dress, then come down to a breakfast with all of us. I buried into my freedom, reading and walking, pottering around the garden whenever I felt like it. Sometimes, when I walked into the living room, there was a hushed conversation.

'Oh yeah?' I questioned.

Jack winked, 'We're having a private chat, aren't we, Frodo?'

On New Year's Eve, Jack and Reubs decided to make banana bread. It should have been a totally normal sight, the two of them weighing ingredients and then mixing, but we are now so far removed from normality, this act of baking bread was exceptional. I stepped up to Jack and landed a little kiss on his cheek. 'From the bottom of my heart,' seemed a peculiar saying until I met him.

As I walked away, I knew what was going to happen: Reubs moved in and planted a wet one on Jack's other cheek.

'Oi!' I turned around with a false affront. 'What do you think you're doing?'

I walked back to mark Jack with another kiss.

'Oh, here we go,' Jack complained.

We repeated the routine, and each time Reuben's enjoyment blossomed some more. His mood lifted. His personality swelled. Each kiss and repeat cast a happier smile.

'Now I'm telling you for the last time, young man. He's MY boyfriend and that's final.'

Reubs squared up to me and replied, 'Well, he's my Samwise Gamgee. Put that smoke n pipe it!'

Jack and I fell about laughing. Flour went everywhere. Reubs stood there, lips turned inwards, with a face that told us his circuit was complete. The electricity flowed. Their banana bread was delicious, of course. It was barely out of the oven for twenty minutes before we had eaten it all, still warm, with cups of Yorkshire tea and milk and honey.

Reubs and I have spent more than fifteen New Year's Eves together. We were on Princes Street in Edinburgh, the year of the crush, holding on to each other for dear life and spilling onto the side streets into the New Town. We once went to a James Bond Party in London, with our friend Kas dressed as Reuben's Bond Girl and me as Le Chiffre. But this year was all a bit too much for him. At ten-thirty, Reubs took his leave.

'Night night,' I said. 'Next year is going to be better, trust me.'

'I hope,' he replied.

Before leaving us for the night, Reubs passed us a customary piece of A4. He turned it upside down and kissed us both lightly on the cheek. Jack knew we had to wait for him to disappear before turning the page to reveal that he'd used crayons, not his usual bold felt-tips, and his lightness of touch rendered the image barely visible, as if it was fading into the page before our eyes.

If I stay in bed looking through the skylight, unhelpful thoughts ricochet like marbles down a run. This morning, like every morning, I came straight downstairs. Last night's dinner plates are stacked up by the sink. I nibble on leftover treats – the calories of crisps and chocolates and cheese are settling around my belly. I should really throw it all away. Return to discipline. Structure. No alcohol, no cigarettes. But those intentions don't last long because I'm soon scratching through the odds-and-sods drawer in the kitchen looking for an old pouch of rolling tobacco.

I head out for a cigarette and disturb a robin. It's the only life in the garden, with its burnt-orange belly teetering on the hazel. There's little further evidence of warmth in the valley. All is hushed, like a sustained breath. These are the still hours before the day begins. Although I feel lonely now that Jack has gone back, I do enjoy this time idling while Reuben sleeps, it gives me time before the hardest part of the day. The time when I rediscover that I am Sisyphus, and that the boulder of our brotherhood has rolled back to the bottom of the hill. My body, still aching from yesterday, has to get ready to start again.

Sometimes I sit on the top step, where I have never sat before.

It seems perfect for this moment. I'm waiting for despair to topple like a Slinky, down each step into the front room. I peer back through Reuben's bedroom door: the angle of his back at odds, between rise and fall. *Faire la grève*, I decide. I'm on strike. Let's see how Reuben fares on his own today. How far uphill will he go without me?

I am trying to keep focused on him, leading him with a constant, calm love. But this kind of love is not always a feeling. Sometimes it is a decision. I have lakes and oceans of real love for him, but there are times when it is lost in all the frustration and anger and sheer desperation. That's when I have to *decide* to love him. I remind myself what his life could be, and how each and every day we can take tiny steps towards it.

Yesterday, I let Reuben wake up and join me for breakfast in his own time. He arrived at past 2 p.m., in dressing gown and slippers, and sat answering my questions using gestures or signing Makaton, his voice hidden in the recesses of winter. But he hasn't lost his voice. I've heard it. His layers, his routines, his deliberate movements, his voice: these are all parts of his life that he can control. He has chosen not to talk, in the same way he chooses to put so many clothes on, buffering himself from the world.

Time slowed at the kitchen table, and I lost myself watching every whispered word form, imagining the drawings come alive: every lion, the shading of every sheep, every splitting heart, every hobbit, every Whoopi Goldberg, all of them looped in perpetual slow motion, inside the cinema of Reuben's mind. Looking closely, the expressions in the eyes of these characters have started to haunt me. His art is instantaneous, and I'm so grateful that he is making these marks on the page. But many of them also make his fear visible. Drawing by drawing, what he's been through becomes more undeniably real.

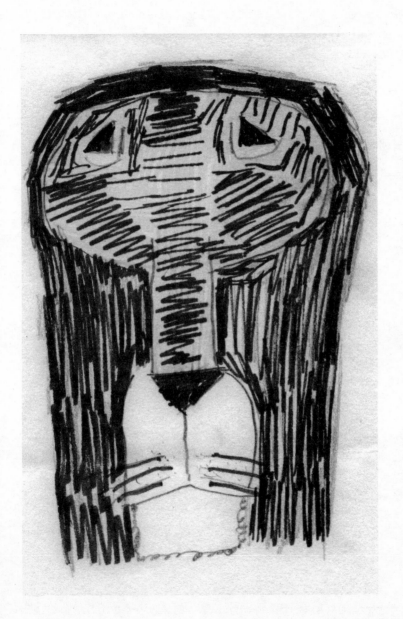

What
a eVein

Sleep
Well

I am wire
love you
Frodo

Happy New
Year
2021
Family

I miss Jack. I miss the warmth of the Andalusian sunshine. I miss blue skies. I miss coffee that is strong enough to restart your heart. I miss the early olive harvest. I miss seeing the grey heron by the river and shouting 'Buenos Días' to Antonio through the olive groves. I miss my other life, and as the weeks pass I find it increasingly difficult to know whether I'll be able to return to it. More than anything else, this morning I miss Archi Boy and can't shake the image of him alone in the cold from my head.

Standing out in the garden, finishing my cigarette, I still can't believe Archi has gone. That's probably the real reason I let Reuben lie in so long the other morning. I was scared. I didn't know how he was going to take it. I put it off as long as possible.

A couple of days after Jack left, a message pinged into my phone from Nacho on the farm. *Sorry to disturb Manni, but Archi didn't come home last night.* Jack had gone to the coast for business meetings, so wasn't back home yet. I pictured all the dogs: Beau, BB, Duna and Archi. Archi rules the roost up there, and knows the place better than any of us.

I texted back, *What do you mean he didn't come back?*

Nacho replied, *We were out walking last night, he ran off. I called and called but he never came.*

Archi often goes off on adventures but he always comes home before dark. I called Jack and he managed to get back before evening, and found Nacho pacing the drive, not making sense. Jack turned to the dogs and said, 'Take me to Archi.'

They understood. Of course they understood. They are the four musketeers. Jack followed them through a hole in the fence into the olive grove. Duna led the pack, and halfway through the grove, Beau and BB hung back. Duna carried on to take Jack all the way to the tiny little body of Archi, his spilled blood frozen to the top soil.

It was dusk by the time I plucked up the courage to tell Reuben about Archi, but after nearly forty-eight hours of waiting and posturing, it was Reuben who held on to me while I cried. There were a pair of ducks on the pond, just a few metres from where we were. I pointed them out and we sat and watched them paddle and dip their beaks into the dark water.

Before bed, Reubs wanted to cheer me up so he cleared the table and blew out the candles. He even found his voice to ask, 'What we do tomorrow bruvr?' The words left his mouth loud and clear, without stutter or pause. My eyes flicked up to focus on his face. It was fleeting but I saw it, the light as it sped through his eyes. He was there, in the room. I saw Reuben. I heard Reuben.

'We could go to the farm shop,' I suggested.

Reubs bunched into his favourite corner of the sofa and started drawing, felt-tips working busily. Occasionally, he would pause and lift the sketchpad to allow himself a good look at the picture before carrying on, adding a bit more yellow here or some more words there. When he was sure it was finished, he tugged the page out and put it in front of me, the right way up. I looked at it while he manoeuvred himself away to make a mug of hot milk and honey.

It was a portrait of Archi Boy wearing his green collar.

Before heading upstairs to bed, Reuben came back over and brushed my cheek with a gentle goodnight kiss. 'Do you love me?' he whispered, shuffling up the three steps of the kitchen.

'I love you, Reubs,' I replied as he disappeared around the corner.

I poured myself a second glass of wine and raised it to Archi, celebrating his life. But I was also celebrating Reuben. If I hadn't cracked up, it wouldn't have given him the space to comfort me. Because these past weeks have been all about finding ways to make him feel better, he hasn't been asked to reciprocate, to express kindness and care. Yet these qualities are as much a part of being Reuben as his felt-tip drawings and his broken glasses, his *Joseph* tote bag and Simba cuddly, his tummy-rub aftershave, his love of Whoopi Goldberg and dreams of living in Narnia.

I finished off my wine and watched the ducks on the pond again. When they vanished behind the reeds I stood up to get a better

He's Dead.
He Was My Friend.

x eat Archi ~~~~~~

~~Peom~~

Just
Celebrate
his life
brother

~~mama smotimala~~

Dont Worry
You got m~

love you

Spain

~~Poem~~
Peom

sleep we
tonight

look. 'Don't be afraid,' I said. 'Stay as long as you want.' I was feeling pleased last night. Out of all that worry about Archi, I was foolish enough to think that maybe we'd cracked it.

But it's morning now.

The wine is finished and the ducks have gone.

Time for Sisyphus to rise, head up those stairs and knock on Reuben's door.

Nearly every morning we begin like this, sneering at the blinding light. He covers his ears whenever I say something encouraging, all positivity tutted back into its box. The morning is heavy at our feet, and with each day that passes, my strength is waning. I'm sure it was easier before Jack took over. I didn't think about it. I just got on and did it. Maybe it'll get easier again, but having that break makes the mornings feel harder than ever.

Usually, if I heave Reubs into a sitting position, he sinks back to the pillows unless I hold on. There's always such a disconnect between Morning Reuben and Evening Reuben, as if a night-gardener visits with shears and severs all the growth. Even putting his feet on the floor seems an insurmountable challenge. He stares at his legs as if he's never seen them before, he resists my hands on his. I cannot help him if he does not want to be helped.

Showered, breakfasted, dressed.

We manage to step out before 11 a.m. and head up the lane. We don't need anything from the shop, but I want to get out into the bracing air and have some sort of transaction with life outside of the cottage.

Reuben wants to stay on the lane but I take him through the fields. 'The slower you walk, the longer it takes,' I tell him. 'Don't think about all the steps you have to make, just think of the next one. I'm not going anywhere. I'm here. But you have to learn to walk alone. I can't walk with you all the time.'

As we walk, a dull panic starts in the root of my belly, tearing my insides down to the bottom of my spine.

We stop at a puddle and look at our reflections, incongruous yet oddly connected. What a pair. We look like two statues, the front of our wellies half underwater like emerging submarines. Reuben has reached an impasse, and I have too. Our gazes are cast in mud-bronze and we concentrate on not looking at each other. My mood has come down like a curtain. Normally, I am practised in techniques to lift it, but today there's nothing I can do.

His wellies are sinking deeper into the mud. He's on the verge of tears and I wish he would cry. Open the flood gates, let it all out. The shop is a marathon of obstacles away. I urge him to try. I beg him to take one step but he is rooted. He stands like a diver on the 10m high board who has been thinking about diving for so long now that he's completely lost his nerve. The impossibility of stepping over the edge. The impossibility of going back. He's convinced that he's not capable. I refuse to accept it. But then he buckles and I move in to hold him before he collapses.

'Shall we do it together?'

Relief floods his face as he takes my arm.

Clay clods our feet as we reach the bottom corner of the field by the river. I go back to silence. I can think of nothing that can alter the way he feels, or the way I am descending.

There is no way Reubs can negotiate the final stile. I support his bulk over and onto the road. He looks at the tarmac but there is no celebratory relief. I stroll ahead without him, go inside the shop and realise that I have no idea what to buy.

I browse until I end up with a pot of tomato chutney. Because I'm out of money, I pay for it using Reuben's debit card and the purchase makes me feel worse. The glass jar is too cold to touch so I zip it into the pocket of my kagool and head back outside.

I think of my bank account and the money I've borrowed to save my business. Jack's generosity is clear and unwavering; I can't ask him to help any more. We try to contribute towards bills and housekeeping at the cottage, but even these are now becoming more difficult to manage. I need a job, not a jar of tomato chutney. I can't keep depleting his funds. That is some of his disability allowance gone. It's not right that he's having to support me.

Although I want to reboot and start the day again, when I exit and see Reubs standing outside, the black dog of depression lunges at me, driving its fangs. I feel pain and see a white flash of emotion. I become the cruellest brother. The most selfish person alive. I move straight past and leave him standing.

I walk and burn with guilt, with disbelief at myself.

I have abandoned him.

It's not even midday but my day is unsalvageable.

I don't turn back.

I charge down the lane hoping not to see anyone, then head straight back into the cottage and into my bedroom, pulling the duvet over my head to hide from the light.

I feel bereaved. I must go and find him.

How will he get home?

I must get up.

I cannot get up.

The inside of me screams.

When I wake up, the rage seems to have left. I lift my head and cast an eye through the darkness. It's not late but Reuben is already in bed. He either sleeps or pretends to. Thank goodness he's here. Thank goodness he got back. What the hell was I thinking? I pad downstairs and see the remnants of a sandwich on the counter: crusts, a pot of jam, butter. He hasn't put things away but at least he made himself something to eat. At least he found his way home.

There's a drawing on the kitchen counter, a split heart on yellow card. Beside it is a teddy embroidered with the word LOVE. Where did he get it from? There's a price tag attached to the ear, £3.99. He must have walked the whole mile to the petrol station alone, and then that same mile back.

Love Will
Find A Way

brother

I have a replica of the medieval labyrinth from Chartres Cathedral in northern France. It's laser printed, to scale, on a large piece of material so that I can travel with it folded into a rucksack. It's my talisman. I got it done many years ago, after I walked the real thing, carved into stone in the main nave of the cathedral, an emblem of pilgrimage pressed into the floor like the indentation of a giant ink stamp.

Friends and family and clients have all walked my fabric labyrinth, pacing through the route in and then following it as if the walls were real, making rhythmical U-turns as they wind towards the centre.

Reuben walked it once at The Corner. I watched him from an upstairs window, head bowed, pausing to trace out the next section in his mind. Everyone who had walked it before him paused in the centre for a moment, before stepping off the fabric in a straight line, returning to two dimensions. But not Reuben. Once he was in the middle, he began retracing his steps, still in three dimensions. If there was only one way in, then there was only one way out. Why hadn't I thought of that before? He sees walls where there are none. I watched him taking baby steps to work his way out, taking the same amount of time it took to get in, working in Reuben's dimension.

In the golden light of the afternoon, I want a quick stride alone so encourage Reuben to head off to the field at the top of the hill. 'Take a photo,' I suggest. 'Show it to me when you get back.'

He dresses as if he's going mountaineering and we head off in our different directions. At the river, I pass a man standing at the bridge with a camera on a tripod. A long, heavy lens points in the direction of the water.

'Afternoon,' I say. 'What are you waiting for?'

'There's a kingfisher,' he replies. 'I haven't been able to snap her yet. Or him. I just really love kingfishers.' He seems almost embarrassed by his own words.

As I walk on and do the loop, I keep thinking about the man patiently waiting, lens balanced, poised for a moment that may never come. Just the possibility of the bird is enough, the prospect of its beauty streaked across the riverbank.

On the way back, as I near the bridge, I am bursting to say how wonderful it all is. His passion. His patience. More than anything, I want him to know that I understand. But I say nothing. I smile, nod my head as knowingly as I can, carrying on towards the cottage. I chastise myself for not making more contact, for not speaking those thoughts. I almost go back but the moment has passed. I stride up the lane, walking up the hill towards Reuben, walking with determination, walking from my core.

When I reach him, he shows me the pictures he's snapped on his phone. One of his wellies, one of the ash tree on the field edge, one of the stile he clambered over when Jack was here.

Since Jack left, I have been reducing Reuben's dose of Fluoxetine. One pill every other day, then one every third day, fourth day and so on until today, the very last one.

I suggested that he should make his own breakfast this morning, 'Why don't you be in charge?' He agreed, heading for the cupboard with his *msli* bowl. Once it was full, he turned towards the fridge and steadied it while he took out the blueberries. One by one, he arranged the tiny fruits, forming a complete circle. A Ring.

He then took similar care to unscrew the vitamin pots and place each pill in the same order as they are every morning. He couldn't muster the tension to squeeze and twist the lid off the turmeric and black pepper, so he asked if I would do it.

I was about twenty-five when I hit my all time low. Help wasn't at hand, or more likely I didn't know how to ask for it. I ran away to Spain. I ran to colour. I ran to the blue skies and orange trees of Seville, and the Sevillanos eased sunshine back into my life. A change of scene helped me through. A move, if you're fortunate enough to be able to make one, can save a life.

Antidepressants do give people a ledge of safety to hang on to, so I'm not completely opposed to medication. But I am worried about the prevalence: that little green-and-yellow pill gets administered like aspirin in some health services. In Reuben's case, they were prescribed responsibly but then not scrutinised. In a sector that seems risk averse and paranoid about 'best interest' decisions, not once did I see a carer or anyone in management asking themselves whether it was in Reuben's best interest to keep taking them.

Dr Aaberg has supported my decision, and a friend warned me what it was like coming off them. She described how it took her several months, so deep was her dependence.

'Tell him from me,' she said. 'He's very brave.'

He swallows each tablet with a gulp of elderflower cordial, then stares at the last little green-and-yellow in the packet. He pops it out and stares again at the empty foil pill sheet. Though we've been preparing for weeks, he still looks nervous. I am too.

He looks at me and asks, 'Why, bruvr?'

I don't know how to answer.

'We've talked about it, Reubs.'

'I've got my Mummy,' he says.

I'm not sure what he means.

Does he feel like I'm punishing him? Am I depriving him of something vital that Mum would reinstate? I don't know what to say or do so turn away from the table as everything blurs.

He keeps talking to himself now that I've backed away.

'I do it for love. Fa mi ly.'

In it goes.

I don't see it but can picture the gulp as the cordial goes down.

I head back towards him and kneel by his side, waiting for his eyes to lock into mine.

'What, bruvr?' he asks.

'I am so proud of you, Reubs. So unbelievably proud.'

We hug. I cry.

He smiles and asks, 'Why you always a heap, bruvr?'

'You are very brave.'

That night, as my brother sleeps in the room beside me, all is quiet except the doubts in my head. I am ashamed of myself. If I can abandon him in the road like that, what else am I capable of? We really have to get this right. There's no way I can leave Reubs again until we find and then settle him into a new life. But how long will this take? Months? Years? I'm definitely not going home by the end of the month. Jack sent me a message last night: *This is turning into a nightmare. What the hell are we going to do?*

I don't like imagining Reuben's future. Inevitably, projecting him forward in time brings me to his life expectancy, which is mid-50s for people with Down's. But we are at a crossroads now and I have to think the most difficult of thoughts in order for us to move on. Reubs is the closest I'll ever have to a biological son. It's easier to love him than to let him go. And no matter how many circles I draw on paper or in my mind, there are always going to be two fundamental alternatives. One: we commit to Reuben living with us for the rest of our lives. Two: we find him an environment where he can learn to be on his own two feet, and I can learn to be apart.

As I lie in bed, the valley hushed in darkness, I try my hardest to imagine Reuben's happy future. I start breaking his needs down into subtitles in my head: Safety, Routine, Pride, Friendship, Purpose, Community, Love. Jack and I could give him most of those things, but even if Reuben was by my side for the rest of my living days, would that turn out to be the best thing for him? Shouldn't he find his own way, in another care home or with a host like Becky in Emminster? Yet the quiet voice is in me, whispering that we should wait. I've learned to listen to these instincts over the years, even if they haven't always been right. We have time, so long as my hope is still intact. And I do believe that Reuben will have a full and happy life again. In the darkness before dawn, with this resolve, my worries begin to thaw.

The morning brings clarity and I make the snap decision to sell my car. We need the money, and this is a decision I can control while we wait for the things I can't. I call Fernando in Spain, my business partner, my friend. He's been covering for me at work while I've been away. He loves Reuben and understands the struggle, particularly because he has a disabled nephew, Sacha, whom he adores. He really knows the weight of worry and it's such a comfort to hear his voice.

He agrees to help, fielding enquiries and arranging viewings. I load photos and descriptions onto a website, Fernando guides me on the price. Once the advert is live, I feel better. The car will sell quickly. My clients used to love the sliding doors, but I don't need it now and can find something else whenever I get home.

'Thanks, Fer,' I say. 'That's a weight lifted.'

'Don't worry. *No te preocupes*. Whatever work comes in, I can handle it. You concentrate on Reuben. All will be well. You'll see.'

While I'm on the phone, Reubs heads up the lane on another watering mission to our neighbours. He's been there every Monday and Thursday on his own, making sure all the plants have a big drink. Jane and Neill offered him five pounds a week while they're away – it's so good for him to be given a chore by someone who isn't me. These last couple of days, he's brushed me aside whenever I remind him what he has to do.

'Know what I'm doing, bruvr.'

He hasn't had a paid job since he was fired from the Waitrose in Newbury, where he stacked bananas and milk for three hours twice a week. It was the first time he had ever worn a uniform – he was very proud of that orange clip-on tie. One day, feeling peckish, he spied a huge bowl of his favourite food: coleslaw. He made his way around to the back of the deli and proceeded to shovel gigantic spoonfuls into his mouth, right out of the fridge display cabinet. Needless to say, he was reported by a customer and was fired on health and safety grounds. Dad had to escort him to talk to the manager.

Manager: 'Reuben, are you a member of a trade union?'

Reuben: 'No, I have Down's syndrome.'

Reubs is gone for well over an hour before he comes back along the lane. As he gets within range of our wi-fi, a WhatsApp pings into my phone, *I. need. Alarm Code. brother.* Shit. I didn't think to top-up his phone with credit so he had no coverage up there. Luckily, he hadn't gone in and tripped it. But he must have been standing outside in the bitter winds waiting for me to reply.

'Oh Booba! I only just got your message! Have you been standing outside all this time?'

I bring him close and he is chilled right through.

'Come here. I'll warm you up.'

I remind him of the code, he repeats it.

'Got it now,' he whispers.

'And now what?' I ask him.

'What we do, bruvr?'

'Well, we need to water the plants don't we? Do you want me to come up and help you?'

'Well… yeah,' he replies as his face relaxes. 'My bruvr you do after me.'

'Somebody has to,' I tell him.

'Nah, is fine. We bruvrs.'

We head up to Jane and Neill's together, reciting the alarm code, over and over, until I'm convinced Reubs has memorised it. I notice that he's wearing my scarf again, the one that my friend Sophie D knitted me for Christmas.

'Who said you could take that? Cheeky.'

'I like it. Cosy,' he whispers.

'Well, you ask for it. You don't just take it.'

He hasn't said anything about his own scarf, the one I threw out, so I really don't mind him wearing it.

He moves alongside, leaning in close to say, 'Sorry, bruvr. Can I have scarf?'

'Just look after it, OK.'

It always feels strange stepping into somebody else's home when they're not around. The trust they have in you doesn't diminish the sense of trespass, and although the rooms are full of their personalities, the house is hollow without them. In the kitchen, we both notice things we'd not seen before. A photo on the wall, poems stuck to the fridge with magnets of lighthouses and Cornish pasties. The matching yellow and blue checked material of the oven gloves. Reubs spots a framed quote from *Lord of the Rings,* something Gandalf says to Frodo. Reuben's face collapses into a smirk. I take it as my cue and say it aloud in my best wizard voice, 'All we have to decide is what to do with the time that is given us.' But my delivery falters as I notice the peace lily on the table.

'Oh dear,' I say, pointing to it.

'What, bruvr?'

'Well, I've seen healthier peace lilies!'

Reuben scrunches his face into a knot, 'Odd.'

The pride and joy of the kitchen is a mass of limp leaves and lifeless flowers, hanging over the edge of its wicker basket. There's a pool of water around its base.

'You've drowned it, Booba!'

The knot on Reuben's face draws tighter.

It's time to run through everything once more.

We walk around the house counting the plants and checking they are all still alive. There are seventeen in total, not including four cacti. To make sure this doesn't happen again, we number each pot or basket, then draw a map and weekly tick sheet for all the plants, each one labelled with *a little* or *a lot (but not too much)*. Reubs then fills the watering can with the extra long nozzle and we do the rounds again, making sure he practises before he pours. Just a drop for each cactus is difficult – when the water appears at the end of the nozzle, it takes Reubs a while to react and pull back, leaving a pool soaking into the soil.

'Don't worry, brother,' I reassure him as we lock up.

I carry the lily home to see if putting it out in the sun might help. As we walk back down the hill, I hand Reubs a crisp five pound note for the week. Money earned. Routine. Responsibility. His lips turn inwards as he folds it carefully and slips it into his wallet. He's a little lighter on his feet.

For lunch, we sit in silence and eat scotch eggs and cheese. Reubs eats all of his food for a change, and then takes his plate to the sink. I make him wash his hands before he folds clothes from the drying rack into two piles: one for him, one for me. I spy him smelling the T-shirts. He takes the clothes upstairs and spends the rest of the day in his room, while I read downstairs.

As the light wanes, it finds every dust particle, every smeared fingerprint on the living room glass. I cleaned the other day, but this afternoon every surface, including the air we breathe, seems smeared by traces of the last weeks.

After a couple of hours outside, I check on the peace lily but conclude that we need to replace it, and deposit the dying plant out on the compost. I call Reubs down and together we drive off to the garden centre to pick out a replacement. At the check-out, I remind him, 'Not too much water this time.'

Indicating to leave the garden centre, Reuben asks me if he can go to Portland Place. His request strikes like a pendulum.

'Near, bruvr,' he adds.

It's true, we are close but he's caught me off guard.

'What do you want to go there for?'

'I know,' he replies.

I want to say it's too late in the day or we should at least ring them beforehand. But I don't. Despite what my feelings are right now, Reuben has expressed himself. He has intervened in the day. He wants to go, so he will go.

I indicate the other direction, change lanes, and a look appears on his face that I've not seen for ages. He's a man with a plan.

We park outside and I help Reuben get out of the car, then hover at the front door waiting for him to press the bell. I stand right behind him, in case he needs me. But I also don't want to miss this moment, not for all the tea in Yorkshire.

Emma appears in the doorway and her face fills with obvious delight. Reuben doesn't bother with Hellos or How are yous. He just tells her he loves her, and what else can she say other than 'I love you too.' There's a brief hesitation before he decides to turn around and wander back to the car. I follow him, smiling and nodding, not saying very much as we clamber in.

He wanted to set the record straight.

No hard feelings.

'Now home, bruvr,' he says.

I manoeuvre the car out so we can drive away, and Reuben has a huge grin on his face.

It was only this time last year that we first heard about Portland Place. Mum, Dad and Reuben had moved out of Jack's cottage to be in the middle of town, and they were living above a department store on West Street. Sam called to tell me about it and I talked to her as if Reuben wasn't in the room.

'What's it like?' I asked.

'It's within walking distance of the centre of town. There are seven residents. Sorry, tenants. There are seven tenants and it's an assisted living facility, so Reubs would be encouraged into a more independent lifestyle.'

Mum and Dad needed to head back to Norwich, but there was just about enough time for us to settle him in.

'It sounds promising,' I said.

'It does. And once we get him into the system, it'll be much easier to find another place, later down the road if we need to. Places like this don't come up very often.'

Over the years, lots of people have wondered if the natural place for Reubs was with Mum and Dad. That's what Jack's mum, Angela, thought. And it's a fair question that becomes more complicated the older he – and my parents – get. Even now, whenever I try to talk about it, explaining how they are getting less able to care for him, Reubs can't comprehend it. He completely refuses to engage with the idea of either of them ageing, let alone passing away. On one occasion, when we were talking about it, an anger flared up in him, the likes of which I'd not seen since I refused to let him have a fifth helping at an all-you-can-eat in Malaga.

If he can't comprehend mortality, whether his own or my parents', just think of the shock he would experience if he was living with them and one of them died. Whose world will he occupy when they're gone? Reubs needs to be on his feet, with a new place of his own and an established circle of support – and please, just one friend. Surely that would be better for him in the long run. He will miss Mum and Dad, of course he will. But the impact of their absence will be considerably less than if he were living in their world, within their care.

After we'd been to see Portland Place, we called a family meeting in the flat. Jack and I, Mum, Dad and Reubs. The heating was off because the landlady had told my parents the bills were astronomical, so we all sat in the kitchen in our coats, throwing Reuben's future around like a hot potato. I still wonder how Reubs felt about it. We laid down the various scenarios for him, one by one. I remember his eyes trying to focus as the conversation flowed too fast for him to follow. I'm sure he was worried. We talked about Mum and Dad's return to Norwich. I explained why it would be bad for business if I missed the start of the Easter tourist season. We all knew that Jack still needed to recover from his time as Reuben's carer. Our lives must have seemed so full of obligations, all of them without Reubs. When we moved on to talk about Portland Place, we presented it as an idea but really the decision had already been made.

Mum and I had been to see the room without him, which was a good thing because the carers had just finished hoovering up the sadness of the sudden death of the previous tenant. The mood was very sombre. All the carers had been deeply affected, which, at the time, spoke volumes about their compassion. This was positive. And it wasn't an ugly room. There were sash windows facing south that caught the low winter light. It had potential. We started to envision making the space cosy for Reubs, painting it and changing the curtains. Mum and I thought we'd surprise him with an Aslan theme and trawled Pinterest for inspiration. And it worked – Reuben's face lit up when he saw the mural for the first time, covering an entire wall behind his bed. Aslan was always there to watch over him, along with cuddly Simba, bean-bag dog and the *Good Sleep* clipboard.

Reuben moved to Portland Place at the beginning of February. Even though Mum and Dad didn't approve, he hung his rainbow flag up in the sash window, and at long last it looked like he had a place he could call his own, stamped with his personality. We could visit him whenever we wanted. He was encouraged to go into town with other tenants. There were plenty of opportunities to socialise through the clubs and events we'd found.

By moving Reuben into assisted living, we were relinquishing our responsibilities as carers and stepping back from everyday decision-making. Often, family members are happy about this, relieved not to be in charge any more. I know this because, over the years, more than one carer has approached me (inside and outside of Portland Place) to say how touched they are by the concern we have for Reuben's welfare. Many families, they tell me, find it easier to walk away. But I have struggled with that. I have wrestled with myself for years about whether we, his family, should be responsible for

Reuben's daily life and his choices, or whether social services ought to be. More or less overnight, once Reuben was in Portland Place, we were no longer part of all the conversations.

But February ticked by and we all kept in touch easily on WhatsApp. He continued with his twice weekly activities at the day centre and his dance sessions with Anna, although he still didn't really participate in either. He was also struggling with the idea of sharing a home with other people with 'special needs'. But he enjoyed popping into town and stopping off to see Mum and Dad on the way. On paper, Reuben's new life looked promising. But life had a surprise waiting for us all, just around the corner. It wasn't just Reuben's life that slipped into a black hole.

Jack and I were in Spain when the first wave of Lockdowns were announced across Europe. Mum and Dad were no longer allowed to go back to Norwich, but because the tenancy on the flat was up they had to move into Jack's cottage. They were only ten minutes' drive from Reuben, but they could only park in the road and wave through the window while talking to him on his mobile, assuring him that everything was going to be alright. These are the moments that Mum used to disinfect her hands and have him push his fingers through the narrow gap at the bottom of the window, so she could trim his fingernails.

We all retreated uneasily into the new reality and Reuben was no different. He never left the house because he wasn't allowed to. He became withdrawn. He began to wither. He packed away his rainbow flag and kept it in the bottom of his wardrobe. He stopped texting me. He wouldn't take phone calls. The little voice he'd rediscovered since his breakdown, rebuilt under Jack's diligent care, started to vanish. Then he stopped talking altogether.

Every time I called Portland Place, the carers told me he was quiet but fine. I could see that he was on his phone until late into the night, so obviously lonely, and often when I called to speak to him at 11 a.m. he was still in bed. The idea of him sitting in that room tormented me. I thought about him night and day. Even if he couldn't or didn't want to reply, I sent him messages to tell him Aslan would always protect him, that I would come and get him, that everything would be over soon, and we could be together. The idea of a reunion seemed to give him strength, and that's when the Aslan mural started appearing in the background of every selfie or video call, those enormous, luminous eyes peering over Reuben's shoulder. I can't believe how much I've grown to despise the colours of that room, particularly the mural.

I don't want to die, brother. His fears were marching again. I could hear the terrible drumming of feet.

Everything achieved the year before, all the props that had been removed – the hats, the scarves, the hoodies, the pills – had reappeared. I'm sure many of the carers tried to put a stop to Reuben's slide, perhaps the care provider did too, but by the summer they had a ruin on their hands. Reuben had become a shell of his former self.

In August, when I was able to make it back to England for the first time, I remember sitting in the car after a visit and watching Reuben through his bedroom window. I saw one of the carers sitting on his bed, talking with him, leaning in like a friend. Something must have happened in one of the other rooms, though, because they left abruptly and Reubs just sat there, staring out towards the street, unaware that I was watching.

How could the needs of seven people be met by three carers? When you hear talk of resources being stretched, what people are really saying is that not enough money has been invested in the people on the front line of care. No matter what excuses are made, what language is thrown about in explanation, it has everything to do with the willingness of private care providers and the government's failure to fund those who need it the most.

They were happy to administer drugs, though. Earlier that summer, one carer took the decision to continue with Reuben's prescription of Fluoxetine without consulting with us. I was out when the GP called on the house phone to review whether or not he needed it, and they didn't try getting hold of me again.

The only other contact the doctor's surgery had for me was my Spanish mobile phone, so perhaps they weren't allowed to call internationally. The GP called the care home and spoke to one of the workers instead. Together, they decided to keep Reuben on 20mg without further review. The GP asked this person to inform me of their decision, and they failed to do so.

It was at that moment that my doubts were no longer abstract. The anger became real. It had a focus: someone failed to involve me in the decision to administer antidepressants. To me, it felt like they were saying that they knew better. This is unlikely to be true, of course. It's more likely that somebody forgot to say something or call me back. But the story of Reuben's life is full of moments like this. Having Down's syndrome should make him stand out in a crowd, but we'd rather look away, avert our eyes and whisper behind his back, like those other mums at the school gates in Headingley. But it's not OK for anybody to do that. It's understandable, but not acceptable. And what definitely isn't OK or understandable is why people within the care profession behave in the same way. Reuben was in his room at Portland Place, all those hours and days and weeks, staring out of the ground-floor window. But he was never really there.

Before this, I had not been at peace with the care being provided, but I hadn't wanted to throw accusations around. From then on, I refused to be intimidated by what was in essence a lack of communication. I had to raise my game, too. I began to intervene with phone calls and emails, daily. The carers probably felt as if I was putting them under surveillance, and even more pressure than they were already under. No doubt, at the time, that was exactly what I'd hoped they would feel.

And where was Reuben in all of this? How was he feeling? What was he thinking? Could he see past his isolation?

One evening, when we organised a family Zoom, a staff member helped Reuben connect on a Kindle that Nathan had sent him. We were excited to finally see him on the screen, and at that moment when everyone joins, the second between seeing their name and seeing their face, there'd usually be bright smiles, warmth and greetings as pixels turned into human love. But that night, when Reuben's gaunt, blank face joined the screen, it was a shock for us all. There was no recognition. His eyes were dark pebbles. A face mask covered his mouth and nose. He was completely hidden inside himself, and we grappled with fragmented conversation. It was so painful that leaving the call was a relief. I felt a deep grief, but at that point I didn't want to share it openly with the rest of the family. Minutes later, Reuben texted us all a video of himself weeping, rubbing tears from his eyes with a clenched fist.

'My family,' he whispered. 'I miss my family.'

It was agony to watch. He cries so rarely. It takes a lot to push him over the edge. My tears followed his, but I also felt a strange sense of relief. He had cried. They were real tears. If there was something in him that could break, it also meant he could heal.

He's fishing in the drawer for his green-and-yellow pills.

'They're all gone, Reubs,' I remind him.

'Pretend,' he replies without looking at me.

He pushes an invisible pill through the foil and holds nothing in his hand before popping it in his mouth and swallowing.

Let him pretend, I think.

Let him stick to his routine. It'll pass, and today is not the moment for rocking the boat. My only job this morning is to get him up and ready and out of the door to the day centre.

I woke him at 8 a.m. to have him ready by 10, but his resistance was like dragging sacks of sand across gravel. To save time, I came straight down and neatly lined up his vitamins on the table. His routine became mine. I made him sandwiches for lunch, and it felt so good putting them into Tupperware and clipping the lid shut.

I didn't realise how much I needed this until Angie called. She had developed a soft spot for Reuben while he was at the day centre last year, and always goes above and beyond the responsibilities of her role to make sure we feel supported. She rang yesterday afternoon and I really wasn't expecting it.

'Reubs is OK,' I told her. 'Up and down, you know.'

'And how are you, Manni?'

'I'm fine,' I replied. 'Fine.'

She paused before asking the question again.

'Are you really OK?'

Maybe it was her genuine concern that cut through, or perhaps it was the sheer and sudden relief of being given the opportunity to be honest with another person. Her question broke me. I crumbled, falling silent as I tried to blink tears back into my eyes.

'You're not OK, are you?'

I couldn't find enough voice to answer. I started shaking my head, even though she couldn't see me.

'Right. That's it. I'm processing for a carer's burnout.'

Struck by the official language, I panicked.

'What does that mean?'

She told me how there'd be a room in the day centre where Reuben could spend some time, drawing alone if he wanted or interacting with the staff, while I had some time to myself. She went on to explain that she was also going to contact social services about funding, so we could turn it into a daily visit from ten in the morning until two in the afternoon. I counted the hours on my hand – one, two, three, four hours. For the first time in three months, I was glad that there was somebody else in charge, a professional, someone with so much empathy and experience.

'I'll organise transport, Manni. It'll be a bus just for Reuben, but I'll need a few days. Can you bring him till I get it lined up?'

Reubs doesn't finish his breakfast, and I struggle to put his shoes and coat on. He doesn't want to go. I look at his face and I see a real anxiety in his eyes, his gaze tight with distress. I realise that we have to backtrack. I haven't explained enough. I haven't prepared him. I can't simply shove him out through the door

I take his coat off and we sit on the steps.

'Booba, sorry mate. Is it all a bit too much? A bit too fast?'

He looks at me with a sense of relief.

'New stuff is difficult, I feel that way too. But it's not really all new, babes. It's Angie. It's the day centre. Remember? It's the same building, the same people.'

'Will I come back?' he asks me, pointing to the kitchen floor with his glasses.

I giggle, 'No, you're never coming back, Reubs. You're going to live there for the rest of your life.'

'Shut up, bruvr.'

'You will only be there for four hours. Well, three now because we're late!' He counts out the numbers with his fingers, one, two, three. 'Then I'll come and get you. And we'll come back here for a peaceful afternoon.'

'Ah,' he exclaims. 'Not long.'

Why had I just assumed Reuben would understand?

Why was I so frightened of explaining it?

I tell myself off for not running him through it sooner. I was far too busy wondering what I'd do with my free hours. But once he has taken himself through the process of the day in his mind, he seems much happier. The muscles in his face relax.

It's way past 11.30 a.m. when we pull into the day centre.

The building used to be a primary school, with high-pitched slate roofs and a playground that wraps around it. There are no children playing here today, no skipping on tarmac. Only staff cars and a bus parked at the doorway.

'Press the buzzer, Booba.'

He follows my instruction, peeling a glove away from his hand and gently pushing.

Angie appears, smiling from behind the double doors. Her face looks a little distorted through the safety glass.

'Good morning handsome,' she says to Reubs, her voice lilting with genuine affection. Reuben smiles and waves away her compliment with his glove. 'Oh I've missed you,' she tells him. 'Where have you been all my life?'

'Sorry, we're late,' I say.

'You don't have to apologise,' she assures us. 'Right, let's get you in, out of the cold. I hope your brother made you something delicious for lunch because if not, he'll be in big trouble!'

She winks at me as Reubs follows her into the building, down the corridor, past the office window with its sliding glass and left into his very own room.

I stay put as they disappear behind the double doors, feeling bewildered. Angie has just relinquished me of responsibility and I almost cave in without it. I turn around slowly and don't really know what to do with myself. I say good morning to the bus driver scrolling his phone with a thumb. Over two whole hours until I have to be back here. What am I going to do? How am I supposed to spend the time not worrying about Booba? I have completely forgotten what it feels like to plan for yourself. Shall I go somewhere? In all the excitement to get Reuben here, I'd forgotten it was my birthday.

I drive off in a bit of a daze and finally decide to head to the harbour, which looks like a postcard of itself from the 1970s. Everything seems dated. The primary colours of the fishing boats pop in the sunlight, oil slicks the water. There are more places closed than open, but I get my coffee and sip through the plastic lid.

I dangle my feet over the edge of the harbour wall and imagine lines connecting the buoys under the surface of the water. I count the boats moored in the harbour, and choose my favourite. A gull lands to my right, another to my left. They close in as if I had chips. I talk to them. I give them names. I start worrying about Reubs. I wonder if he is happy. I wonder if he is safe. I wonder if he will only eat half of his packed lunch. I wonder if he is talking to anybody.

Is this what carer's burnout feels like? I have the opportunity to be by myself, just for a couple of hours, but feel terribly guilty. Fuck. My head starts racing to places I don't want it to go to, my heart starts beating faster. It's that coffee, surely. I'm on the edge of a panic attack. Can I hold it back?

An elderly couple stroll past, keeping just far enough away so they're not obliged to say good morning or see the look in my eyes. I budge back a little and find an empty bench behind me. It feels safer here, away from the edge of the harbour wall. I close my eyes against the shape of the sun, and its glow helps the spirit level in my head. Shit. That was scary.

My head still feels flushed with blood when I get back to the day centre at 2 p.m. Smiling through the mist of my thoughts, I thank

Angie for intervening and giving me some time

'Nothing gets past me,' she says. 'You looked shocking, my darling. When else were you gonna get yourself some proper rest?'

'I thought I did a good job at hiding it,' I confess. 'Was it really that obvious?'

'To me, yes. But look. Please call me whenever. And I mean whenever. Day or night.' She gives me her personal mobile phone number and I tap it into my phone.

'And I've sorted the bus,' she adds, turning to address Reuben. 'It will be there at ten o'clock on the dot, so make sure Manni is ready. No lazing about in bed, OK.'

'Angie, I don't know what to say.'

'You don't have to say anything.'

I'm quieter than usual on the way home, and Reubs must notice because he puts his hand on mine as I change gears. I don't speak all afternoon. I'm not sure whether it's because I can't or whether I don't want to. Reubs seems worried. He asks me if I'm OK and gives me a hug. I only eat half of my scrambled eggs, and after supper I take some of Reubs' felt-tips and draw a big red heart in the centre of a page. I write along the bottom edge, *sleep well brother love you turn all the lights out*. I then give him a kiss on the cheek and hand the paper to him face down. I make myself a mug of hot milk and honey and shuffle upstairs, where I stand on the landing until Reuben calls up from the living room.

'Bruvr!' he says in giggles, just like he always used to, with a full froth of amusement escaping from the pit of his tummy. 'What you like.'

After that awful family Zoom call with Reuben, the idea of him being stuck in his room at Portland Place haunted us. My elder brother, Matthew, kept commenting how dark his room looked. That video message of Reuben crying into his phone will always be burned into us. But things were about to get even worse.

The six months that Mum and Dad were near Reuben turned into eight. They had managed to rent their house out to a friend in Norwich, but news of the wooden floor buckling from rising damp in the living room put pressure on them to go back. Then there were Dad's appointments for myasthenia gravis, which had been confirmed again after weeks of cancellations. They couldn't delay their return any longer. Meanwhile, Jack and I weren't allowed to leave Spain to see him, so for the first time in many years Reubs was about to live without any family close by. It was too difficult to discuss without being with him, and we were all so worried about how he'd take it.

I still don't know, to this day, whether any staff at Portland Place took the time to sit with him and explain. It came as no surprise, when we did manage to organise more calls and messages, that his gestures were diminished, more and more void of any emotion. I kept sending messages and cards and presents, while friends and family sent him care packages which were kept in the front porch for 72 hours before Reubs was allowed to open them – there was one package, with a jigsaw puzzle inside, sent by a friend in America, that spent two weeks in the porch before Reubs was given it to unwrap. He must have felt so utterly cut off. Despite the support and love that arrived on phones and on computer screens, in envelopes and small packages, Reubs suffered from the lack of physical contact and affection. Care providers of homes and sheltered housing all over the world couldn't adapt quickly enough, and by the time virtual networks of support and community had been established, much of the damage had already been done.

This is when Reubs started hiding his food. It was Emma who had noticed it. She saw what was going on before it became too routine, and thankfully she emailed to let me know that he was stashing his meals in his tote bag or pockets, later throwing food into the bin in his bedroom. Emma was also the one who weighed him at his all-time low, 55 kilos. The other carers did respond to this, and rallied around to make sure he was eating enough food. A friend of ours, Mary-Lou, also started making batches of Reuben's favourite gnocchi, with portions of rhubarb crumble for pudding. She left these meals by the front door of Portland Place, and they were a big hit. I got a WhatsApp from Reubs: *got Post Card brother Gnocchi. more Crumble. you Something love you brother*. He gained two pounds in a matter of days.

When we were allowed to leave Spain, I came straight back to England and was allowed to make daily visits. I was always asked to go through the alley first, at the side of the house. 'We'll bring him round the back,' they said. How I hated that phrase. It was as if he and I weren't really meant to be together, as if there was something criminal in being seen. On that first visit, I couldn't sit for long on the cold, rigid bench and stood up to start pacing the paving slabs. 'My Bruvr,' he mouthed to the staff who held him close in case he toppled. We extended our arms but couldn't touch. We locked eyes and blew kisses through masks, holding back like boxers before the bell.

A carer I didn't recognise showed us up to the top terrace, where a swing bench faced another metal seat with last night's rain collected on it. The back door closed on its fire-secure hinge. I waited until we were alone before speaking.

'Hey, Reubs. I've missed you so much.'

I looked at him, expecting our bond to rise and make itself felt. But he looked away. Perhaps my eyes were too questioning. He wasn't ready. It's far easier to be with strangers. Hiding is less complicated. There was a flutter of recognition, but no real connection at all. The space between us was empty and I didn't know how to fill it.

'I love you, Reubs,' is all I could offer.

He looked away and raised his shoulders in a shrug.

Did he not believe me?

That first visit didn't last long. It was cold and uncomfortable, and all he wanted to do was go back inside.

'I'll come tomorrow,' I said. 'I'll come every day.'

The back door creaked open as they led him back to his room.

During that summer that's exactly what I did. I visited him forty-six times in the forty-six days. There was just one Sunday when I almost didn't go. I wasn't in the mood. I wasn't breaking through and was tired. It was raining. It could have been the day when Reuben needed me most. If I didn't show, what would've happened to him? I had to go. It was too risky not to.

Before I arrived, Reuben had been allowed to linger in bed until late morning and the first question in my head as I walked down the alleyway was why didn't he get up earlier? There was nothing for him to do, that's why. I later found out that he was often finishing his breakfast as the other residents were sitting down for their lunch. Why was he allowed to do that? He was still drawing, at least. But even that was starting to fizzle out.

I don't doubt that the carers looked after him, but were they able to *care* for him? A quick search on Google tells me that the English word 'care' comes from Old English *caru*, which itself is a blend of Old High German *chara*, meaning grief or lament, and the Old Norse word for sickbed, *kǫr*. When I saw him that day, I was grieving for Reuben, no doubt about it. I lamented what he used to be, and wondered how, at the very least, I could help the staff at the centre give him a reason to get up and out of bed in the morning. I *cared* for him, and I *care* for him still.

I am aware that I was a demanding family member, kept apart from my brother by circumstances that neither I nor the carers or the care providers could do anything about. I was asking a team of overworked, underpaid people to care for my brother on a much deeper level than the demands of their days allowed. In many ways, their hands were tied. They were working within an old, outdated approach to care, entrenched at Portland Place and a thousand underfunded homes like it. There was no way they could adapt to the pandemic and continue to ensure Reuben's best interest. It didn't take long to realise that we had a battle on our hands.

Sadly, heartbreakingly, there are countless residents of care homes, assisted living flats and sheltered housing all over the UK who do not have a family to fight their corner or defend their rights and needs. Perhaps that is partly why the Mental Capacity Act of 2005 developed the principle known as 'best interest'. If Reuben's care assessment concludes that he lacks the capacity to make his own decisions, or if there are no family members to help him, then those decisions are taken for him by a whole host of individuals involved in his welfare.

During those forty-six days that I was able to visit, I asked to be more involved in whatever best interest decisions were being made. I was determined to find a way that the system of care at Portland Place could be scrutinised. Gradually, I discovered that the root of the problem was not at Portland Place itself, not among the carers who worked there. It was at the head offices of the care provider, with which I had never had any direct contact until I insisted on starting a weekly session with them online, to start tackling the problem of Reuben's isolation.

These conversations quickly became quite crowded. Reuben was there, as was his social worker, social worker's manager, several carers, a care home manager, an adult learning-disabled psychologist, Dr Aaberg the psychiatrist, a senior worker at the care provider, a speech therapist, other therapists, and us, his family. What bothered me most about those sessions, wasn't that most of the people involved didn't really know Reuben personally. It was the fact that, had I not asked to have been part of Reuben's support group, I would not have been invited to join. I would have carried on being excluded. The minute Reuben stepped into Portland Place, there was nothing about the system of care that enabled his family – who had been his primary carers for so long – to engage in the slow, complicated process of defining what Reuben's best interests really were, let alone plan how to meet them and then ensure that they were being met.

*

As instructed by Angie, we're at the garden gate by 10 a.m. It was a struggle but we made it, and as we wait for the bus I run through all the positive parts of the day again with Reubs, starting by saying he'll be rid of me for another four hours, then explaining why it's good to get a change of scenery and see other people.

'You'll be safe and cosy,' I reassure.

As the bus approaches, Reuben recognises Marie on board.

He points and pulls down his mask to show me his smile as she waves back. They show genuine affection for each other as the door opens and Reuben is ushered on, perhaps both of them reminded, briefly, of the life they used to have. Marie is one of those people who appear to be wrapped in goodness. Her face always breaks into an easy smile, and I thank her as she fastens Reub's seat belt and adjusts his mask so it is covering his nose.

As they drive away, I can see that Reubs has moved seats so he can wave. It takes so long for him to convert the thought of waving into the action of waving, that I think we've missed saying goodbye. But just before the bus disappears down Annings Lane, there it is, a raised hand flapping about through the back window.

I stand in the lane until a sense of release seeps up. I have another four hours. I have four hours for *me*. I'm giddy with possibility, and run back into the house to rip off my dressing gown and get ready to go for a long walk. I already know that I want to follow a route I've done a hundred times before. I want to see if it feels different today, without him walking at my side or knowing that he's at the cottage waiting for me to get back. A sense of excitement warms through my body as I get my walking boots on. Perhaps we both need to remember what it's like to miss each other.

Shutting the front door, I remember Dr Aaberg saying that I mustn't be too ambitious. But clearly his ambition for Reuben and mine do not match. I have no doubt he cares – and perhaps he's right, I shouldn't be too hopeful that my brother will return to who he was. Dr Aaberg is nothing but sincere, full of empathy and expertise. But I'm Reuben's brother. I saw him learn to walk. I've played and laughed with him for over thirty years. I have seen him give speeches to hundreds of people at a wedding and win karaoke competitions in front of strangers. I've seen him reach heights no one ever dreamed of. I've still got high hopes. I'm not ready to stop dreaming for his future, and I'm bound to be more ambitious.

Recovery will be slow, I understand that. It may never be complete and I will probably need to adjust my expectations, but at the same time I'm determined to nurture that space in Reuben's mind where he can wander freely without fear.

Maybe we'll never see the Reuben of old completely back in the room, but I am convinced that fighting for the small changes, the tiny steps, will shift him away from the reality of his depression. Every step he takes, every day we get through together, is ground that we have gained and a step towards him rediscovering the confidence to speak again.

Over these last weeks and months, every walk has left and returned to Reuben. Always, whether I am with him or without him, I am walking the labyrinth of his past and future, through the folds of the landscape, the ridgeways and the holloways that bring such intimacy to being here. I've been a walker since my teens – when my mind is jumbled, this is how I help myself untangle it all. Every year – except for two – since 2001 I have walked the Camino de Santiago, either as a guide or because it has become such an essential part of my year. I love the route. I love the ritual of wearing the pilgrim's shell and swapping my nationality for a pilgrim's passport. Every walk has become a small pilgrimage for me. Sometimes I carry my burdens too heavily, and each step becomes penance for a sin that I have never even committed. But every walk always has promise. Every walk is a commitment.

When Nathan and I took Reuben along the Camino, he was coming up to his twentieth birthday. I was thirty years old, Nathan was twenty-five. Three brothers striding out. As you walk the Camino, you naturally gather a wider pilgrim family, of all ages, genders, languages, cultures, politics, religions. Give or take a few kilometres, most people walk a similar distance each day, so you reconnect with the same people at lunch stops or dinners, forming your own, loose band of merry pilgrims.

It's one of the most rewarding parts of the experience, the surprise of strangers and how you weave in and out of each other's paths and lives so effortlessly. I'm pretty sure it has always been that way, back into the twelfth and thirteenth century, when use of the Camino was at its peak, and the artefacts of this diaspora began spreading along the route – monuments built by aristocrats and royalty, entire towns settled by pilgrims who never went home, convents and monasteries that were founded by the devout, hospitals that were opened for the weary and infirm.

None of this collective sense of history and pilgrimage happened for us brothers, though. Our journey was different. We did meet people but conversations were usually left unfinished, and we rarely saw the same faces twice. Pilgrims weaved through us, smiled, chatted for a little while and then, with apologies, needed to get going. We heard it over and over again. 'I'd love to hang out with you guys but I really have to continue.' (Probably true.) 'I'm getting cramp.' (No way of telling.) 'I'm getting cold so I really need to hit the road.' (Off you go then.) 'Maybe we'll see you tonight?' (Fat chance!) 'If you guys make it to Astorga tonight, I'd love to buy you dinner.' (We didn't make it to Astorga that night.)

I get it. It's fine. Don't feel bad. Reuben walks a third the speed of most people. We were the last to leave and always the ones who never arrived, having to stop somewhere in the middle of each official stage. By walking so slowly, we missed out on Camino friendships and community. At the start we didn't notice or mind, but as we clocked up the miles, the strain of isolation began to show as Nathan and I were locked deeper into Reuben's existence.

His slow, quiet ways were showing us something that nobody else on the Camino could. Over days, we started to experience the world through him. We walked at his pace, stopped when he stopped, to look at the flowers in his *Secret Garden* or notice the same animals of Narnia and the trees of Middle Earth that dotted his path every day. We weren't taking Reuben on a pilgrimage, he was leading us. But late one afternoon, three kilometres from the next town, Reubs sat down in the middle of a dusty path.

'Reubs, what are you doing?' I asked.

'I'm done, bruvr,' he replied.

'You can't be done. We're not there yet.'

'I'm done,' he repeated.

Nathan and I looked at each other. We had packed a tent just in case, suspecting that something like this might happen, and pitched it right there for the night. After that, Nathan and I started to feel frustrated by Reuben's pace. We didn't tell each other this – neither of us wanted to admit impatience. Instead, we bickered and grew more and more exhausted by the day.

At our wits' end, we very nearly abandoned our pilgrimage – twice. When a huge argument loomed, at the next fork we agreed to carry on walking to the same place separately, along different paths. Nathan took off one way with our miniature schnauzer, Monty, and I pulled Reuben along another.

I walked an even lonelier path that day. Sometimes, being with Reuben is like being by yourself. He demands nothing from you in conversation. He can stay happily silent for hours. Often, I glanced down to remind myself that he was on the end of my arm. As we walked, I came to the sad conclusion that this is what life must be like for my brother: he meets people, casts his nets of friendship, full of love and aspirations, only for those nets to be hauled back empty. People simply cannot or do not want to slow down enough to get to know him. He only sees people again if they wait for him, or if they come back. It's never up to him. This is one decision he can't make. If he does, it tends to lead to disappointment, which gets harder the more you experience it. He still dreams of true friendship, I'm sure of it. Yet any true or intimate human connections with peers seem to have evaded him.

On the Camino, Reuben's reality hit me. I kept gazing over at him, wondering how he did it. How could he be so brave? My love for him swelled. I didn't have to imagine his emotions any longer. As we stood there in the middle of a field, an ancient path beneath our feet, we were both alone, isolated by our particular pace of life. I imagined the hundreds of thousands and millions of people who had passed that very spot throughout the millennia. Ghost pilgrims. On the Camino, at least, you are never really alone.

Without malice, never with judgement, Reuben walks with an open heart. He never expects, he rarely asks for anything. It is our job to anticipate his needs, to know what's best. But this is the tricky bit, because what he needs and what you think he needs are not always the same thing. The only way, I've realised, is to keep asking the questions and be patient enough, slow enough, to wait for the answers.

'I miss my Nathan,' he said finally.

'I miss him too, Reubs. It's alright. We'll meet up with him tomorrow. He'll be waiting for us, I'm sure.'

When all three of us were back together, reunited, we hugged as if we'd been apart for weeks. Those twenty-four hours were just the oxygen we needed to carry on. From then on, we managed to settle more easily because we accepted the rhythm as it was. We were still far from Santiago, but we no longer wished to be somewhere else, with someone else, or further along the path. And along the way, Reuben established his own routine. Each evening, normally while Nathan and I were figuring out dinner, he sat on his bunk with his felt-tips drawing a wardrobe into Narnia. Every night the same: another wardrobe would appear. Usually, he gave the finished artworks to one of us. But I remember one evening he left a picture on the bunk of a young man from the United States, who approached me just before lights out.

'Hi, I think your brother left this on my bed,' he said, showing me the drawing.

'Did he? Bless him,' I replied.

He faltered, almost embarrassed to ask. 'But what is it? What does it mean?'

'It's a wardrobe. It's from *The Lion, the Witch and the Wardrobe* by C. S. Lewis.'

His face blanked.

'It's a book. A story about children finding their way to a magical world, called Narnia, through the back of a wardrobe. My brother is finding the Camino tough, so at the end of every day he draws a wardrobe as a sign of hope – one day soon he'll find a Narnia.'

Even though the room was barely lit, I could see that the man's eyes were full of tears. 'Fuck,' he whispered as he disappeared into the shadows of the dorm.

We never saw the man again, but we learnt on the Camino grapevine that Reuben's drawing had reversed his decision to abandon his pilgrimage. Before meeting Reuben, he had decided to quit. He was tired, mentally and physically. The wardrobe had been a sign for him to continue, to finish what he had started. When we told Reubs about it, he replied with an uncanny glint in his eyes.

'I know,' he said.

From then on, whenever we arrived at a pilgrims' refuge, we would discover that somebody had reserved a bed for Reuben. This went on for the rest of the journey. Every evening, a guaranteed bed. We never found out who they were, so we called them the Camino Angel. Perhaps it was that man who was about to give up, or somebody who had heard about it along the way.

Then towards the end of our journey, we walked with two young women from England for a day. They were not in a hurry either, it turned out. So we ambled at Reuben's pace, glimpsed some of his magic, and although we parted company the following morning, they left a trail of letters, gifts and sweets along the Camino, like a series of talismans showing us the way home, hooked over bent nails, lassoed over gate posts, stuck to noticeboards, or dangling from low branches. Reuben loved it. He spent the remainder of his Camino seeking them out, and the anticipation pulled him forwards, up hills, through valleys, even into the crowds of Santiago de Compostela.

Getting to know Reuben is an act of patience, possibly even an act of devotion. At my usual speed, it would take two or three lifetimes to get to know my brother properly. If you take your time, perhaps it would only take one life. But let's be honest, hardly anyone has the time. Sadly, our lives are too busy. We're constantly trying to keep up with everything and everyone else. Being able to step away from our usual lives and walk the 210 miles of Camino with Reuben, was a privilege. Nathan agrees, those twenty-five days were fundamental in shaping the rest of our adulthood. The experience changed us, and forged an unbreakable bond between us brothers.

It's almost dark when the bus arrives back at the cottage. Marie brings Reuben all the way to the back door.

'He's had a good day,' she tells me.

'Thank you, Marie. I can't tell you what this means to us. We were going a bit bonkers, weren't we, Reubs?'

Reuben points at me with his broken glasses and we all laugh.

'See you tomorrow,' Marie chimes as she runs back to the bus.

I peel Reuben's many layers off and give him a hug.

Is that a tiny twinkle I see in his eyes?

'I miss you, bruvr,' he whispers.

'I have missed you too. Did you have a good day?'

'Did have luffly day, bruvr. Do you love me?'

'Sometimes,' I jest.

'All the time!'

'It's not easy to love you all the time, Reubs.'

'And you.'

'You're right there. I'm a nightmare.'

'Nah. You my bruvr.'

'We're getting there, aren't we?'

'We do.'

Reuben is at St Mary's when I catch up with him, taking another photo of the church for Jack. He left the cottage an hour before me, and when I catch up he hooks his left hand over my arm. There's no day centre today, so Reubs can stick to his routine of watering Jane and Neill's house plants. It also means we can keep our routine of fish and chips on a Thursday.

He begins to drag and my back twists after just a few steps – I can feel my sciatica twinge.

'Booba, I can't pull you all the way to the beach. It hurts my back. You can rest your hand there but walk on your own.'

My voice has an angry pinch to it, which isn't intentional.

'I am sad and lonely,' I say in my best Aslan voice. 'Lay your hands on my mane so that I can feel you are there.'

A few days ago, I had made up my mind to call Sam and let her know that we are not going to take Becky's offer of a space for Reubs in Emminster. I hadn't felt the courage or conviction to say anything before, not until this morning after Fernando called to let me know my car has been sold. Knowing my bank balance was about to crawl back from its overdraft freed me to worry about other things; I thought of Becky and decided to call Sam and get it over with.

'It's not that I don't think Becky is capable,' I explained. 'I think she's great. But knowing how intense it's been lately, I just think that it's too much for one person. I don't want that for Becky.'

'I understand, Manni, but Becky would do a terrific job.'

Sam is constant in her support. She's so patient. She works tirelessly and selflessly. Her stamina and commitment are incredible.

'It's been bugging me for days,' I confessed. 'I just can't help thinking there's a better option. He needs more than one other person. I'm holding out for that.'

At least I know what the *wrong* path is, even if I still don't know what the right one looks like or what direction we need to go in. Perhaps I shouldn't have waited so long to tell her.

'We'll need to get our skates on,' Sam retorted. 'What about Fox Hill, in Stourcastle?'

She had mentioned it before.

'Are there still places?' I asked, as if booking tickets for the ferry.

'I've not been up there myself but I've heard nothing but positive things. It's proving to be popular,' Sam replied.

There was a pull of dread in the pit of my stomach.

'Have we left it too late?' I asked, sounding desperate.

Sam promised to make some inquiries, and I promised to really engage Reuben in his future. But before I talk to him, first I'll have to convince myself that being put back into care is the best thing for my brother.

It might be one of February's windiest days, but the earth is dusted with snowdrops, and the presence of sun draws people out of their homes. The car park hums with activity. Against the racing clouds, the beach curves like steel into the distance. The sea is rough so we stay well above the tideline; I lie on the sand and pebbles, Reubs stands and stares at his feet.

I point along the beach, 'This has to be one of England's most beautiful beaches. Don't you think?'

There is no reaction. His eyes flit between pebbles and he adjusts his rainbow beanie, pulling it further down around his ears. He raises and lowers his eyebrows. I think he does it to feel the tickle as his eyebrows brush against the material of his hat.

'Your Samwise Gamgee loves it here,' I tell him.

Still no reaction. I might be able to bring my brother to the beach but I can't make him look at the horizon.

*

As we walk east, I notice a man watching us from the rocks above. He seems to be working on the sea defences of a little wooden house perched above the beach. Is he staring at me? Or is he staring at Reubs? I wave to defuse my doubts, but feel uncomfortable when he waves back.

Reubs takes my hand as we make our way gingerly towards the sand. He wobbles on a rock and leans into me for support. There's a change in his facial expression, a deeper level of concentration is needed to navigate without falling. Once we've got over the other side and onto the flatter stretch of beach, I take his beanie off and he watches it disappear into the pocket of my kagool. We turn our faces to the sun, close our eyes, take several deep breaths of sea air.

The tiniest of smiles forms at the edge of Reuben's mouth. A huge grin spreads across mine. What bliss! Neither of us notice as a huge wave crashes, but I spot it foaming up the beach and selfishly sprint away at the last second, leaving Reubs stranded in the frothy aftermath.

I release a belly laugh and bring Reubs close to hug his chill away. 'Bruvr!' he says, still a whisper, but there is a fresh edge to his expression.

He gently whacks me over the head with his soggy gloves.

'We better sit in the sunshine to get you warmed up,' I tell him, handing back his beanie.

We take a few selfies and a little video of us running up the sand in slow motion. I rotate around Reubs, taking portraits as he squints into the sunlight.

We head back towards the rocks and the man by the beach house stops what he's doing to wave again, this time more intent on making contact with us. What does he want? We can't avoid him because the path to the restaurant runs right alongside. I wonder if we might know him – he's a tall, elegant man, with a calm determination. I don't recognise him but stop as we get nearer.

'Does he look after you?' he asks Reuben, gesturing to me.

I tell him we're staying at Annings Lane and that we try to get down here every week.

'My son, Toby, has Down's syndrome,' he explains. 'He loves the beach. He's twenty-six. How old are you, young man.'

Reuben's eyes begin to sparkle.

He tells us his name is Phil. We introduce ourselves and tell him we're brothers. He wants to know more, so I begin to tell him and thoroughly enjoy the unexpected warmth of our conversation. When I've finished our story, he chats to Reuben more than me and manages to find out when his birthday is and what his favourite films are. Reubs relishes the attention.

'Hope to see you both again,' Phil says as we wave goodbye.

'Tell Toby we said hello,' I add as we part company.

I feel foolish as we weave through the parked cars to the footpath. You would have thought, by now, I would have learnt to read how people gaze. I suppose doubt is ingrained in me from all those stares in the playground and the streets when we were younger.

'He was cool,' Reubs says to me.

I stop and stand square to face him.

'He was, Reubs. Very cool. He thought you were cool too!'

'Did he?'

'He did, Booba. And he'd be right. You're one of the coolest people I've ever met.'

Negotiating the route to the restaurant is tricky for Reubs, but I leave him on his own and wait at the top, sitting on an empty bench. There are dozens of people milling around, waiting for tea or a sandwich or fish and chips. I see the tip of Reuben's rainbow beanie appear at the top of the steps. It's a full two minutes before his whole body follows. He seems to be resisting, but that fight in him is gradually weakening as he allows himself to be happier.

'Hungry?' I ask.

He points at me and mouths, 'You?'

It's Liberty who takes our order.

'Any chance of some fish and chips?' I ask.

'Coming right up. Sparkling lemonade for Reubs and still water for you?' She knows us so well.

We've been heading down here for the last few Thursdays, whatever the weather, so we can indulge ourselves in this salty, vinegary routine. We always sit on the same bench. Yet another Brother's Bench. As ever, Reuben eats half of his and wants me to carry the other half home.

'You can carry it yourself,' I tell him today.

He folds the brown paper around the food and manages to squeeze the lumpy package into his day bag. The wind has picked up since we've been on the beach, and we are glad for the shelter of hedges as we turn and walk home towards Annings Lane.

When I visited Reubs at Portland Place that difficult summer, there were days when I thought I'd lost him. He was so deeply locked away. I searched desperately for different connections – from the things we talked about when we were together and what he ate, to the DVDs he watched and the photocopied family photos of our past lives in the Stanmores and Reading that I left with him. On one visit, from that swing seat in the garden at the back of the house, I suggested we go into town for a little walk. It took all my powers of persuasion to convince him. His dull gaze held only shadows as we shuffled down the garden path and out onto the street, unsteady on his feet, edging along. Months of inactivity had affected his balance, and more than once he had to stop to assess his footsteps along the pavement.

I waited for him at the entrance to the allotments and pointed to the middle field, 'Let's walk to that bench, Booba.'

Thinking back to that day, through all the other days and hours that we've been together, I realise that Reuben's recovery has always needed to be shaped by his capabilities, not the expectations of me or anybody else. That doesn't mean I shouldn't have ambitions for him, set the bar high. But so much frustration and damage happens in that space between expectation and ability. It is important to have aims, to set sights on future possibilities, and to then gently stride out towards them, taking one step at a time if needs be. 'Look, over there. We'll walk to that bench.' One step, two steps, three.

We sat down that day and gazed across at the allotments.

In the quiet, a silly request emerged in my head: 'Reubs, say sausage for me.'

One of the common physical attributes of Down's syndrome is a large tongue. Macroglossia is its medical term. This inhibits his diction and vocalisation, and Reuben's pronunciation is typical. Certain words, like sausage, are spoken as if through a bird's nest. If you push your tongue to the roof of your mouth, round your lips and squeeze the word through the gap. That's how Reubs says it.

Throughout his childhood, we three older brothers enjoyed his differences, celebrating them, turning them into laughs rather than tears. He had always enjoyed the attention and played his part with an acute sense of comedy. But not that day on the bench. While we sat there, he looked completely defeated. Maybe there was a buried memory, but either it was so deeply covered or the mechanism for reaching into the cinema of his past had broken.

When he didn't turn and say 'sausage' for me, I cried.

He reached out his hand for me to hold.

'We're not supposed to hold hands, Booba,' I said.

It felt so good. His palm in mine.

He lowered his mask and lips to make a slight popping sound as he tried and failed to find the words, 'N... O... W... Dry tears.'

He was still in there, buried beneath a pile of Reuben rubble. This tiny gesture was a sign of life. I clung to it and didn't want to let go. I dried my tears with my free hand so as not to leave his grasp.

When a man approached, all wide strides and smiles as he walked his dog, I felt guilty and dropped Reuben's hand. I didn't want to break the rules. That's what our government had told us. The man might be all smiles now, but maybe he would speak to someone and Portland Place would find out and report me. I imagined getting fined by the police, for holding my brother's hand.

As the man disappeared through the allotments and across the river, I looked left and right to check the meadow was empty.

'Reubs, we can have a quick hug.'

He looked up, brighter than I'd seen him all morning.

'Don't tell anyone. It's a secret.'

As I embraced him, he expelled an emptiness and melted in my arms. I could have held him for hours. It was his first hug in months. When the smiley man in the tracksuit bounced back over the footbridge, I let Reuben go. It was enough, though. That embrace made us both feel lighter, and from then on, whenever I came to visit Reubs that summer we made sure we went back to the bench, come rain or shine. We called it Brother's Bench. Even now, whenever we're out walking, on the beach or shopping in town, we keep an eye out for a Brother's Bench. They're everywhere when you start to look.

It takes us over an hour to dawdle our average speed of thirteen metres a minute. Earlier, I was happy to walk as slowly as him. There really was no sense of urgency. But the day has turned and the skies are menacing, I want to get us both indoors. As we're going downhill past Dairy House, despite my unease, Reubs stops and motions for me to continue alone. He wants to walk the last section by himself.

'You sure? If a car comes,' I tell him, 'get right into the hedge. It could rain soon.'

I stride out ahead, leaving him behind.

Near the cottage, I check the weather forecast on my phone to see what we have in store tonight. It doesn't look good. There are red warnings all along the coast as the storm comes in from the south-west, gusting off the Atlantic.

Reuben takes off his coat and kicks off his walking boots when he gets back in. He sits on the sofa and takes his chart out of the orange folder, just to make sure that the day is going as planned. He studies the words to find the right box, to mark the fact that we've made it. *walk to beach*, tick. *fish and chips*, tick. What's next? *drawing on sofa*.

I play the soundtrack to *The Secret Garden* loud enough to dissolve the sound of the wind outside in the dusk, but occasionally a gust makes the doors tremble. Reuben is distracted by it, looking up from his felt-tips as if there was a large beast in the living room. He notices me looking at him.

'What you staring, bruvr?' he asks.

'You. I'm just staring at you.'

'Shut up, bruvr.'

Another gust turns his head towards the garden window. The weather has been so beautiful all week. Should I say something? Will acknowledging the stormy weather just make it worse?

After supper, I load the dishwasher and check my phone again, as if the wind will drop by looking at the forecast. Reubs is definitely uneasy. Circumnavigating fear only helps it fester, so I decide to help him face it.

I walk over to the sofa and take his hand.

'Reubs. Look at me.'

He puts his felt-tip down. Maybe he knows what's coming. At first, his glance seems to bounce off me and recoil.

'Were you scared that night at The Corner?'

How can he answer that?

He was petrified.

I know that fear is still locked away in him.

If ever I have questions, I ask them. When I have doubts, I talk them over with Jack or a friend. But Reubs needs a helping hand most of the time, a little push to ask what or why. His emotions are just as defined, and I'm sure he knows how he feels. It's just difficult to find the words because they are all locked away in boxes.

'Did you feel lonely that night?'

He lifts his thumb and forefinger, to measure out his loneliness, just-a-bit.

'I'm sorry.'

He tilts his head, 'Just lightning brother. Like *Independence Day*.'

'But that's a film, Reubs. Films aren't real. You know that. You were safe. The Corner is as safe as a fortress, and you had Katie next door. It was just a storm, Reubs.'

'Yeah, like here.'

He lifts his finger and points towards the dark of the garden.

I want to say something but stay quiet as he too considers his response to the silence. He's trying to find another key to open a box. 'I got you,' he says.

I've always assumed that I was capable of loving Reuben more than he is capable of loving me. I think the very nature of disability, or at least of our understanding of it, predisposes us to feelings of superiority. *Dis*ability versus ability. But am I really more able to love than Reuben? I doubt it. There are so many lessons to be learned from this quiet man who sits by my side. I am constantly humbled by the new ways of thinking and being that he demands of me, always asking for a deeper affection and compassion. There is an equality to our love that I've long taken for granted. All this time, I have assumed that he's the only one who needs to re-learn himself.

In darkness, the wind through the trees brings the storm closer. There are layers of sound within the thrashing. I can hear it all as Reuben sleeps. The wind is incessant. I try to settle in my bed but can't. I go downstairs to make myself a cup of tea and open the doors, needing to feel even more engulfed. Each gust takes away a little more of me. I don't really want to sleep tonight.

3

It is 6 p.m. on a Friday night and Reuben is sitting in the kitchen, dressed as a nun. My phone camera is focused on St Roch in his chapel, the most convent-like part of the house, as people begin to log in to the live feed. Pretty much everyone who promised they'd join is watching.

I wink at Reubs and put my thumb up to signal that we're going to start. He tries to wink back but he has never been able to. His face, pinched like a cherub's, tilts with a concerted effort.

I pan out until Sister Mary Clarence (Reuben) enters the screen, hands devoutly poised in prayer. There is reticence in his expression until the opening line – 'I will follow him' – reminds him of the moves. The music holds memories for him. You can see the past and the future meet as the song continues, and yet his choreography is still stiff and half-expressed.

As the beat kicks in, there's a change in his eyes. He starts to flaunt, and I have to chase his movements around the kitchen with the camera, trying to keep my phone steady as I grin and giggle.

It's hard to believe that earlier he was sitting on his bed, refusing to get dressed after a whole week of making props and posters, run-throughs and dress rehearsals. Only half an hour ago he had given up, and I was ready to give up too. I shouted and hollered and pulled out the tools of blackmail and persuasion.

'They will all be watching, Reubs – Mum and Dad, Samwise Gamgee, Tommy Boy. Anna can't wait to see you.'

'Where?' he asked me.

'In their phones. Through the camera.'

I can't wrap my head around the idea of them gazing in from the ether, so I try to make things simpler by explaining they'll all be watching from their sofas.

'Pretend,' I added.

'Pretend, bruvr.'

We made it downstairs just in time for the curtain-up on his Friday Night Musical, and now I'm watching my baby brother spin and twist. Reuben David Coe, a man with Down's syndrome, *not* a Down's syndrome man, dressed in a nun's habit mouthing the words, 'I will follow him, follow him wherever he may go', with a delay of about four seconds between the music and his voice. It reminds me of when we were kids in church and Reubs always used to be one line behind in the hymns – he would belt them out anyway, and Mum had to sit between Matt and me to stop us from spoiling the sacred with our laughter.

As the music slows, I grapple for the bunch of yellow tulips on the kitchen counter and throw them from behind the lens. They may be wilting in real life but they look great on the screen. Reuben pauses in his final position and then takes a bow, letting go with a sparkling smile. The muffled applause and digital whoops join us in the living room, love pouring in.

'APLAUSOS!' I scream, my voice cracking with joy. 'That was amazing, Booba. Well done that man.'

'Ingya,' he says.

After we wave our audience goodbye, blowing kisses with promises of seeing them soon, everybody leaves happy that they've had a glimpse of the old Booba. I turn to him and ask if he's happy.

'I am,' he replies.

'Good. We want you to be happy, always. If you're ever not happy, will you let me know?'

'I will, bruvr.'

He pulls his habit up and over his head, making for his favourite corner of the sofa for a well-earned rest.

'Well done, Reubs. You were brilliant. I love having my brother back in the room.'

It may have only been five minutes of his life, but tonight I'm full of hope that something was triggered, a memory muscle, a reflex, something that might reconnect Reuben back to himself.

Back when Debs, Reuben and I were all living together in what became known as 'San P Palace', we managed to strike the fine balance between supported living and independence. It was a team effort. And we had a little community. When Debs and I were busy, friends used to take Reubs out for lunch or dinner, and the neighbours would check in on him. The personal trainer at the gym used to watch out for him as he clocked 1 km on the treadmill, which later became 2 km, 3 km, 4. Our friend Victor bought Reuben a motorised tricycle and – I find it hard to write this now – my brother used to cycle (yes cycle!) around San Pedro de Alcántara on the bright blue cycle paths, wearing a lime-green cycle helmet that Debs thought looked ridiculous.

It is *this* version of my brother that I think of more than any other. This is the Reuben that Dr Aaberg never met. He was independent, creative, funny, full of energy and so mischievous. When I get a clear glimpse of this Reuben, as I have done tonight in his nun's outfit, it convinces me that we're on the right track.

Even at those heights of being himself, he was still reluctant to identify with other people with Down's syndrome. Debs and I would occasionally try to encourage Reubs to make contact, and we went on doing this until one afternoon, while we were having lunch in Passion Café, a family walked in with a son who was Reuben's age.

'Look, Reubs,' I gestured towards the family's table.

Reuben's reply was emphatic and wise, 'And what?'

I blushed with embarrassment. Here I was, trying to throw Reuben together with 'his kind', and he was quite rightly digging his heels in and letting me know that he didn't want to be defined. In his own quiet way, he told me to stand down.

Many years ago, our family friend Hugh asked Reuben a very

interesting question. 'Reuben, are you Down's syndrome or do you have Down's syndrome?' *To be* or *to have*? Reubs thought long and hard about his answer. 'I have Down's syndrome,' he replied.

If you have Down's syndrome, does it mean you have to identify yourself as being Down's syndrome? Is *having* Down's different to *being* Down's? I refer to someone who *has* Down's syndrome, rather than someone who *is* Down's syndrome, because my brother asked me to.

A few weeks later, while Reubs and I were sitting on the terrace of Peggy Sue's American Diner, close to Marbella's Old Town, the tables turned. I thought the restaurant might remind him of *Back to the Future*, with candy-pink booths and black-and-white chequered flooring. As I ordered some drinks, he went inside to check it out. When he came back he said, 'There's a girl who has Down's syndrome inside, bruvr.'

I smiled and couldn't let the opportunity pass, '*And what*?'

He grimaced – I had him cornered, and he hates that.

I let the moment sink in before gently suggesting, 'Why don't you go in and say hello, Reubs?'

He thought about it for a few minutes and then thought about it some more. I watched as the idea formed slowly in his mind.

'I think I will,' he said, popping his drink down.

Time seemed to stop completely as I watched him approach the family at the back of the diner. He stood there and smiled when he reached them, and through the large window I could see the family saying something that prompted Reuben to wave at the young girl (we found out she was called Janie). When she saw Reubs, her face lit up with an internal light. He then stepped forward and started gently stroking her head. Out of place, out of time, two people with Down's were sharing what can only be described as love.

By this point, I was standing and leaning for a better look. The manager, Dani, came over to ask if I was alright. He put his hand on my shoulder to steady my crumpled frame, then took me to one side to weep against the window of the shoe shop next door.

Afterwards, Reubs strolled out of that diner as if he'd just collected an Oscar. He was almost levitating. He came over and grabbed me. 'Come here, bruvr,' he said as he took me into his arms. On our way home, we were chatting about Janie and I asked why he sometimes ignored other people who have Down's syndrome.

'It's hard for me.'

'So, it's easier just to ignore it?' I asked.

'Yes, bruvr.'

'But you didn't tonight. You went straight up to that little girl and loved her.'

'I know, bruvr. I know.'

'I am so proud of you, Booba,' I told him as I squeezed his hand.

'Ingya.'

On Saturday morning, dawn brings full sunlight into the cottage. In the front room, dust dances through the angled rays.

I wake Reubs at 8 a.m., now he's used to getting up for the bus to the day centre. While I'm waiting for him to come round, I notice his nun's outfit in the corner, poking out of a plastic bag. Yesterday's fancy dress. Last night's disguise. My memories burst out in the form of a giggle. He yawns and stretches his arms, 'Why you laugh, bruvr?'

'Just remembering something. That's all.'

We bought that nun outfit in Spain. It was around the time that I was so busy at work that I was flying out of the door before dawn and crawling into my bed straight after rushed dinners. Reubs and I hardly saw one another, and he never demanded anything from me. On a rare weekend when I didn't have to pick up or drop off clients, I tried to apologise.

'Booba. We've hardly seen anything of each other.'

He rolled his eyes, feigning annoyance, 'You always so busy!'

'That is why we are going to do whatever you want to do today.'

While I went to get ready, I told him to think about it and tell me when I got back downstairs.

I showered. I dressed. As I brushed my teeth, I was imagining all manner of things he might suggest: tenpin bowling, DVD shop, cinema, all-you-can-eat buffets.

'You ready to tell me?' I asked him when I got back.

A huge grin filled his face.

'Go fancy dress shop, bruvr. Buy nun's outfit.'

His sleepy gaze meets mine while I'm reliving this memory.

'Aslan is on the move,' I say and he looks at me as if he knows what I mean.

This winter, we have experienced water in all its forms: rain, sleet, fog, hail, ice, snow, river, lake, sea. Moisture clings to every day of every week. Thinking back, we've rarely been dry. But slowly, almost unperceived, spring is taking back the year, thrusting the greenery through the crust of the earth.

'How are you this morning, Booba?'

He lifts thumb and forefinger together.

I interrupt the gesture, 'A little bit happy? Well, that's great.'

He tuts, makes a face and then corrects himself.

'Well yeah. A little bit happy.'

A huge smile rises into my face like a hot air balloon.

'And little bit tired,' he adds.

Before I can stop him, he reaches for the face mask underneath his pillow (so that's where he hides them) and puts it on, yet another shield to hide behind.

As it's a bright and sunny day, I suggest we go to the market. The idea meets with total nonchalance until I remind him that there are several stalls selling DVDs.

'Mss Dobtf I nefg,' he whispers.

'Take your mask off. I can't hear what you're saying.'

'Mrs Doubtfire, bruvr.'

'Well, we better go and look for it. You never know.'

He pauses, then whispers a new thought. 'I got good idea, bruvr. You buy for me and I stay here. Tidy a bit.'

'Not happening. We're going together. End of story.'

A tut. A scowl. A forced yawn. I ignore all three.

'How many lives do we get, Booba?'

He slowly raises the index finger on his right hand.

'But it's my life, bruvr,' he says.

When we step out onto the front drive, he's moving so slowly I wonder if he's doing it deliberately to goad me. Doesn't he want to get better? But he is, I remind myself. He really is. And he's never going to get any better if I give up on him, so easily slipping into that habit of low expectation. Nor will he improve unless he wants to, which is the part of him I can't always reach.

'Can you close the gate, please?' I ask.

In town, the early birds have got all the spaces, so we park near Lidl and walk in. Reubs takes my arm and steps gingerly into the centre of each paving slab. People step into the road to get around us, and some cast a caring smile. Other eyes pull that pitying gaze. Do we really look that bad?

As we pass a shop window, I stop and look at our reflection. I'm unshaven. My hair is a gravity-defying mess of grey. Reubs clings to me and looks at the pavement. We do look like a sorry pair. I bet people are wondering: what's the story there then?

I give Reuben ten pounds as we edge down South Street, just about far enough from the DVD stall so he can see the shelves of multicoloured plastic.

We arrange to meet at a café back on West Street.

'In thirty minutes?' I suggest.

'Not long,' he replies.

'You want longer?'

He lifts his hand and pinches his fingers. A look of decisiveness comes over him, an expression I haven't seen for a long time.

'OK – see you there in forty minutes, then. At one o'clock.'

He lifts his hand to stroke my face.

This is the first time Reuben has been on his own in town for nine months. But he's reached that stage now, he can walk alone. If I keep imposing my will and decisions on him, even if that's just holding his hand through the high street, it might repress him. It's a fine balance between making him feel safe and allowing Reubs to rebuild enough confidence and feel empowered by his own decisions. He must not fall back into lethargy. The hardest bit for me is trusting that he can do this. Will he get to the DVD stall and back again? Finding his way will engage his memories, remind him how to navigate the streets.

I don't just walk off. I can't. I do that weird and creepy thing of crossing the road and spying on him just to make sure. There he is, mask on, hat on, scarf on, hood up, gloves off, as he looks carefully along the spines of the hundreds of DVDs. The fact that he wants something, anything, is a major breakthrough, and my heart beats with a sea-swell of pride.

But as I walk away, I wonder if I'm doing the right thing. Is it too early? He won't get lost, will he? I glance back one last time and see him handing a DVD to the man on the stall, even enjoying a bit of market banter.

I have to trust him. I don't have a choice. I need to open that space for him. I head back up South Street where everyone seems so chirpy, as if the warmth of the sun has given them permission to enjoy themselves. There's a singer performing in the square, so I hover for a while, moving away from Reuben but still staying on the same street, listening to the songs of heartbreak and applauding with the rest of the crowd who are balancing cups of coffee and bacon baps on their knees. As she starts another song, I drop two pound coins in her guitar case and head off down West Street.

I find a seat in the café, order coffee and a croissant, then just as I'm sitting myself down Reuben appears in the doorway, bang on 1p.m., as if he were waiting outside for the clock to strike.

He tackles the steps before slumping into the seat by my side.

'And?' I ask him.

'And what?'

'Did you find it?'

He reaches into a paper bag and pulls out *Men in Black II*

'Oh,' I respond. 'Haven't you got that one?'

'I think. I did.' He curls his tongue with the pride of a purchase.

'You didn't find *Mrs Doubtfire*?'

'I will.'

Mist clings to the valley. Above, looking as if they are suspended above clouds, Jess's sheep have reached the top of the field. They have almost completely stripped the turnips. Checking the flock's progress has become my morning habit, a field calendar that marks the passing of time. It feels like ages ago that they were level with my eyeline at the bottom fence, just starting out.

Jack and I had a strained conversation on the phone last night. I know he would much rather our little family were together again. He would make it work, just like he makes everything work. He would find a way to have Reuben back in his life. Sometimes, I underestimate just how much Samwise Gamgee misses his Frodo Baggins. I forget just how much Reubs means to Jack, and how invested he is in Reuben's future. They fulfil something in each other that cannot be replaced or replicated.

Everything is made worse by distance. Jack and I have been apart for nearly four months now, and the strain of separation makes everything more complicated. Neither of us really admits how much we miss the other. We are burying those feelings. And he knows what it's like when you start running out of steam. Even if you should stop and take more time for yourself, you don't, you dig yourself in and get through one day, then the next. My mood swings from compassion to anger, through lethargy to determination.

'What the hell are we going to do?'

That's the question neither of us has the courage to ask.

Of course, Reuben is hoping our life here can go on forever. This is becoming his home. Each time he says he wants to stay here with me, my emotions drop an octave. If only I could ignore responsibilities and the complexity of it all. All the housing options in town have led nowhere. And when I turned Becky down in Emminster, that put a stop to other possibilities of Reuben living with host-carers. I still have so many doubts, and while I turn them over and over in my head, Reuben sits on his bed and draws. He sits on the sofa and draws. He sits in an armchair in the living room and draws. He is almost forty years old and his life revolves around felt-tip pens. Lucky him.

After speaking to Sam, I looked online to discover that Fox Hill was purpose-built for assisted living. It is one of the first projects of its kind in the county, it boasts on the website. There are design plans and images too, showing how the architects have replaced common rooms with gardens, removed long corridors and walls and turned the community into something more open and spacious. It's part of a scheme called 'Integrated Community Learning Disability Services' – not the snappiest of titles, but what it sets out to do seems much more progressive than most care housing. I also love the fact that it's called Fox Hill. Reubs could draw a fox. He could add a cuddly one to his pillow-props.

Before Sam got back to us, I made the decision to drive Reuben to Stourcastle for the day, to get a feel for the town. If we liked it and they didn't have places, at least I would be keeping my promise to Sam, engaging Reuben – and myself – in his future. We went a couple of days ago, after Reubs had done his watering at Jane and Neill's. The drive was north, through the chalk downs, inland from the coast. Reubs was asleep within minutes, which annoyed me at the time. He was missing the beautiful drive and seemed generally uninterested in our day out. I even opened his window to give him a blast of cold air, but that only woke him up long enough for me to offer him a swig of water. He twisted his torso away from me, so I couldn't see him drinking, then put the bottle back and closed his eyes.

I always wonder what he dreams about. Does he dream about the past? Do the memories of the day jostle in his head at night? Maybe he'll drift back to when he was younger, waiting for that bus in Teletubbyland – that's what we called the Rec ground down the road from the red brick house that Mum and Dad bought in Thatcham, on the housing estate in the new part of town. Reuben was still at school in Reading, some ten miles away, and the school bus would collect him from the bottom of the alley, fifty metres from our house. Every day he had to go up and over Teletubbyland on his way to the bus stop, where the developers who built the estate covered the rubble and waste in soil and seeded it with grass, leaving us with what looked like perfectly formed burial mounds in the middle of suburbia.

Reuben loved Teletubbyland, and on one particular day, he had to pick up the pace because he was running late. Mum and Dad hurried him out of the door and urged him to run for the bus. 'Running Reuben' is an oxymoron, so inevitably he took his time in Teletubbyland, walking up and down the mounds, in his own world. He missed the bus, of course, and my parents didn't realise he'd missed it until three hours later when Mum made her way back from the shops. She spotted him at the bus stop, standing to attention. Martha, our cat, was waiting by his side.

'Hello, my mother,' Reuben beamed as Mum pulled the car up alongside the curb.

'What on earth are you doing, darling?'

'I am waiting for the bus,' he replied proudly.

'Get in, yer silly billy. The bus left hours ago!'

'Oh.'

He wasn't alarmed or in the slightest bit worried about the bus that never came, content with his thoughts drifting through Teletubbyland. 'What am I like!' he said as he got in the car.

When we arrived in Stourcastle high street, I tapped Reuben awake. 'Look at this. It's lovely. A café. Fish and Chips, and a bakery.'

'DVDs?' is all he wanted to know.

We parked the car behind the Co-op, grabbed some sandwiches for lunch, and wandered back along the high street towards the river. We found a bench in the public gardens, where the old railway used to run through the town. It's a delightful spot. Reuben unwrapped his piri-piri wrap and started nibbling.

'What do you think, Reubs?'

'Like the film,' he replied. '*Railway Children*.'

We fell into silence while we ate, but after a few minutes, Reuben stopped chewing and took his broken glasses out, pointing at the mural opposite the bench.

'Look. Like us. Bruvrs.'

There was an uncanny resemblance to his own drawings, and he recognised this straight away.

'Well, what do you know!' I exclaim.

Two giant hands meet in the middle of a bursting sun, and along the wrists and arms are written the names of those local residents who fell on the battlefields of the Second World War.

I explained what the mural was for, and he looked thoughtfully on as his jaw moved up and down mechanically, in gradual pursuit of swallowing. I finished my sandwich and started to wrestle with the idea of Reuben being here. I wondered whether it was a good town or not, and whether my brother could live in a place he had no connection to. Half of me wants to listen to Jack: grab Reubs and run back to Spain. We could make it work. He could spend the weekdays with Jack, get involved with the Down's syndrome association in Malaga, find his feet in a community. Jack is ready for the responsibility, but am I? Am I ready for the worry? I want someone else, apart from Jack, to worry with. We can no longer do this on our own.

But Reubs is the most precious human I know. I can't just leave him and run away. The guilt would never leave me alone. I know myself. Unless he is happy, my own happiness will always be overshadowed by a feeling that I have failed him. There will be nowhere to hide.

'Luffly, bruvr,' Reubs said as he finished his wrap.

I grabbed his hand to steady my own. There was so much I wanted to say. But I couldn't say it all at once. I did tell him why we were in Stourcastle, though. I wanted him to know why we were there. I told him about a place called Fox Hill, but didn't say that it could be a new home for him. By leaving that bit out of it, I am still hopeful that Reuben will find his own answers to the difficult questions we both face.

We didn't stay long. We didn't go too close. We stayed on the other side of the road, peering across.

The main buildings at Fox Hill are old council offices that blend with a new building. It's an easy walk from the town centre. All the wide front doors are painted in primary colours.

When I asked what he thought, Reuben shrugged.

Heading back to the car, I was determined to find things he could connect with. I pointed out the historic buildings and the glimmers of the river in the distance, but he wasn't interested. The one thing that caught his eye and caused him to stop in his tracks, was a charity shop. He didn't go inside, but through the window he could see two shelves of DVDs right at the back. His eyes sparkled. I hoped there was a copy of *Mrs Doubfire* in there.

'They've got a good selection,' I said. 'We'll have to come back.'

He shook his head and smirked, 'My bruvr.'

He then grabbed his right ear lobe and gave it a gentle tug.

'Ear by here.'

How he has clung to this phrase. It allows him to avoid saying No, when either he doesn't want to hurt somebody else's feelings or when he would rather be left alone. But as with many things, viewing the meaning through him turns the phrase into something more complex. *Let's play it by ear* starts to look less about being easy going, and much more like a mechanism for escaping the pressure of interacting with other people, and all the hopes and dreams, demands and expectations they might have for him.

Ear by here.

*

A dear friend from Spain, someone I hardly see any more, sent me a text last night. He just wanted to know how Reubs and I were doing, so I gave him a quick update and mentioned Fox Hill because I was still processing our trip. His reply tripped me up, and I can't get it out of my head: *A tug on heart and conscience. I pray you can find a solution where inspiration, care, devotion, sympathy and love come up to your standards. You have done your very best... never forget. Sending you deep love and good wishes, Guy P.S. How is Jack coping? Longing to get pissed and walk in the hills with you both.*

I spent the entire night with Guy's words in my head, aware of myself and the shape of the room, trapped by thoughts that hardly go anywhere. Jack might not be here but I forget sometimes that he must be suffering, just as much as us. Reuben and I have each other, whereas he's alone. When I tried to switch off, all my efforts to find an avenue of sleep just kept me more awake. I could process the thoughts, but just as they started to go somewhere, the notions and arguments got vaguer, so it was impossible to draw any conclusions and move on. Instead, I had to go back to the beginning again and again, to think about how Reuben needs me, to wonder how much of this need is his, and how much of it is about me being needed. Life needs purpose. Purpose helps us escape the purgatory of ourselves. It also makes us happy. To be wanted, to feel the gaze of unconditional love.

Throughout his life, Reuben will always need me. Rather than being a liability, is it possible that this is, in actual fact, the greatest of gifts? A gift that will never diminish. Aren't responsibilities what bind us? Don't they assuage the weight of the human condition? I decided not to have children, but I do have a brother who needs me. He keeps me grounded and keeps me sane. So why on earth do I want to give this gift away? Why would I want to distance myself from a source of happiness?

Because being here, caring for Reuben, has also separated me from Jack and my life in Spain, which are other sources of happiness. Why can't these sources of happiness combine? They did before, when we were living together. A friend once sent me a text that read: *The bond you, Reuben and Jack have is amongst the most beautiful I have ever seen. People are affected by your unity. Why would you ever break that up? It will be really hard for Frodo to lose his Samwise Gamgee and his Gandalf the Grey. You were born to be together.*

I am so torn. I patter downstairs before dawn to put the kettle on, and for a change I carry the cup of tea back up to bed, careful not to spill any on the stairs. I plump up the pillows and sit thinking, gradually realising that what I am experiencing are the crushing blows of guilt, and I cannot reconcile them.

One voice says that I should never again abandon Reubs to the care system. The other voice tells me it's high time Jack and I got our lives back – we have been separated longer than we've ever been separated before. And this isn't the first time one of us has been with Reuben. This has been going on for over two years now, taking it in turns to support Reubs on his road to recovery. Selfishly, I want the freedom of our relationship back. We deserve that, don't we? Neither Jack nor I are getting any younger, and I feel we have sacrificed enough. Dr Aaberg thinks that social independence would be Reuben's best chance of a fulfilled and happier future. It's not natural for him to be living our lives.

My thoughts keep spinning.

I've struggled to let go of the image of Reuben in my head and in my heart, the person who walked the Camino with his brothers and lived a life of independence with Debs and me. That Reuben is not the person I stole away from Portland Place. But the real Reuben isn't the person in my head either, and my failure to completely rediscover him frustrates me.

None of us are born to be alone. We are formed and nurtured to be part of a community, part of a tribe. It is through these people that we discover and express our sense of identity and belonging. It may be painful at first, but I know what the healthiest option is for Reubs. He needs to find his own way.

Jack is the first person I call.

'The uptake has been quick,' I tell him. 'There are only four flats left out of seventeen, and it will soon be full. Social services will still need a profile of Reuben. A committee will decide if one of the flats is suitable.'

'Or is it the other way round?' Jack asks, sounding more subdued and cynical. 'Will the committee decide whether Reubs is suitable for them?'

His resistance isn't personal. He's doing it for Reuben, and it's not me he's questioning. Already, things are moving too fast.

'Here we go again,' he says. 'What kind of care will Frodo get? What do we know about the provider? Can we ask for references?'

He always asks the right questions.

If I am being asked to file a report about Reuben, shouldn't we expect the same of the carers?

'I'm not sure, Manni,' he says. 'Why doesn't he just come back?'

'Sam says it's a good place. It's progressive. There's nothing like it around here. It's different to everything before.'

My tone is unconvincing, but who am I trying to convince? Myself? Jack? Reubs? Jack has already lived through the disappointment of seeing Reuben slip away, and neither of us could bear to live through that again. He's being pragmatic, I know that. His bluntness is an expression of love. And he would genuinely rather bear that responsibility himself, than trust a care system that has already failed Reuben twice.

Because Jack isn't here, he will trust me. But I'm going to have to do much better to convince him – and to convince myself.

Jack's abstention forces me to ask again, who is this really for? Samwise only thinks of his Frodo. I am thinking about myself and my work and my collapsing business. I am thinking about my friends and the life I have made in Spain over two decades. I am thinking about my relationship with Jack. Is that all so wrong? After months of separation, I want our relationship to find an even keel again. Should I be willing to sacrifice all that for my brother? Does it really all come down to whose happiness is more essential?

Is my happiness less important than Reuben's?

Is his happiness any less important than mine?

If he does stay here, while I go back to Spain, will that actually make me happy? If he comes with me, will being in Spain make him happy? It didn't last time.

Will I really be able to leave Reuben in a town, the name of which he can't even pronounce, and walk away?

By the time I put the phone down to Jack, the idea reeks of abandonment. Look what happened the last time I left him. It was at the end of the summer, after our time on the Brother's Bench and those forty-six conversations over forty-six days, when he became noticeably lighter and brighter and more nimble on his feet. His focus shifted out of his room. He was more able to stretch his imagination and remember all the family and friends and loved ones, all rooting for him and sending him love. But when I left Portland Place at the end of the summer, who picked up the slack?

As I boarded the flight for Malaga, I knew that the distance would do nothing to ease my guilt. I expected to be overshadowed by the worry of Reuben's mental health. Before the summer, my concerns had been fairly abstract. The video calls and Eddy's photo of Reuben at his window confirmed my suspicions. But after those visits, seeing him and knowing the reality of Reuben's day made leaving that much harder.

Those couple of months back in Spain passed desperately slowly for me. Jack could see my frustration mounting. The unanswered emails to the staff and the care provider, the phone calls that Reuben would never pick up, text messages with no reply. I was only half living in Spain. Part of me was back with Reuben, inside the rooms and corridors of Portland Place. How could I get on with my life when I knew my brother was regressing again?

That's when Reuben's message hit my phone. It was the brightest part of the day, the November sun was at its highest. *brother. do. you. love. me.* It was like running head first into a brick wall. I was completely floored. Five words. Five fullstops. No question mark. Because this wasn't a question. It was a silent protest, a call to arms. Just five words that laid bare everything that was wrong with Reuben's life and the care system he was trapped inside. There was only one possible response.

There's no way I can tell Reuben about the places at Fox Hill, not yet. I need to hear from Angie first, that grounding voice. She is one of the few people who truly understands our dilemmas, and who can always see all sides of the argument.

She's busy at the day centre when I phone, but she can tell that I'm desperate and clears some space in the afternoon to talk.

'Oh, Manni. It's so difficult to know what to do.'

Even hearing her voice starts to calm me down.

'I can only tell you that Fox Hill is the best of the best. I have heard wonderful things, and only wish we had one in this town. How many places are there?'

'Four. I don't know how many others are applying. It feels a bit like entering a bidding war, and still I'm not sure if it's the right thing for him.'

'But you have a very strong case with Reubs. If it has been designed to give tenants true independence, that is exactly what he needs.'

'But is he ready? Is he strong enough, Ang?'

My voice breaks at the end of the sentence. I have to sit down in the armchair by the front window.

Really, the question is this: am I ready?

'Look, Manni,' Angie reassures, 'let's think hypothetically. If Reubs gets a place, and I really hope he does, you can still pause to make the final decision. It's a process. If you don't apply, you won't find out. And I don't live that far from Stourcastle, so I promise I'll go up and see him at least once a month.'

'Will you?'

'I wasn't going to tell you this, Manni, but I've such a soft spot for Reubs that I've talked with my husband about him coming to live with us.'

'Don't!' I gasp.

'It's true, we have. I love Reubs. I really do and he's not getting rid of me that easily. So rest assured that whatever the outcome of all this, I will be here.'

I am broken by the goodness of this woman. I cannot believe she is willing to take on the responsibility of Reuben's welfare herself. I don't know what to say.

'Now, you get your head down tonight,' she urges. 'Get some rest. Things will be clearer in the morning.'

As I put the phone down, Reubs appears at the top of the stairs.

'Who that, bruvr?'

He must've heard me. I'm kidding myself thinking I can't talk to Reuben about his own future. I can't keep talking to people without him in the room.

'Who do you think?'

'My Angie,' he replies.

I pause to take a deep breath before asking, 'Do you love me?'

'I do, bruvr.'

I climb the stairs and motion for Reubs to go back into his bedroom. I ask him to sit down on his bed.

'Why do you love me?' I ask.

'I just do. That's why.'

'And you know I love you.'

'I do, bruvr. My bruvr.'

'Hold my hand, Reubs.'

He reaches and we sit looking into each other's eyes.

'What?' he says as if he knows what's coming.

'Do you trust me, Reubs?'

'I do, bruvr.'

'Good. Because the people at Fox Hill want to meet you, and I think that is amazing news. I've thought about this a lot. So much. And I think you could be really happy there.'

'Fox?'

He lets go of me and puts both hands above his head, to make two ears that wag with his fingers.

'Fox,' he repeats.

'Exactly, Booba. Foxes are clever and wise.'

'Like *Fox and the Hound*,' Reuben adds.

'*Fantastic Mr Fox*,' I echo. 'You can find happiness, just like Tod did in *Fox and the Hound*. And that is all I want for you. For you to be happy again.'

He looks away and I follow his gaze out of the bedroom window.

Jess is in the field with her collie, rounding up the sheep. Reuben watches her too. There are two animals separated from the flock, and we both anticipate the moment she gets them into the pen and shuts them in with the others.

Reuben turns back to me and says, 'Well, yeah.'

Where does he get his courage from?

'They would like to meet you. To just say hello.'

All the tension begins leaking out of me. I was prepared for him to be angry or unsure, but his response is neither of these things.

'It might not work out,' I add. 'It might not. They might take someone else. But unless we have a look, we'll never know.'

All too often I have seen Reuben disappear when he walks into a room. It's not because he wants to, or because people can't see him. It's because people are unsure how to engage with him and his differences.

'Would your brother like a drink?' I get asked.

'I don't know,' I reply. 'Ask him.'

'Is Reuben hungry?'

'I don't know, ask him.'

'Will Reuben be alright in the garden? Out there by himself?'

These questions are well-meaning but show a lack of exposure. The amount of people I meet who have never met or socialised with someone with Down's syndrome is surprisingly high. Has it always been this way? Historically, have people with Down's been hidden away, tucked out of sight?

Reuben came to meet me in Paris once, to join a group of students I was guiding for an American travel company. It was 2007. He was twenty-four and flew as an unaccompanied minor from London, holding a sign saying SORTIE. His suitcase was green but in the lights of Charles de Gaulle, Terminal 1, it looked blue so he missed it. There were 171 people on that plane that day and not one of them thought to help Reubs out, so he ended up ambling around the airport, totally lost. I was on the other side of security waiting for him and becoming more and more agitated. An hour passed. Another hour. They wouldn't let me in to find him. I lost my rag. I ranted and raved. I threatened to call the President of France. Eventually, they confiscated my wallet and agreed to escort me through the terminal building. He wasn't difficult to find. I spotted him straight away, far off at the back end of the building, a lonely shadow in the dim luggage hall. He was sitting on a bench flipping through the pages of an illustrated

Brother's

love Will Find a
Way

Sleep Well love you
lie in

Whoopi's
as Deloris

Sleep Well love you
brother

Mr Beaver

Sleep Narnia
Well
brother They say Aslan is
love you on the move

Samwise sam

am miss you

love you

Frodo

long time

Gandalf The Gray

9-30 lie in

love you

brother

sleep well

am father's favorite
son
am special am Joesph

Joesph Brother's
my brother's

Joesph

Jealous my coat
Iassqbhar

Matt   Manni   Nathan
Reuben   ~~Judah~~   Levi

tommyboy
Joesph give Benjamin ~~Zebulun Naphtali Simeon~~ ~~Dan~~
long hug

love you
sleeping
Well brother

The Mission

make everyone
and World emotinal

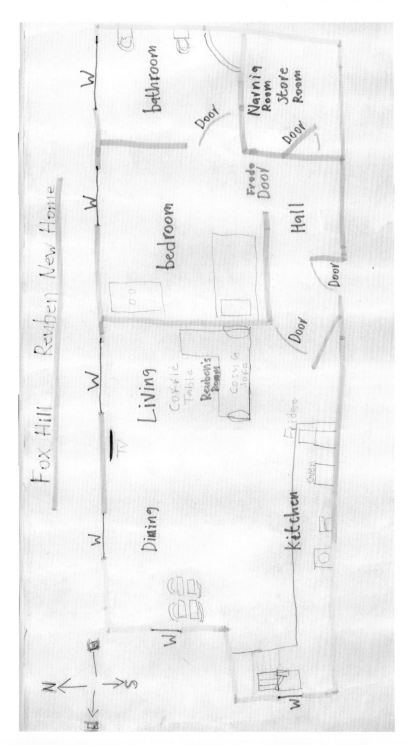

Good Things about fox hill

look's Abew for me

Finger X

~~~~~~~~

Play by ~~heare~~ ear

am miss my family

am home now
I s it Bredy

Fox

Sleep well
brother
love you

Peace Lily

For brother

card

No matter
Where I go
you Will always
be my brother
emotinal
For you

am miss you brother
love you

Red name

Brother. Do. you.
love. me.

Book Tour

brother's
Tour

Stage

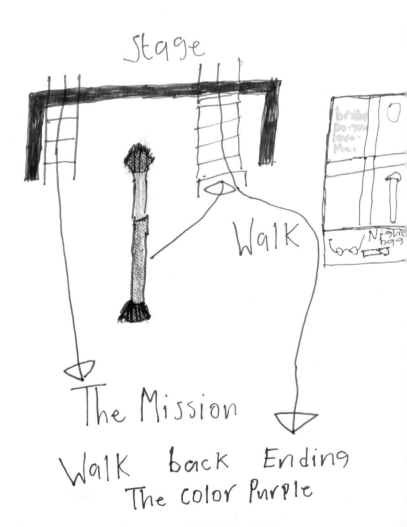

Walk

The Mission

Walk back Ending
The color Purple

Rainbow beanie
hat

PumBaq

love you

sleep well

Lion king

The Lion, the Witch and the Wardrobe, as cool as a cucumber.

'My bruvr,' he smiled.

I trembled as the fear of losing him rushed out like the tide.

'Don't worry, bruvr. I'm here now,' he told me.

But I'm guilty of the same neglect, and so is Reuben. I remember taking him to a Christmas party organised by Bumblebees in town, at the Women's Institute Hall. The carers were festooned with tinsel and elf hats. We were welcomed like old friends and Reuben had a present from Santa Claus. There was a young lady there with severe disabilities, her head braced in support cushions that were fixed to her wheelchair. One of her carers took her out onto the dance floor for a boogie to the Christmas songs.

'Come on, Reubs. Wanna dance?'

His eyes looked at me in despair. Although it was a privilege for us to be there, to witness an outpouring of festive cheer and generosity, both of us felt uncomfortable. I could tell that Reuben wanted to do a runner. He didn't want to be there. He didn't want this to be his tribe.

The young lady was being gently spun around in her wheelchair, first in one direction, then the other, and just as dancers find a spot where they perform pirouettes, she locked her eyes on me in the middle of each rotation.

'Who, me?'

She wanted to connect with me, and I wondered if I should approach and wish her a Happy Christmas. I could've asked her name and told her mine. But I didn't. Instead, I used Reuben's long face as an excuse to leave, thanking the team and making an exit.

We stopped in The Anchor for a drink afterwards. I needed a pint to drown my shame. By failing to acknowledge her, I had made her disappear. I was mortified at my own ignorance. Why didn't I go up to her? Was I embarrassed? Did I feel uncomfortable? Whatever the reason, it's the same thing that stops people acknowledging or engaging with Reuben. The easiest thing is to walk away.

No wonder Reuben just wants to disappear sometimes, to hide away in his room where there are no disappointments or demands. He's safer in there, hibernating. It's no surprise that leaving it behind dazzles him. In the warmth of spring, stepping back outside must seem full of risks and dangers, because it means he will have to find different ways to avoid the pain.

Before we set off, I give Reubs the cuddly fox that I bought online. He clutches it as we pass the old mill and bump over the bridge into Stourcastle. Getting nearer, driving down the high street, I can hear his breathing becoming more anxious.

Ever since he took that last yellow-and-green pill, there has been a new edge to his breath. I notice its shortness more in the mornings. His movements have become a little bit slower, too. Our hugs have been longer. Reuben's circuits must've been so welded by antidepressants. Pills that I agreed to.

I know my brother is wired slightly differently to me. His trisomy 21 affects every cell in his body. But Reuben was one of the happiest people I have ever met. All I want is to fill his life with opportunities again, not Selective Serotonin Re-uptake Inhibitors.

It feels like Reuben's future and past are boring towards the present, right here, right now, as we drive towards Fox Hill. There is no margin for error. His care is so complicated, and because I'm struggling to make these decisions on my own, I spoke to Dr Aaberg. He said it was a positive step, which has definitely helped give me courage. But the most reassuring thing he said took me back into the past, to the day I drove Reuben away from Portland Place, when the doubt was crushing and I wasn't at all sure whether I was doing the right thing. Dr Aaberg cleared his throat before saying it, 'I'm sorry we didn't get things right the first time.'

It's a March day held down by drizzle, but there is so much colour and goodwill here that we barely notice the rain. The daffodils are out, shaking raindrops. As they welcome us inside and start giving the tour, the care team direct all their attention to Reuben. The first thing he spots is a huge box of DVDs under the stairs.

'Oh, you like DVDs, do you Reuben?' asks Ivy.

He nods.

'A lovely guy just dropped them off for us, so help yourself.'

He looks timid at first, but soon gets over it and dives in to pull out *Patch Adams*, while I stand in the stairwell making polite conversation with Ivy, Tess and Meredith. His lips disappear as he slots it into his day bag. He loves Robin Williams. *Hook* is one of his favourite films. Reuben would make a great Pan.

'Tess is on the float team today,' explains Ivy. 'She can take you up to see one of the flats, OK Reuben?'

We are here because of Sam and Angie and Dr Aaberg. We are here because of necessity. But we are also here because deep down, despite the fears and the angst, I have clung to the idea of finding Reuben a home of his own.

As we approach the empty flat and pause outside, waiting for Tess to unlock it, I'm struck by the realisation that it's the first time Reubs has ever considered a front door of his own. I'm nervous and excited and want to say so, but keep my mouth firmly buttoned.

'Now,' says Tess. 'I'll show you Flat 12 because it's my favourite. It's just to give you an idea. If you get a place, it might not be this one but it would be similar.'

His eyes follow her around inside.

Even on a murky day in March, the main room spills with light. The first thing Reubs notices is the TV aerial socket on the far wall. He leans into Tess and whispers, 'It's all new.'

'It is, sweetheart. It's brand new. You would be the first person to live in it,' she replies.

I raise my eyebrows to let Tess know that he means a different kind of new, and she just about catches the gesture.

'Oh, I know, darling,' she says to Reubs. 'It's quite a lot to take in isn't it. But I tell you what, if you come here, we'll look after you. You'd be really happy.'

'Well, we got cottage,' he tells her.

Tess doesn't know Reuben's story yet. Nobody at Fox Hill does. Perhaps she's heard it all before; that's why places like this exist, to try and repair what's broken. She stands with Reuben at the window and points towards the building opposite.

'Over there, that's the day centre.'

Reubs looks at me and says, 'Not far, bruvr.'

I borrow an old phrase of his, one we haven't heard for ages, 'Well, what do you know!'

After visiting the flat, the team tells me there is a mother in the building whose son has just moved in. She is willing to talk. Her son, Stewart, is out at the day centre and I find her in his flat, arranging the last pieces of furniture that she's bought for her son's new home. She shows me inside and is happy to answer my questions. We talk about the building, the care team, the care provider behind the care team.

'What a set-up,' I say.

'I can't tell you how relieved I am,' she tells me. 'Stewart will soon be 25, and do you know what? When I drive away, for the first time in his life, I won't be worried about him.'

The emotion of what she's just said overwhelms her completely, the exhaustion of being a single mum colliding with relief. I join her in tears. We sit there weeping, two strangers in Stewart's flat. It feels wholly appropriate, though, because we both know what the other has been through to get here.

'I'll be rooting for you both,' she says. 'Make sure his Pen Picture gives a compelling argument. It'll all come good. You'll see.'

'Pen Picture?' I ask.

'You'll need to write a profile for Reuben. They'll then match his needs against the facilities and the ethos here. They call it a Pen Picture.'

*

I take Reuben's hand and we walk towards the high street. I want to remind him how close it is and for him to imagine being a man about town again. I pretend to wave at people we know and impersonate their replies with different voices: 'Alright, Reubs?' 'How you doing?' 'Good to see you, Reubs.' He goes into all three charity shops but comes out empty handed from each – there's really only one film he wants to find. We buy sausage rolls, still warm from the oven, and walk down to the church to find a bench to sit and munch.

Reuben nibbles on the pastry taking sparrow-sized bites.

'Samwise would love it here, Reubs,' I say. 'Mum and Dad would too. Imagine Mum with all those shops! And guess what, if you come here, then Tommy Boy will come and see you.'

'Here?' he asks, the half-eaten sausage roll is glistening through the brown paper bag on his lap.

I need some space for the words to unravel.

The day hangs formless in front of us, so I send Reubs to the village on an errand. 'Your mission, Bond Reuben Bond, 0021, is to make your way to the Post Office before closing time. Once there, you will buy food for lunch.'

'What food, bruvr?'

'Whatever you fancy,' I tell him.

'Well, something,' he replies.

I nudge him out of the door and tell him to call if he needs me. I have the whole cottage to myself. Finally, I can make a start. I open my laptop and begin to type.

Starting out, I'm determined to capture as much as possible. Reuben's needs, Reuben's dreams, his weaknesses and strengths. But as I write, it feels like I'm exposing him. I feel like a police detective writing a psychological profile. What gives me the right to describe him? A Pen Picture should really turn the mirror on me, on all of us, to explain why he needs to be sheltered at all.

I must concentrate, rein myself in.

Instead, I come up with the idea of describing the way he makes *me* feel. I can only really know this. And the more I write, I realise just how much these past months has fused us together. While I'm explaining how it made me feel to watch Reuben dance, go for a walk, wash-up or buy that DVD, it feels like Reuben's voice is in my head, whispering his story. I'm also struck by how vulnerable we all are. I don't think that my needs are more or less significant than Reuben's. Perhaps his are heightened, but I'm pretty sure what I describe as Reuben's weaknesses are also my own.

When I start to repeat myself, I know the words are drying up.

I read back what I've written, tidy it a little, and start to go through my emails and messages from Mum, Dad and Nathan.

I had phoned Mum and Dad to describe our first visit to Stourcastle, then again after our meeting with Fox Hill, and they had agreed in principle that if a place was offered to Reuben, we should accept it. 'Sounds like just the place for Reuben,' Dad said, and I agreed with him. If we had to design Reuben's perfect town, it would be somewhere very close.

'Has it got a theatre?' Dad wondered.

'Do you know what, it has.'

After months of uncertainty, to have their support was a huge relief. But even if he was offered a place, only half the battle was won. I would still need to convince Reubs and myself that accepting it was the right thing to do.

I start copying and pasting from Nathan's email:

Reuben needs a sense of community, some responsibility and a healthy routine and it's my adamant belief that he'll bounce back to the little character his brothers and friends know so well.

I now feel like a headteacher compiling a school report. But I'm not. I'm a brother typing to explain the complicated needs of his younger sibling. I snatch a bit from Mum and Dad's email too:

As Reuben's elderly parents, we think Fox Hill would provide an excellent opportunity for our son to feel free to choose and to make his own life choices . . . We know it is a new location for Reuben, but we feel the ethos is so appropriate for our son that once he has overcome the newness of things, he will respond in a creative way.

Towards the end, I begin to write about the seeds of his breakdown. I write about the storm. I speculate how that terror germinated, burrowing and growing until it smothered him. Can they help disentangle Reubs? I really want the committee who reads this profile to feel as if they know who he is. But they won't. They can't. They would need much more than this sketch. There's no way I can paint layer upon layer of understanding and insight, memory, nuance and detail. I just hope it's enough.

Squeezing in my concluding remarks, I wonder what Jack would add to the Pen Portrait. *I'm not sure, Manni. Why doesn't he just come back?* I am amazed at his unflinching commitment to be part of Reuben's future, but I have to put his thoughts to one side and keep writing.

It is easy to conclude that overbearing care does not suit Reuben's sense of well-being. It's more of a question of helping him to do something himself rather than doing it for him. At Portland Place, he totally lost his skill set as the carers did most things for him. He even forgot how to use a knife and fork. I believe we need a 'We will not do anything for Reuben that he is capable of doing himself' approach to his care. In the cottage, Reuben is in charge of bins, he hangs washing out, folds it when it's dry, vacuums, empties the dishwasher, does the Post Office run, helps me prepare dinner, and even waters the neighbours' plants. His skill set has improved massively and there is much room for growth and improvement. It is key that Reuben is encouraged and supported to do all these things for himself, rather than have them done for him.

I feel Jack's presence as I save and close the document. The onus really is on me, but I remind myself that the decision is not made yet. As Angie said, this is part of a process. We can't engage in the idea fully unless we start moving towards it. We need to wait and see what comes by submitting this application. If it's what Reubs needs, a life of his own outside the cottage, without me, then this could be the first step towards that. It could also be the only option we have right now. And the difficulty is that there's never an absolute knowledge of Reuben's needs. I could say that *he* needs independence, it will be good for *him*. But again, it feels like I'm describing myself. *Reuben at Fox Hill is what his brother needs, it will be good for him.* Perhaps the difference is that I can act on my will and wishes, but Reuben can't. Of course, he'd rather nothing changed and that we lived in this Narnia forever. Maybe he'd even be happy, at peace with this brotherly hibernation. But it might not be best for him. Besides, he can't do that without me. He can't be here on his own. And I can't keep going indefinitely.

This inequality makes me feel uncomfortable – I have the power to decide his future. He doesn't do that for me. I can include him in the process, I can talk to him, walk him around Stourcastle or Fox Hill, introduce him to people and places, drink coffee and eat croissants in cosy cafés and let him buy DVDs from the charity shop. I can make him feel as comfortable as I can, and even if by some miracle he agrees to all this, it still doesn't mean that it is his will or wish. He agrees because he has to. He goes along with it because he has no other choice. But even if he doesn't want to go, and expresses this clearly enough to me in whispers and drawings, he would still then rely on me or somebody else to live out the consequences of any reality. He can't live alone in the cottage. He can't cook all his own meals. His will, wherever it leans, is always bound to others. Bound to me, bound to Jack. Bound to Mum, Dad. Bound to carers. At thirty-eight years old, Reubs is still totally dependent on all of us. His life has never been (will it ever be?) a complete expression of Reuben. It is a constant collaboration.

There comes a day when parents cut their children loose, put them on a train destined to a new and brilliant future, while they stand on the platform waving goodbye to the very centre of their universe, suddenly filled with the angst of an empty nest. But parenting never ends. How terrible it would be if it did. Instead, the role morphs as children become adults and parents themselves. Growing up, we're all encouraged to be ourselves and to express our individuality. Yet who we are is a web of ongoing relationships. There is probably no such thing as individuality. We all rely on one another, most of the time. My will isn't just bound to Reuben's. I'm bound to Jack. I'm still bound to Mum and Dad, to some degree. I'm bound to our neighbours and friends. This village, any town or city is a universe of interactions and infinite communities. Freedom, individuality, both are an illusion. Being ourselves means being with others, relying on them, committing to them, so we can enrich each others' lives with laughter and love.

When a baby with Down's syndrome is born, this lifelong commitment deepens, and is often shaped by a life lived in permanent childhood. That's just one of the reasons Reubs is so special. I will always be a big brother to Reuben. Because his needs are constant, my obligations are permanent. I will always have his back. Of course, it's true that being his primary carer is hard work. But it's just as mentally tiring not seeing him, constantly worrying and wondering if he's being looked after. Being here, there are the practical things of course, the constant list of chores that by the end of the day have me reaching for the wine. These things push me right up against the idea of myself, so I don't feel like an individual any more. I am no longer free. But when I am away from Reuben, living out there in the world as only myself, being 'free', I do not find anywhere near the depth of love and warmth that I have when I'm with him.

We have made huge steps together. My brother is back, if not yet completely formed. Yet there is still the potential for self-neglect, because he won't have me badgering him all the time, telling him to tidy up, eat more, walk further, scrub harder. Part of letting go is also relinquishing my rights to be a bossy, loving brother. Stepping away is not about loving less, I must remind myself of this. It is about learning to trust again. I must remain doggedly hopeful, otherwise my doubts will leak into Reuben, and I cannot let that happen.

By the time Reubs returns from the village, almost two hours later, I have finished writing. With the words still echoing in my head, I watch as he puts lunch on the kitchen counter. An onion, a carrot and a swede.

'And what am I supposed to make with these?' I ask.

'Well, something. And this,' he adds, putting a Mr Kipling Battenburg next to the vegetables.

'Champion.'

'Did my best,' he says glumly.

'And your best is brilliant, Booba. Really. Well done. Did you see anyone you know? Terry and Jan or Jane and Neill?'

'No.'

'Were they friendly with you in the shop?'

'I think.'

'Am I going to make something delicious with your purchases?'

'I feel.'

I get up to ponder the ingredients but draw a complete blank. Instead, I turn the oven on to 180°C and get two cottage pies out of the freezer.

Even today, coming out as a gay man can be complicated. Back in the 1990s, it certainly was for me. My parents' generation were still immersed in the stigmatising media coverage of the AIDS crisis of the 1980s and 1990s. In particular, the Section 28 legislation that Margaret Thatcher and the Conservative government introduced in 1988, prohibiting the 'promotion' of homosexuality by local authorities (including in schools), forged a lingering shame that we all absorbed in subtle ways.

I took my parents out for dinner to share the news, haunted by the months and years of mounting dread, and started a journey fraught with pain. It was a great shock to both my Mum and Dad. (Jack always quips with a grin, 'How could they not know? You used to knit your own ties!') My parents' Christian world order went into disarray. Their son no longer aligned with their faith, nor their teachings. I was patronised, criticised, ostracised. Not only by my parents but by many of my Christian Union friends at university. They boycotted my twenty-first birthday party because it had a Jean Paul Gaultier theme, and they felt they needed to make a stand and be seen to do 'what was right'.

It was all so wrong.

It became one of the most difficult periods of my life.

With my parents, where there had been unity and intimacy, a chasm opened up, and there was very little emotional material to help us build bridges. Our philosophies were so at odds that it took a very long time for us to find any compromise. We scrambled for many months, then years, to find it. It was arduous, and for too long I lived with feelings of worthlessness and self-doubt. Reubs was witness to that. He was only eleven but he remembers my parents' sadness. He remembers their tears. He remembers me leaving home and moving abroad. It makes his own coming out process even more exceptional. I am still impressed by how intelligently orchestrated it was.

We were enjoying a day out visiting a National Trust house and gardens. He was twenty-one, I was thirty-one. We had stopped in a village to buy drinks in the local shop. Reubs began when we got back to the car, 'Looks like village Little Britain, bruvr. Where Daffyd lives.'

I had to add the line, 'But I'm the only gay in the village.'

It kind of did look like the TV show, but I didn't notice the similarity as much as Reuben's need to talk. It was his opener, and I knew he was trying to start a conversation.

'What do you know about gay men, Reubs?'

He shrugged his shoulders. He was showing such courage to talk to me so candidly, so I made it easy for him.

'Do you like men?'

He turned his head, looked at me with an intense gaze, smiled and replied, 'Well, yeah. Like you.'

This was the first time we had ever spoken openly about sexuality. I was so proud of Booba for trusting me, and skilfully working his way through to this brave expression. 'Shall we find a lovely restaurant and order a bottle of wine?' I suggested.

'Well, yeah.'

We were two brothers talking about our deepest emotions over lasagne and a bottle of cheap rosé. We felt so grown up. Reuben's coming out was a beautiful and exciting process, just like every coming out story should be. It's a moment when somebody steps into their true identity. How is that not a cause for celebration? So often, coming out stories are surrounded by the fear and trepidation of peoples' reactions, in their schools, amongst friends and families. You would think that nowadays 'coming out' should be easier, but I know many, many cases, close to me and far away, where this has not been the case at all.

I don't remember the name of that Berkshire village or that restaurant, but the weight of that moment endures time and place.

Reubs and I had always been close, but from that afternoon we were bound by an even deeper sense of loyalty and commitment.

'Don't want Mum and Dad sad,' he told me.

'This is not about Mum and Dad,' I reassured him. 'This is about you being who you are. What you feel. Staying true to the feelings you have in your heart.'

He put his right palm on his chest.

'That's the one. You just remember what Mufasa said to Simba.' I found my best Mufasa voice, 'REMEMBER WHO YOU ARE.'

He went on to have flings with guys, played Alice in *Alice in Wonderland*, watched every Whoopi Goldberg DVD, dressed up as a nun, and he even gave shows in drag. He was a staggering example of living authentically, and was an inspiration to so many. Reubs had embraced his identity, spectacularly. My parents weren't the only ones who wondered whether he was trying to emulate me, his older brother. My argument against those crackpot theories was always that he loved all his brothers in equal measure. 'Loving a gay brother does not make you gay.'

Reuben also wanted to be loved. He wanted to know what it felt like. When we discussed it, I once said, 'You'll be better off with someone with Down's syndrome, Booba.' His reply was a swift 'Nah, I like Brad Pitt.' Don't we all, sunshine. 'But let's be real,' I carried on. 'You need to find someone who understands you.' Then he said it, the first time ever: 'Am Downs on the inside, not on the outside, bruvr.' I hugged him close and told him he was more handsome than Brad Pitt. From then on, I yearned for him to meet somebody. 'Come on universe,' I would beg. 'Make me the happiest brother alive.'

In 2015, when Jack and I first moved into The Corner, Reuben flourished. We formed a trilogy of incomparable security and love. But I knew he used to look at us and wonder when it would be his turn to find someone. As he's grown older, I think he began to see the possibility slipping away.

After his breakdown, when he moved back with my parents, he

also had to live inside their world system again: their Christian beliefs, their hymns, their home-group prayer meetings. Reubs, in his vulnerable state, moved away from the self that had taken him a lifetime to establish. It's hardly surprising that brushing up against this culture again, having reverted to an almost childlike dependency, resulted in a sort of de-programming of his own beliefs. Not only did he have to process the fact that he has Down's syndrome, he also had to realign his sexuality, to exist within the cultural norms of his parents. He didn't want to make Mum and Dad sad.

All this week, I've been waking up at random times of the night thinking, 'Shit, I should have added THAT! I should have told them about THAT.' The committee met a couple of days ago, a decision has probably already been made. Should I have sent flowers? Should I have made a weepy appearance? Was his Pen Picture enough?

A pang of loneliness hits like a stitch. What I would do to have a friend on the sofa to chat all this through with. Talking would go a long way to unlocking my fears. It's important, isn't it, for Reuben to find his own way, rather than have me at his back all the time, pushing him gently uphill.

What I would do to have Jack in the room, I haven't seen him for so long. Our relationship is as strong as a fortress, but I text the question knowing he'll probably joke, 'Are you feeling needy today?' I still need to know, *Do you love me? xx*

Of course I do! he replies.

How much?

Enough

Enough for what?

Enough for you not to worry xx

Last night, after another instalment of Reuben's Friday Night Musical, I felt euphoric, and still did when I woke up this morning. It was so much easier than before. There was none of the last-minute resistance and battle to get Reubs to his stage in the kitchen on time. I was so pleased that early in the week we had decided on a *Joseph* theme, because finally it meant the Dreamcoat our friend Nico made from scraps could be taken off its hanger. Reuben rejected it when it was made, which disappointed Nico and me. He was in Portland Place at the time, and I just knew that the coat would have its day.

The cheap smoke machine and disco lights arrived in time for Wednesday's walk-through, and I fired them up in the living room just to watch Reuben's face fill with wonder. Something really clicked as he started directing himself between the table and the living room. After the rehearsal, he decided to embellish Nico's Dreamcoat, and wanted to add to the costume by wearing his golden Pharaoh hood and the other *Joseph* outfit we had made in Marrakech. He looked incredible. And although the performance only lasted five minutes, it was a complete joy for me and the others watching. His performance was still very slight, but some of the moves that Anna had introduced were creeping in, combining with his old favourites, and I knew that in his mind these were all great leaps and stretches across an imaginary stage. I completely forgot to buy flowers, though, so while he was enjoying his applause at the end, I handed him a potted plant instead. He bowed and smiled with the aplomb of a West End star. As the music rose to its finale, he hit the last beat with a bowed head.

Curtain down. I pressed stop on my phone.

The magic was over.

I take Reubs a cup of tea and sit on his bed waiting for his sleep-fog to lift. As he becomes more awake I start chatting about the show, but he doesn't want to talk about it. He acts as if it never happened, and he makes it very clear that he doesn't want to be reminded. Is this really the same young man who was dancing around the kitchen in a Dreamcoat last night?

Do I really have to start over again, every single day, rolling the boulder of my brother uphill? I try to hide my disappointment by changing the subject.

'Looks like the sun might come out today, Reubs. What do you feel like doing?'

No reply.

'Let's get you up and in that shower.'

'I did,' he retorts. 'Last night.'

'Did you? And did you wash your hair?'

He tries to see his fringe by lifting his eyes up, 'I think.'

I pick up scattered clothes.

'Saturday today, Reubs. Cleaning day. Get up and strip your bed. I need to get these sheets in the wash.'

He looks at his quilt and lifts the corner to see the bottom sheet. He counts the pillows, daunted by the task. Anyone might think I'd just asked him to trim a football pitch with a pair of scissors. I tell him there's no rush but still put the chore in the middle of his morning, 'Whenever you're ready, Reubs.'

But I can see that it's too much this morning. Too soon. Too early. I should let him be, for a little while longer. Just because I'm ready to start my day, doesn't mean that he's ready.

I begin downstairs: vacuum the living room, the hall, the downstairs loo. I mop the kitchen floors. When I'm done, I climb the stairs to find Reubs standing in the corner of his room, wide-eyed, dressing gown on, the day bag slung over his shoulder, paintbrush in his hand, staring hopelessly at the crumpled sheets on his bed.

'Not to worry, Reubs. Is it too much?'

'Well… yeah.'

'Do you want me to help?'

He jerks his head to look at me, 'Well… yeah.'

I carefully lift the quilt and show him as I undo the buttons at the bottom. He finds them tricky so I show him how to line them up and push through the holes.

'Here, Reubs, you do one.'

He takes the quilt carefully in his hands and finds the edge of the stitching. He holds his head to the side, concentrating as he eases a button through the slit.

'Well done, Booba. See! You can do it.'

'Littew by littew, bruvr. Littew by littew.'

Something similar to a smile brushes his face, but vanishes as he looks backs towards his stripped bed. Behind him, I spot the crusts of a sandwich pushed under the mattress cover, hunks of half-eaten bread under his pillow, a squashed banana poking out of his day bag. He hangs his body in shame.

'Reubs, what on earth are you doing?'

The extra decibels in my tone are too much for him. He covers his ears, and I should stop but I don't.

'How many times!' I rage. 'Do not bring food in your bedroom.'

Demanding that he cleans the mess up, I come dangerously close to insulting him and know immediately that this is all too much. Too much for Reubs, too much for me. My reaction is so distorted. I'm not even cross about the breadcrumbs or him eating in his room. This sudden anger of mine comes from a much deeper place. Staring at him and the way his body cowers on his bed, I'm transported back to Portland Place. I see my brother alone and afraid, right back in that pain. He's breaking my heart and yet I'm still lashing out, 'You better clear up every single last bloody crumb. Do you hear me?'

I bolt downstairs to the kitchen but have no idea what to do with myself when I get there. I just stand by the table as my mind boils over. I catch my bitter reflection in the doors to the garden, arms raised and tightly crossed, my face contorted in the glass. Who have I become? The only thing I can think of doing is heading out of the back door and up the lane. I want to keep on going forever, but stop in the top field to let out all I have in my lungs. The gushing air is like a punctured tyre.

I wrestle my phone from my pocket and call Nathan. He's six hours behind but I call anyway hoping that he'll wake up. And he does, whispering because Kate and the boys are still sleeping.

'Hey Manni, what's up?'

I am always honest with Nathan. I have no problem sharing my weaknesses with him.

'I feel awful. I just lost it with Reubs.'

'You called to say that?'

'I mean, totally lost it. Like never before. About nothing. Literally over crumbs. I caught him stashing food in his bedroom and eating it on the quiet.'

'Where is he now?'

'Back at the cottage. I came out for a walk.'

'Mate – don't beat yourself up. I'm not surprised you've blown a fuse. I would have blown weeks ago. You boys are living an intense situation. I feel frustrated being so far away.'

'I just don't know what to do. If this place at Fox Hill comes up, should we take it? I know Jack doesn't want us to.'

'Does he not?'

'No, he doesn't. He'd rather Booba comes back to Spain.'

'But we have to find a way to get Reubs to stand on his own two feet. This Fox place sounds great. When will you hear back?'

'The next couple of days.'

'Why don't you just wait for that? No decision has been made. Just hang in there. Listen, I've gotta go. The kids are stirring.'

'Thanks, Napes.'

'And Manni, please don't beat yourself up.'

When Nathan has gone, I take a few more deep breaths before starting back to the cottage. I want to apologise to Reubs. He must be told that my anger has nothing to do with squashed bananas and breadcrumbs, and has everything to do with how narrow both of our lives have been these past months. Even with the routine of his tick sheets and charts and his trips to the day centre and Anna's visits to the cottage, despite how much more we are walking, how committed Reubs is to watering Jane and Neill's plants, and how brilliant and wonderful the Friday Night Musical has become, the many threads of our lives and our brotherhood are wrapping ever tighter around us.

As I weave through the kitchen, aiming for Reuben's bedroom to begin my apology, I notice a felt-tip card facing out on the haberdashery cabinet, leant against the fruit bowl. He has beaten me to it.

I run upstairs and fall onto his bed, crying from the deepest part of me. Reuben strokes my head and rubs my shoulders.

'Thank you for my card, Booba.'

'It's fine,' he replies.

'I'm sorry for shouting earlier. You didn't deserve that.'

'We will have luffly evening.'

'And I know you must be a little bit scared.'

'Well, a bit.'

'I'm scared too.'

'Do you?'

'For sure! A new home, a new town. New people, new everything. It's totally normal that we're both feeling apprehensive.'

'What's that mean, brother? Ahensive?'

'Nervous. A little bit nervous. But we'll always have each other, Reubs. So I don't want you to be scared. Alright?'

'Alright, bruvr,' he reassures me.

'And I really am sorry for shouting at you,' I repeat.

'Nah, nah, nah. Done now. We do have luffly evening,' he says again, graciously.

I sit at the garden table with my morning coffee, putting off calling Jack. The air is still sharp. I wrap my new scarf from Sophie D around my neck and put on another layer. The sun tingles on my skin and my limbs seem to lengthen as winter recedes. I've brought out a stack of drawings that Reuben's made of these past months, through winter and into spring, all of them heavy with felt-tip ink. As I look through them, they seem to have a musicality that reveals itself through the repetition of certain characters and words, themes and colours. They remind me of a trip to the Alhambra I made with somebody who had synaesthesia. He wanted to be as alone as possible, so I took him on a Tuesday in February, at 3 p.m., the quietest time of the year. He hoped to find out if the neural pathways in his brain would respond to the ceramic tiles that adorn the walls and floors. As he walked through the grounds and into the different parts, particularly in Salón de Embajadores and Palacio de Comares, where the geometrical designs and primary colours are the most intense, the man filled with music. There were no melodies, he said, just chords and harmonies swimming in his head.

One by one, I really look at Reuben's drawings and find it impossible to see them without my own associations. Are the chords of sadness in me or the drawings? The symphony of his struggles might not be there. Only he knows what he felt when he put felt-tip to paper, and I feel like a bystander peering into a soft and colour-filled world.

↑
Brother's

love Will Find a
Way

Sleep Well love yo
lie in

Whoopi's
as Deloris

Sleep well love you
brother

Mr Beaver

Sleep Narnia
Well
brother They say Aslan is
love you on the move

Samwise Sam

am miss you

love you

Frodo

long time

Gandalf The Gray

9.30 lie in

love you

brother

Sleep Well

am father's favorit
son
am specialam Joesph

Joesph Brother's
my brother's
Joesph
jealous my coat
lassqohar
Matt   Manni   Natha
Reuben   ~~Judha~~   Levi

tommyboy
Joesphgive Benjamin ~~Nancy thing Poo~~
long hug

love you
sleeping
Well brother

The Mission

make everyone
and World emotinal

I gather his drawings into a neat pile on the garden table and put them to one side. It's now time. I can't delay it any longer. I dial Jack's number.

When he answers, I start telling him that I read the email when it first came in this morning, so I already knew he had been offered a place. But I right-clicked the unread option because I wanted Reubs to feel like he was the first to read it, hovering the mouse before opening a door to his future. Nerves got the better of me, I explain to Jack, so I started ham-acting when Reuben came downstairs, as if I was a contestant waiting for the judges' scores on *Strictly*.

Reubs looked at my laptop and pointed.

'Does that mean?'

'It means they really like you, Reubs. They also think you're a perfect fit for Fox Hill. And guess what? You remember that flat that Tess showed you? Flat 12. They're giving you that one, Tess's favourite.'

Although my fist punched the air, it moved in slow motion because I wasn't sure if Reuben would share my sense of relief and celebration. 'You got a place, Reubs!'

A flash of panic washed across his face.

'Am nervous,' he said.

I grabbed his hand. 'Me too, Reubs. It's good to be nervous. It means you're growing. A flower opening.'

I re-clenched my fist to demonstrate, opening and stretching my fingers like petals as wide as they could go.

I didn't tell Jack that a place was available for Reubs as early as 19th April. It's not even a month, and for now I don't think pinning dates to it will help. Neither did I mention to Jack that I only just about held it together long enough, and that after the bus for the day centre had collected Reubs, I crumpled at the kitchen table, warm tears and conflicted emotions pouring. That's when I picked up Reuben's drawings and went outside for a cigarette.

Talking to Jack, holding back some of the details, I lose myself and start to confess instead that I'm feeling both terribly guilty and relieved. As I speak, I'm increasingly distracted by the sharp realisation that I might have to say goodbye to Reubs, the most precious part of me. I have spent all this time preparing him to be ready, but I'm hardly ready myself. This time, our time, this precious hibernation is coming to an end. It's a shock. Suddenly, reality is pressing at the edges.

I must be gabbling because Jack hasn't said a word yet.

'... it was such a lot of work putting his Pen Portrait together.'

I pause but the line is still silent.

'It's good news, isn't it?' I ask.

'What do you want me to say?' he replies. 'You know my feelings.'

It's true. I know that Jack's faith in the system is weaker than mine. Is another shambles inevitable? Fox Hill looks like the model of twenty-first-century social care, but the quality of this care will only be as good as the people that give it, as it always is. Despite the excitement and newness of the housing, what will happen when the cost of living keeps going up and the lovely carers we met last month move on to other places or other sectors? Seeking out better pay or a more convenient commute to work? Their hearts might be in it when Reuben moves in, but if they're not treated well or paid properly for their hard work, the agency staff or younger carers will start coming in, breaking those relationships and the continuity. Am I ready to put my brother back into a system that is so volatile? Am I ready to trust again?

After talking to Jack, I tap out a quick sequence of texts to Nathan and Matt, Mum and Dad, sharing the news. They're all part of it, and I desperately need to hear from them. What do they think?

Mum's reply arrives first, *Brilliant. Exciting.* Matt's text comes in next, while I'm putting Reuben's drawings back on the shelves in the living room, *So pleased for you, Reubs. Your own pad!* I keep the phone close to me as I wait for Nathan's response, but because of the time difference don't expect it until later. None of the replies are enough, though. I need much more, so call Mum and Dad's home number. Mum is out shopping when Dad picks up. He's watching the birds on the feeders while we talk.

'Most care homes limit people like Reubs,' I say in a moment of clarity. 'They strip people of their ability to make decisions. They strip any sense of belonging to a community. I think this place is different.'

'Praise the Lord!' Dad exclaims, then corrects himself. 'Oh, I'm not allowed to say that, am I!'

'No, you're not. Well, of course you are! You can say whatever you like. That's your truth.'

We carry on chatting about how empowering it could be for Reuben to have a sense of ownership over his flat. Since we've been together, Reuben has been taking on new challenges. He's been going on more long walks. He's dancing with Anna. He's starting to resist me less, when I throw ideas for the day his way. Fox Hill should mean he continues to become more active in making his own decisions, and this I'm sure will continue to unlock him.

After talking to Dad, I make myself some lunch and write back to Fox Hill, thanking them for letting us know, saying what wonderful news it is. I also write to Angie and Sam – they both already know, so I write thanking them for their enduring support and kindness. Nathan's message pings back in the early afternoon, just before Reuben gets back. It reminds me of yet another part of Reuben that had vanished, *You're a lifesaver Manni Boy. Yah!! Reubs. Can't wait to come and visit soon. Don't forget that he's the Mayor of Nantucket!!x x*

The Mayor of Nantucket. I had completely forgotten.

Reubs was staying with Nathan, Kate, Seve and Leo in a house that belonged to Kate's grandfather. It was only a few years ago but seems like another lifetime. Reuben was so independent then. Not only did he fly over on his own, but over the six weeks he worked three different jobs every day: he squeezed oranges at a juice bar by the harbour, gave tours of the tower at the historic

First Congregational Church at the top of town, then spent the afternoon as an usher at the Dreamland Movie Theatre.

All of his summer jobs were voluntary, because he didn't have a work visa, but the movie theatre paid him in free passes, which he diligently collected and kept in an envelope. Sometimes, he didn't get home until 9 p.m., exhausted but full of chatter and cheer. A friend of Nathan's called one day to say, 'I've just seen Reubs singing and dancing all the way down Main Street.'

They nicknamed him the Mayor of Nantucket after that.

At the end of the six weeks, when it was time to head back to England, Reuben handed the envelope to Nathan, packed with the passes he'd been collecting.

'This is for you and sister-in-law,' he said.

That image of Reuben dancing down Main Street lingers. I hold on to it until the bus from the day centre pulls up on Annings Lane. Marie helps Reuben out and walks him to the back door. I ask them how the day was and what they got up to. She tells me about the puzzle they did together, and how Steven and Reuben hung out again. I ask if he's told her the news about Fox Hill. He hasn't. He hasn't told anyone. I fill her in and describe the town and the flat we saw.

'That's brilliant, Reuben,' she says. 'Congratulations, sunshine! What an exciting adventure.'

He tugs at his left lobe. 'Ear by here,' he says, then shuffles off to his room.

Marie and I look at each other knowingly. There's a glisten in her eyes. Of course there is – I'm not the only one who will miss him. She swallows hard and disappears back down the garden path to the waiting bus.

I close the door and follow Reubs upstairs, where he's avoiding eye contact when I knock and walk in.

'Why didn't you tell people at the day centre, Reubs?'

'I like it here, bruvr. Just you and me. I like this *flew*.'

He points out of the window and turns dramatically towards the farm. I sit on the bed to be nearer him.

'But this is not real life, Booba. This is a brother's dreamtime. It's a special dreamtime, so we can get strong enough to move on.'

He fixes his gaze on me, compelling me to continue.

'Your life is like a film, Reubs. There are lots of scenes, one after the other. Some scenes are happy. Some scenes are sad or angry. But the film always keeps going and going. Your next scene is about to begin, and we should celebrate that.'

For Reuben, though, there is nothing to celebrate. To him, getting a place at Fox Hill just means losing everything he's grown accustomed to here. I've got a lot of work to do before he accepts any change. It would help if I could convince Jack to change his mind. Before sleep, I text him to say goodnight. He returns my kisses and forwards me a message from Reuben: *Tell. your. boyfriend. ear. by. here. Samwise. Love. you. Frodo.*

When Jack and I moved into The Corner and began to explore the valley, it was the path to Land's End, in the depths of the gorge, that became our favourite walk. Archi showed us the way, and down there he taught Beau and BB to be *campo* dogs and lose their urban fancies. Jack and I both wanted Reubs to come and see this beautiful, serene place, but each time we attempted the walk he would turn back where the path climbs above the river and narrows past a hollow in the landscape, below the fig tree, where a badger family lives.

'Luffly,' Reubs would say. 'Go back now.'

On one of Mum and Dad's first visits, when Dad became enthralled by the silence at Land's End, we all decided to go. Even Mum committed to the walk. It felt like a family expedition. It was one of those rare spring days when the sun pelts out warmth but not heat, where beneath the shade of the fig tree, there was still a chill in the air. Mum held Reuben's hand.

'Come on, darling. If I can do it, so can you!' she told him.

In total concentration, Reubs edged his way along the narrow path. It seemed to take an age but nobody was in a hurry. We were under the spell of Land's End, where time doesn't exist. At the craggy knoll, before Mad Dog Mile, there was another tricky manoeuvre. 'Scoot down on your bum,' I told Mum. 'Keep your centre of gravity low.'

She did, and on the other side I heard her gasp as she stepped into the wildflower meadow.

'Told you,' I said. 'You had to see this.'

'Do we have to go back that same way?' she asked.

'I'm afraid so.'

'Be fine,' Reubs piped up. 'Looks like a film here, bruvr. *The Sound of Music.*'

I took his hand to lead him up to Thyme Point and then on to The Cove and Land's End. Mum was glad to stop at the river and have a drink. We all joined her, finding a place to sit on the rocks in the sunlight that beamed into the gorge. The oleanders glowed from within. The reeds glistened. Seeing Mum struggle, Reuben had forgotten all about himself, just for a little while.

'Well done, Mum,' he said giving her a hug. 'You did well.'

I keep travelling back to Land's End in my thoughts, usually alone, but often with Jack and Reubs and the rest of our canine family. In these daydreams, Archi will always be alive.

These visions of the gorge bring me such a welcome calm to the days that follow the news from Fox Hill. Time has begun to gallop and there is less space in my head for uncertainty. With Angie, when we talked about starting the process and seeing how we got on, it was a way of exploring the possibilities without being completely committed. This is starting to feel harder. I didn't realise just how much there was to do.

During the morning, I sit at the kitchen table with my laptop to get through as much paperwork as possible before Reuben wakes up. Sam has been amazing. She's been collecting all the information and documents to support Reuben's funding claims for housing and care. The list is endless – we need a care and support assessment, then a care and support plan, a CM54 form for monitoring medication, a full financial assessment with bank statements and details of any savings left from Aunty Eva and the money we raised walking the Camino. We also need a referral and discharge from Dr Aaberg and Reuben's GP, along with the old tenancy agreement from Portland Place, three proofs of identity and one proof of a 'local' connection to the county, and a statement from the Learning Disability Team in town. Add to that all the follow-up emails with Fox Hill, especially when Tess intervened to make sure that Flat 12 was reallocated to Reuben because he needed a shower more than a bath. There were also conversations that needed to be had with the small network we've created here over the last five months, from the day centre and Anna's dance sessions, to his speech therapist and all the friends that need to be updated. I still need to call the council and tell them to give the allotment to someone else. Mum and Dad have agreed to help. Nathan is going to put down a deposit for an Airbnb I've found in the neighbouring village, which will be our family HQ for the week.

Reuben is blissfully unaware of what happens each morning. Inevitably, there's no way I can get it all done before I hear him plodding about upstairs. His lie-ins are getting longer and longer, though. If I don't wake him up, he'd easily sleep past noon. As my time speeds up downstairs, Reuben is upstairs trying to stop time's arrow by lingering in bed for as long as possible. Sometimes, like him, I'd rather the days didn't start. But this morning, like most mornings, thoughts wrench me awake and seem so much more urgent before dawn. Will Reuben need cutlery for his new flat? Can I get his old bed from Portland Place?

I go out for a walk after breakfast and look for things that remind me of Land's End – the way the river bends beyond the bridge, the crooked leaning of an oak branch, how soft a particular mound seems in the field. I won't have much time for walks in the coming days. As well as the paperwork that the Fox Hill committee are asking for, there's so much to organise around the logistics of getting him there. It isn't as simple as packing a bag. There's an entire flat to furnish.

Before heading back, my eyes make a full sweep down across the landscape. The labyrinth of Chartres Cathedral comes to my mind, the one that I have printed on cloth. I visualise it unfolding right in front of me, superimposed on top of these familiar fields.

Back indoors, I head straight to my laptop and print out the architectural plan of Flat 12 that Tess emailed. Reuben helps me unravel Terry's long strip of card, holding it flat while I use the kitchen scissors to cut two, roughly equal lengths. The first will be a countdown chart for moving day, the other will be a bird's-eye view of the space Reubs could inhabit. If he can imagine it in three dimensions, like he did the labyrinth, and start planning what should go where, the idea of living in his own flat on his own terms, may begin to take root. He needs more time to let it all sink in, no doubt about it, but after months of our hibernation, spring has thrown us this alternative reality and even if we had all the time in the world, I think Reuben might still be reluctant for change. This way, at least the quickening pace will draw out the conversations we've been finding it so difficult to have, and confront all those questions that I'll probably never have an answer for.

I use the tick chart to explain that Mum and Dad will join us, 'We'll all spend the week together!' I also tell him that Nathan and Kate have very generously rented us an Airbnb, and that he can help choose all the different bits and pieces he wants for his new home. 'We'll go shopping, Reubs!' We'll hire a van, too. And now, once all of this is out in the open, on a strip of card in bright felt-tips, Reubs studies it carefully and I wonder why I didn't do this earlier. On the second sheet, I draw the outlines of all the different rooms of Flat 12 – kitchen, bathroom, bedroom, living area, window – and once it's all down on paper, I hand him the pen so he can begin marking in miniature how he imagines the flat will be.

Fox Hill Reuben New Home

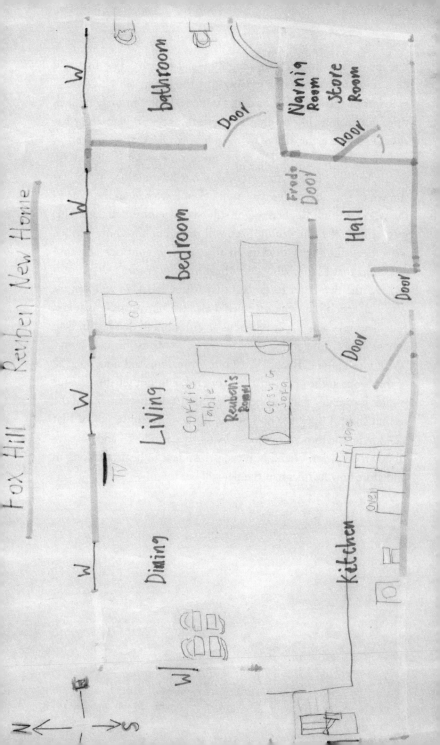

N

S

bathroom

Narnia Room

Store Room

Door

bedroom

Frodo Door

Door

Hall

Door

Living

Coffie Table

Reuben's Room

Cosy Sofa

TV

Door

W

W

W

W

W

Dining

W

Kitchen

Fridge

Oven

Good Things about fox hill

look's New for me

Finger X

~~scribbled out~~

Play by ~~scribbled out~~
ear

am miss my family

am home now
I J it Bredy

I am awake early again, thinking about the day Reuben soared. It was during the holidays, after Mum and Dad had moved to Thatcham. Matt and I had gone to university and Nathan soon followed, which meant Reuben didn't have his brothers around him for the first time since he was born. Not to be outdone, he had enrolled into Newbury College for a year, doing a BTEC in the Performing Arts, and on the way to the pub he was telling me all about his course and the people that he liked. We always went for a drink to catch up whenever I came home, and that night we headed to The Gun. Dad had suggested it, although he'd never been there. 'Not really our scene but there are always cars outside.'

As we walked across the thick carpet to order a pint and a half shandy, all eyes were on us, drilling into our unfamiliar faces. Were they staring because we were strangers? As always, I wondered if they were looking at Reuben. We settled at a table in the far corner and I suggested we leave after our drinks. Reubs insisted we should stay – it was karaoke night, and he wanted to listen. A woman took the mic and started singing 'Tainted Love' by Soft Cell. She had a distinctive voice, which made it even more difficult to guess her age. Face dry and brittle, jeans tight and black boots pointed, a certain hush fell over the room as she sang. When she was done, applause rippled her back to her boyfriend. She sat down and picked up her drink.

'She's good,' Reubs said.

'She was.' I agreed. 'What a voice.'

'I need pen and paper, bruvr.'

I knew what he was planning.

'I don't think that's a good idea, Booba.'

'Get me paper and pen, bruvr.'

I scowled at him.

Reluctantly, I went to the bar for paper and borrowed a pen from a couple next to us. Reuben wrote down his song choice, carefully folding the paper and handing it back to me, then motioning towards the DJ. Obligingly, I walked to the other side of the pub and deposited Reuben's request.

'Righto, we have a late entry,' the DJ announced three songs later. 'Let's see what this guy has got. Give it up for Reuben and "You are not alone" by Michael Jackson.'

All eyes homed in on me, assuming I'd be the one singing. But it was Reuben who stood up and strolled through the sea of gazes, undeterred. When the song started, he missed the first cue. I muttered some kind of a desperate plea into my second pint, and didn't really want to look up. He stood there watching the screen waiting for the loop to come around again.

'Come on, Booba!' I pleaded, but he froze.

He missed another cue.

The woman who had sung earlier began to hum the tune, loudly enough for him to hear. Others followed, and the whole room began to hum along until Reubs found his place in the song and picked up the melody. As soon as he began singing, they stopped so only his voice could be heard above the music, all eyes following his moves, encouraging him on. Everybody was with him, and the support from the audience gave him the confidence to leave the stage and edge out into the middle of the room. Using the length of the microphone, he sang directly to people sipping their drinks. He went right up towards the woman who had sung earlier and pointed at her and her boyfriend as he sang, 'You are not alone cos I am here with you.' He was feeling it. She was feeling it. We were all feeling it. The whole pub rose to their feet at the end as he bowed to their standing ovation.

And who won the prize that night? Reuben did. The woman with the good voice presented him with a rosette, and the landlord offered him a free drink. He ordered an Appletiser, and for the rest of the evening Reubs stood at the bar as every single person in The

Gun filed past to shake his hand or give him a hug. I sat in the shadows, crying into my crisps.

All these years later, while I head out for a morning walk, I can still sit inside that Berkshire pub with its sticky floors. Before the sun has risen fully over the ridge, I relive the way he reversed my expectations and reached out to everyone. At the petrol station on the coast road, while I pay for bread and milk, I am reminding myself that the truth of Reuben keeps knocking me for six. And right on cue, as I'm heading back to the cottage, a message pings into my phone from him: *new. day,* is all it says.

It stops me in my tracks and I stare at the screen, trying to decipher its meaning. I remember that last night, when I went up to say goodnight, he was sitting up in bed holding the floor plan of Flat 12 in his hands, scrutinising it. He put it down on the duvet and picked up the grid of days, his eyes gazing along the row of dates towards 19th April.

A second message appears: *where. are. you. brother.*

I text him back and start walking as fast as I can, breaking into a run for the last few hundred metres back to the cottage. I spy Reubs at his bedroom window and slow down to walk along the garden path. He sees me open the gate and starts to negotiate the window latch. I beam up at him as he opens it.

'Hey, Booba, you OK? Your text, anything wrong?'

'Good. Where are you?'

'I've been to get some breakfast.' I hold up what I've bought to explain myself. 'Are you going to jump in that shower?'

'I did.'

His pride tumbles down from the window like Rapunzel's hair. I don't know which of us has the larger smile.

I make my way upstairs to find out what he's so pleased about: Reuben's belongings are strewn across his bedroom floor. Socks and pants have been tipped from the top drawer. His Technicolour

Dreamcoats, the one Nico made and the other from Marrakech, are folded over his bed. Mufasa and the entire cast of *The Lion King* peer out of his Darth Vader roller case. Flat 12 will not be free for over two weeks, and I've not said a word to him about packing. I've no idea what's going on.

'What are you doing, Reubs?'

A tension emerges from my question, his tongue starts to protrude, his eyes crinkle. I grab him before any more fear creeps in, and as we hug I know that whatever is going on here, I have to play along.

He leans back to tell me that he only wants to pack half of his DVDs, half of his socks and pants, half of his felt-tip pens. He wants half of all his belongings to stay here, with me. I sit on his bed and explain that it's better if all of his things are under one roof. 'Well. Leave some,' he concludes.

Of course, he's right to want an anchor here. All or nothing won't cut it, not with Reubs, not yet.

'Do you want me to help you?' I ask.

'Well, yeah.'

I hold him close, and as our embrace ends I gesture towards the framed photos of Tommy Boy and John Partridge.

'You can arrange all of this in your new bedroom. A new home, Reubs. It's exciting. Wish I was moving to Fox Hill.'

He snatches the opportunity, 'You could.'

'But then where would you live?'

'Here?' he says, pointing to his bed with his broken glasses.

Sun Up

Circle
of
Life

Sun Down

Music
start

The Lion King

4

As the sun rises over Pride Rock, there is a great movement down in the valley, leaves and grasses twitch as the smallest birds and animals scurry for answers to the question they are all asking: *Who will be our next king?*

Far away, in another part of the kingdom, our brave one appears from behind an enormous rock and begins the slow walk with elephants, passing giraffes eating from the high branches of an acacia tree. He is fearless, this little lion, you can see it in his swagger. The hyenas don't bother him any more. Even Scar, the evil lion, leaves this boy-lion alone to walk into the fading sunlight.

But as night falls, he finds himself lost in the darkness.

He doesn't seem so brave now. The trees have faces and in the bushes there are things that lurk. Slowly, the stars begin to shift and swivel to form the full face of Mufasa looking down on his son.

Simba, let me tell you something…

The words are written on pieces of paper that I hold in front of the camera, but I'm convinced Reuben hears them in his head.

Look at the stars.

The great kings of the past look down on us.

Remember that those kings will always be there to guide you.

I think the smoke machine is interfering with the Instagram filters, so an elephant hangs in mid-air and lions roar in from the stairs. But I think our audience gets the gist. Africa. The Serengeti. Live stream. Reuben has been dressed as Simba all day. We had a dress rehearsal this afternoon and he hasn't taken it off since.

It's now impossibly hot because Simba is stumbling through the desert. He's lost and lonely again. Oh dear, will he survive?

Remember who you are, Simba. Remember who you are, Reubs.

My grip on the camera slips as my concentration wavers. I have fallen through the portal into Reuben's mind, and inhabiting this landscape with him, even if for just a few minutes, answers all the questions and eases all the doubts. I am no longer standing in the kitchen of an old agricultural cottage in England. I am looking down the kaleidoscope of Reuben Coe, where my brother is untangling my bewilderment at being back on Annings Lane.

We weren't supposed to be here in the cottage. We were meant to be settling Reubs into Flat 12. All our preparations were propelled by the promise of him having that fresh start. He was packed and ready, two weeks in advance. Everything on his countdown chart pointed Reuben towards that future. Surely, when we had to turn around and drive back from Stourcastle, we were going in the wrong direction. The decision to accept Flat 12 was hard enough. By the time we got back here, my resolve was in tatters. All I felt like doing was hiding away in my bedroom. I wanted to stare out of the window across fields, over hedges and dry stone walls, until there was nothing but the sea. Until now, that is.

Wait! In the distance, Simba can see it. There, by the sliding doors, a silhouette of Pride Rock, where he must go and claim his kingdom. He is no longer lost. He has remembered his way. He knows exactly who he is. He points and approaches his destiny, a precarious ensemble of stepladders and clothes' pegs, cables and cords, all holding a screen print of the sunset. Somehow, little Simba negotiates a path through the living room chaos and begins his ascent up the wobbly ladder, to the summit. All the animal kingdom is poised to bow to its new king. Pumbaa and Timon are almost as excited as me. Right on cue, when that glorious final thump of bass thunders through, Simba drops the paper sun and holds his head high to take the applause.

There are no flowers to offer the star of the show, so I hand him a bowl of fruit instead. It's all I can find.

I flip to a new Instagram filter so generic digital birds can swoop around his head in celebration. Along with the forty or so other people grinning at their screens in kitchens or living rooms and offices around the world, I am profoundly aware that we have just witnessed Reuben being himself. There is no greater privilege.

It still felt good to be together again, despite everything. We hadn't seen Mum and Dad for over eight months, and Reuben stared at them as if he didn't believe they were real. The Airbnb was only three miles from Fox Hill, and was the ideal base for the week. We all met there on Monday, and as usual Mum, Dad and Sasha, their dog, arrived with an over-loaded car. The owner of the house, Martin, greeted us with a hamper of Victoria sponge, eggs, muesli, coffee, tea, biscuits and all sorts of other snacks. Reubs went to his bedroom to start arranging his night-time props. I stayed out and talked to Martin, who told me he used to teach children with special needs – on that first day, it felt like he understood the weight of what we, as a family, were going through. He was fascinated to learn about Fox Hill, and had helpful suggestions of where we might find second-hand furniture, which pubs had good food, or what short walks Mum and Dad could take with the dog.

I didn't tell Martin that Reuben might not be moving in to Fox Hill. Mum, Dad and I silently agreed not to mention it. We would carry on regardless. Deep down, I was still hopeful we might be able to reverse the decision to delay his moving-in day. If we could spend time with the leaders at Fox Hill, they would get to know us and appreciate the urgency of the situation. Perhaps they would help turn the tide. Then maybe that man at social services would drop by and discover that RC was a person with a family and story of his own.

With my parents, almost straight away, Reuben showed signs of regressing. Playing the incapable son, he snuggled up to Mum as she read the newspaper on the sofa, while Dad stepped naturally and eagerly into the role of doting parent. I had to keep nipping it in the bud, explaining that the move was already making Reubs more vulnerable again; we had to do what we could to make sure he didn't slip, not even an inch. We all agreed that 'Mummy' and

'Daddy' should be corrected to 'Mum' and 'Dad', but still Reubs would pretend he couldn't do this or that. He is wily. He played them off each other.

Reuben: 'Mummy, make me hot milk and honey?'

Mum: 'You can make it yourself, darling.'

So he went and found Dad, reading in the armchair.

Reuben: 'Daddy, make me hot milk and honey?'

Dad: 'Of course I can, Reuben.'

And so it went.

Thankfully, there was so much to do and organise that there wasn't the space for Reuben's neediness to take root. But to make sure, I called Meredith to ask if he could start going to the day centre, so he could begin interacting with the community around Fox Hill, coming back to his family in the afternoon. She agreed, and on the Tuesday we dropped him off at a building that looks like an old school, with its red-brick extension knitted into an older stone building, where the gym and hydropool are.

On the first morning we dropped him off, the day centre was sun-filled, and Reuben's welcome matched the warmth of the April light. It felt like a place of goodwill and patience, and while they were showing us around, Reuben beamed when he spotted a picture of a lion on the wall followed by a Whoopi Goldberg DVD, *Corrina, Corrina.* 'I haven't seen it, bruvr,' he said, handing it to me. We couldn't have asked for a better start. It felt like breaking new ground. These tiny signs were feeding my positivity. Would they let him move in early? Surely they would. I had a week to win them around.

While Reuben was at the day centre, Mum, Dad and I were able to start making lists of the things we needed. We had four days left and a very tight budget with which to follow Reuben's plan for Flat 12. He needed absolutely everything: forks to flower pots, cushions to coat stand, bathmat to bin. Most of it we planned to get second-hand. The only new thing we ordered online was a sofa bed for visitors. For the rest of the stuff, we spent the first couple of evenings and mornings trawling Gumtree and Facebook Marketplace, getting in touch with vendors before plotting our routes around the county to pick it all up. I rented a transit for a few days, as large a van as I dared, and became Manni with a Vanni.

The plan was to get all this done and move Reubs into Fox Hill on the last day. We would have a celebratory dinner with Mum and Dad in the new flat. Reuben would host us. I would cook. Happy ending. At least, that's what I had to keep believing. Reubs and I would then spend our first night there, me as a guest on his sofa bed. We would then enjoy a relaxing weekend once Mum and Dad had gone back to Norwich. Then, on Monday, the intense ten-day assessment and handover period would begin, allowing the care team and Reuben to get to know each other, enabling me to explain as much as I possibly could about my brother and his care needs, his habits, his routines. Ten days to grasp the intricacy of Reuben. I clung to what the team leader at Fox Hill, Meredith, said the first time I met her: 'We will do everything we can to ensure Reuben lives his best and happiest life.'

It had all been meticulously planned. Over the last month, so much had been orchestrated to make it work as smoothly and as calmly as possible. I had started off by shielding Reuben from all the complications of electricity contracts and the handover of his finances. But he was coping well, diligently crossing off the days on his countdown chart and visualising his moving day, so involving him in some of these conversations and loose ends helped this new reality crystallise, in my thoughts as much as his. Five more sleeps until we see Mum and Dad, four more sleeps, three more sleeps. Then on Friday morning, the phone rang. It was Sam and she sounded unusually robotic.

'I don't really know how to say this. Is Reuben with you?'

He was, so I moved out of the kitchen, beyond earshot.

'What is it?' I asked flatly.

'I'm in over my head, Manni. You know how hard I've been working for you boys?'

'I do, and I'll never forget.'

'Well,' she began, 'one of my seniors has stepped in. A project manager from the local authority. They think it's all too rushed and want to make sure Reuben starts on a good footing. So much depends on it. So they've pushed his moving date back.'

My voice rattled, 'Until when?'

'Early May.'

'What?'

'Believe me. I gave them every argument I could.'

'But my flight home is on the first of May, Sam,' I reminded her unnecessarily.

She, more than anyone, knows why I have to go back.

A silence hung between us that we didn't know how to break. I stared out at the pond and felt sick at the thought of all the hard work we had done, and of all the plans we had for meeting Mum and Dad the following week. I was going to have to cancel, unbook the van and the Airbnb, tell my parents to stay at home.

'Look,' I said finally. 'I can deal with it. But what am I supposed to tell Reubs? And Mum and Dad arrive on Monday. Nathan booked the place for a week.'

'I know.'

'I have to get home, Sam. Do they want Reuben to be homeless? I'm going to lose my business. My work. I don't know how long Jack and I can keep this up.'

'I know.'

Sam has always made our struggle her own, and she understood that my resilience was hanging by a thread. She brought our conversation back to practicalities.

'They want to stagger the arrivals of tenants, so the entire team can learn the care patterns of each tenant independently of each other. There are staff shortages everywhere, as you know. And also there's an issue with insurance.'

'Surely they knew all this weeks ago. This doesn't bode well, Sam. Maybe Jack was right. We haven't even started and already the bureaucracy is pushing us over. It stinks.'

'It's not Fox Hill. It's social services,' she reiterated, her voice close to cracking. 'There's a new manager who's just come along. He's making a mess. We're not the only ones who are upset.'

For confidentiality, to protect his identity, Reuben Coe is RC in most of his files. But in reducing him like this, does it become easier for this senior manager in social services to see a set of initials rather than a person? Had he even read my Pen Picture? He doesn't even know who Reuben is. Why hasn't he asked to meet us, so I can describe the last five months of our lives together?

Neither Sam or I knew what to do.

No plan emerged from our conversation, and before we hung up the emptiness in us both was profound.

This journey of ours has been so much harder than walking the Camino with Reuben and Nathan. The daily routine, the sacrifice, the gradual emotional distances we have moved each day, the discipline and motivation we have had to find, has left me numb with exhaustion. The finish line was close, the final destination. I had found extra energy because, in the near-distance, we could sense the elation of the end. But this drained away too. All of it had gone, moved back by an anonymous hand, shoved away into a new finish line that felt impossibly far away.

I'm done, bruvr.

After speaking to Sam, I sat with my disappointment for a while. I couldn't call Jack, not straight away. What would he say? He wouldn't say *I told you so*. He's not like that. But the decision I had made for Reuben felt wrong, and I felt so alone. I couldn't help wondering if it was a sign of things to come. Jack had warned me about putting my faith back in the system. Before I spoke to him, I needed to get somewhere, anywhere. So I phoned Mum and Dad instead, to tell them what had happened, but also because I needed to plug myself into them.

'That's ridiculous,' Mum said. 'Surely they can't do that. What are we supposed to do now?'

Dad was more measured, 'Oh dear. Are we still to come down on Monday? Or does that not make sense any more? Have you said anything to Reuben?'

'Not yet.'

'You will, though?'

'Once I've figured out what to do.'

'We could carry on,' he suggested. 'He's still going to go there, isn't he?'

'I don't know any more.'

'We have to get the flat ready at some point. I'm sure you're disappointed. We could set off nice and early so we'll be with you by midday, all being well. But it's up to you.'

I didn't agree, not exactly. It just wasn't discussed again, and while I fantasised about the committee of Fox Hill being there when we arrived, so that we could bowl them over with our love, Mum and Dad got ready to leave. We didn't bring it up when we arrived either. We just carried on sharing our secret. None of us knew when it would be the right time to tell Reuben, or whether we'd tell him at all. I think Mum and Dad were waiting for my lead, and I spent the week waiting for theirs. I wanted to hand over the responsibility to my parents. I just wanted to be their son again, not the one who makes big decisions and starts difficult conversations. And while there were still so many things to be done, it was easier to let the truth drift.

By the middle of the week, Mum and I started to enjoy bumbling along in the van. Reuben spent time at the day centre and with Dad and Sasha, while we drove around the countryside collecting the secondhand and the pre-loved – those people who asked were pleased to hear where their unwanted things were going. An oak dining table from an ex-military family. A sideboard from a garage sale. Kitchen stools from a teacher in Eyemouth. We stopped to hoard cups and cutlery from an antiques centre, and we didn't just find things that would do. We found things that were perfect, like a red plate in the shape of a heart that I found in a Shaston charity shop, on a shelf between puzzles and glass vases.

'Mum, what do you think? A key plate in his hallway?'

'We have to get it,' she agreed.

Later that week, we went to Portland Place. Because Reuben officially had somewhere else to live, rather than with me in the cottage, we were allowed to go back there and pick up the rest of his stuff. A message pinged into my phone from Reuben as we were parking. Mum read it aloud while I was steering us in. 'Get my bed, brother.' I asked her to text back to him: 'Brand new start with your old bed. Cosy.'

Only one of us was allowed into Reuben's room, so Mum waited by the van with the hood of her raincoat up. The tenants had been asked to stay out of the way, and the welcome from staff was cold and awkward. I wanted to get in and out as quickly as possible. I avoided eye contact and moved with desperate focus.

All of Reuben's clothes and belongings had been carefully folded and packed into cardboard boxes, including the grey linen curtains. The curtain poles were the only thing still fixed in the room, so I was relieved that taking them down and dismantling his bed was the only real work that needed to be done. I remembered putting the bed and the curtains up. I remembered decorating the room with Mum, and organising the Aslan mural. We had so many good intentions.

The faces of the other tenants watched me come and go with each load. I don't know if they knew what was going on. I wondered if anyone had explained anything. Reuben had lived here for almost ten months. Will they miss him? I wondered. Will he miss them? Perhaps things might have turned out better in different circumstances, but moving the rest of his possessions out of his old room, the whole place reeked of failure. I was feeling terrible, and I felt sorry for the tenants and the care team. I really hope that whoever took Reuben's room afterwards, has had a better time than my brother.

When I pulled the bed away from the wall, I discovered dozens and dozens of coloured pieces of card and paper, most of them with ripped and crumpled edges. They all had felt-tipped words and phrases on them. I picked up a handful and unfolded them to read:

Am little bit tired.
Am fine. Any dream will do.
Relax evening. Dark.

I started to imagine Reubs sitting there, slowly formulating his emotions so he could then write them down:

Brother Matt. Brother Manni. Brother Nathan.
Mummy. Daddy.
Family.
dream. have a friend. we did text
can't find Mrs Doubtfire

They were a mixture of daily routines and lifelong hopes and fears, all written by a young man desperate to be heard. Yet there they all were, shoved down the gap between his bed and the wall. With the mural behind his bed, I wondered if he was trying to feed these secrets to Aslan.

am wish watch strictly my TV
don't like virus
when Mummy Daddy come

These are the truths of his loneliest hours, etched in felt-tip, reading them hollowed me out.

am gay. want everyone know.
get home.
good day tomorrow

All I wanted to do was run away. I bundled the paper into a bag, not sure if Reuben would ever want them back, not knowing what else to do. Shaken, I had to ask a young member of staff for help dismantling the rest of the bed.

Once everything was in the back of the van, I went back to the room for one last look, to check I hadn't missed anything. I stood facing Aslan. 'Thank you for looking after my brother,' I said into his huge, luminescent eyes.

Back in the van I didn't tell Mum about Reuben's secret stash of messages. It would have upset her too much, to see what was on them, to realise they were never read and that nobody except my brother knew they were there.

'Shall we get out of here?' I asked.

'Step on it, Son,' she replied.

This morning, the kitchen is still in disarray. There are felt-tip posters of the Serengeti and scripts with Mufasa dialogue on the table. The three plastic figures of Rafiki, Pumbaa and Timon are in the fruit bowl. A Pride Rock flag is still hanging in the living room, with a bright paper sun attached by string to a piece of bamboo. At some point, the stepladder must have fallen over and spilled the yellow fabric desert across the floor. But I ignore all the mess and continue basking in Simba's triumph, grinning inanely as I head upstairs to wake him.

'Morning, Lion King.'

I sit on his bed, waiting for him to stretch limbs and his eyes to focus. 'That was amazing, Booba,' I say.

He giggles, 'What, bruvr?'

'Last night.'

'Ingya,' he replies.

'How did you sleep?'

'Like a baby.'

He recoils and grimaces but it's too late he's already said, *Like a baby*. It's a phrase from Reuben's past, something he always used to say. When he moves his hand to gesture 'bit-tired' with his finger and thumb, I put my hand up to block it.

'Uh-uh,' I say loudly. 'Nope.'

He tries to do it again, so I put both my hands on his.

'Reubs, leave it there. You don't need to say it.'

'I do, bruvr.' His eyes are pleading, full of morning dew.

'You don't.'

He tuts, rolls his eyes, shrugs.

As I relax my grip, his hand escapes and he almost sneaks it in, bit-tired, but I manage to lasso his fingers into mine. He caves in and giggles.

'What we doing today, bruvr?'

'Well, I thought we could run a marathon, then go swimming in the sea, mow the lawn, paint the house, then watch a DVD.'

'What you like, bruvr?' he smirks.

'Shall we have breakfast first?' I suggest.

'Well, we could.'

'What do you want – eggs or muesli?'

'Umm. I don't know. What do you think?'

'It's not my choice. You'll be deciding everything soon. But I'll let you get in that shower first, you dirty old man.'

He pauses, casting his mind back.

'You always say that, bruvr.'

He remembers it from our time walking the Camino, all those years ago.

'Bruvr?' he asks.

'What, Reubs?'

'Will I like it?'

'What's that, Reubs?'

'Flat.'

How do I reply?

Difficult as it is to answer, the act of asking the question shows me that Fox Hill has become so much more real to him. Even though we had a countdown chart and a floorplan before, our preparation was two dimensional. There just wasn't time to process the changes. No wonder he protested. He just wasn't ready. But after all that fumbling about, after the uncertainty that made me hide the truth from my brother, has the close encounter helped Reuben comprehend it more?

'You are going to love it, Reubs. It's an amazing place and you'll be happy there. It will be your new home. Not mine or Samwise's. Yours. Reuben David Coe. You will have your own keys. Your very own bachelor pad. No wild parties, though. I don't want you getting into trouble with the police.'

'I wish,' he giggles. 'Will I sleep well there?'

'Yes, you really will.'

'Nice flew there?' he asks, pointing to the sloping field outside his bedroom window, now absent of Jess's sheep.

'A lovely view.'

'Can I watch DVDs there, bruvr?'

'Of course. You have your own TV and DVD player.'

'Is it cosy there?'

'Very.'

'Is there a lamppost there, bruvr?'

He's stumped me there. 'Not sure, we'll have to wait and see.'

I remind him that I will be with him for the first ten days, before I fly back to Spain, sleeping on his sofa bed.

He holds up ten fingers.

Flat 12 was ready on Friday, and we were all exhausted. Although the sense of urgency was false, it had given us all the momentum we needed to get through a difficult week. Mum and Dad put their heart and soul into it. They wanted to finish what they came here to do. Dad and I hung the final mirror and assembled the sofa, and it was done. Any talk of unveiling it to Reuben was subdued. I no longer clung to the idea that he'd be allowed to move in, but I still hadn't found a way to tell him we were going back to the cottage. I did want to say something, desperately. But whenever I thought the right moment had arrived, my heart would start pounding and I'd put my head back in the sand to carry on mapping our routes or calling people on Gumtree to talk picture frames or coffee tables.

When I finally accepted that there was no such thing as the perfect moment, especially with so much stuff to still do, I found something else to say. It was important, and I'd been putting this off too. So I was determined not to let it go. I turned off the TV one evening, asked Dad to come into the kitchen, where we all sat at the table in the corner of the room like cabinet ministers about to debate an issue of national security.

I started plainly, 'We've got something to talk about.'

Reuben rolled his eyes, Mum and Dad glanced at each other and must've thought I was about to confess to Reubs. I took a deep breath and began, 'As Reuben steps into his new home. There is something we need to put straight.' I then launched into my impassioned speech about his need to be free and not feel encumbered by his parents' opinions or desires. Mum and Dad weren't quite sure what to make of it. I'd completely wrong-footed them, they had no idea what was coming. I explained that Reubs had inherited doubts from them, and that therefore they were the only people who could reassure him. It didn't matter what I said, or what Jack said. It had to come from his parents. As I finished, a circle of silence pulled us around the table. Mum reached out to grab Reuben's hand. She knew what I had meant.

'You fly your rainbow flag, darling,' she said. 'If you want to.'

That afternoon, Mum drove Reubs into Fox Hill while Dad and I were in the car park, waiting for them to arrive. Straight away I saw all the layers Reubs was wearing: two polo shirts, a jumper, scarf and coat and hat. He then sat in the car and refused to move. I tried to talk to him, so did Dad. Tess gently coaxed, 'Why not just pop up to see the flat? It won't take you long.'

My approach was rougher: 'We've been working so hard all week just to get it ready for you.'

But there was no budging him.

He was staging a protest, and because of how much we'd concealed from him, I wasn't going to argue. I had to concede. It was almost as if he knew. Besides, why the hell should he get excited about the grand unveiling of a flat he didn't really want to move into?

Mum and Dad went up to Flat 12 and I knelt down on the tarmac by the passenger seat of Dad's car. Reubs pulled his beanie further down, over his eyes and asked me, 'Will I be lonely here, bruvr, like Portland Place?'

'No, absolutely not. You are going to have people with you nearly all the time. From morning until evening, there will be a carer there to help you. And the office is just here, if you ever need anything, you can come down. We all get lonely sometimes, Reubs. I get lonely, even if I'm with you or Jack.'

'Do you?'

'Of course I do. But when I get lonely, I have to think that I'm not really alone. I think of all the people I love.' I tap the side of my head, 'Up here, you have to remember, that you're never alone. Got it?'

'Got it,' he replied, but we were both so far away from smiling.

'I tell you what,' I began. 'Shall we make a deal?

'What?'

Days and weeks of this tightrope, then one phone call from Sam toppled us back into freefall. That week had been positive in some way, in spite of what we had chosen to conceal, but I really was done with it. I couldn't take it any more.

'If you're not ready, Reubs, how about we delay moving in for a couple of weeks?'

Reuben's face screwed into a grimace.

'Well, I've been thinking. What's the rush, right? You like to do things slowly. So we could go back to the cottage for a little while. Get used to the idea of Fox Hill a bit more. Then come back when you are ready.'

'Countdown chart?'

'Scrap it. We'll make a new one.'

I watched the ripple of relief travel outwards from his eyes. He pulled his lips in and lowered his hat even further. Still in disbelief he asked, 'So we all go back?'

'Not all. Mum and Dad, no. They will go to Norwich. You and me, yes. For two weeks.' I reached out and held his hand as the whirr of cars drove by on the main road.

He looked out of the car window, considering this odd turn of events. 'Like *Back to the Future*, bruvr.'

My face broke into a smile.

'Exactly like *Back to the Future*. Now, do you want to have a look at your amazing new home or not?'

'Well, just a bit. If you come.'

I helped him out of the car and across the courtyard. From the entrance, we could see Mum and Dad smiling and clapping above us from the window of Flat 12.

My parents did drive back to Norwich the following morning. I hugged them, feeling baffled and deflated. Any joy in being together as a family had been sucked away. Reubs and I waved them off before getting ourselves ready. I tapped out a text message to Jack, *Emotional day, hope it doesn't break us*, then deleted it.

We started back towards the coast and Annings Lane, driving back to square one. So much momentum, thwarted. I wondered if Reuben was more confused than me, or whether he was actually quite pleased to be going back. I wasn't sure if I had enough resolve to stop imploding. Preparing Flat 12 had been the easy bit. Buying stuff, driving a van around – all that was a doddle. The truly exhausting part was getting Reuben ready. The emotional energy it took. I wasn't sure if I had the reserves to go through it all again.

I slouched in the driver's seat and kept wanting to pull over and delay our return for as long as possible. Before he fell asleep, Reuben asked me how long we'd been brothers. I turned the question around.

'How old are you, Reubs?'

'Thirty-seven.'

'Then we've been brothers for thirty-seven years, since the day you were born.'

'Long time,' he said, staring out at the road ahead. 'We be fine,' he assured me.

'How?' I enquire.

'We will. That's why.'

After we had turned off Annings Lane, Reubs closed the gate and carried his Darth Vader case back up to his room. We had left the cottage spotless and it felt so wrong to start leaving traces again, footprints on floors, crumbs on the kitchen tops, fingerprints on the cutlery and glass. These walls and ceilings will never judge us, but moving back caused a friction that was difficult to bear.

While Reuben unpacked absolutely everything, I sat in the kitchen feeling displaced. As he reclaimed his space and dug himself in, I stayed in my emptiness not knowing what to do.

My first thought was to take Reubs back to Spain. Perhaps it was best not to split up our trilogy. Samwise, Frodo and Gandalf the Grey. I would have to cancel my flights; home felt further away than ever. It was Reuben who pulled me back from the void. He sent me a text message from his bedroom, and in that instant it felt like we'd never left.

what we doing tonight brother

It forced me to step out of myself. I went upstairs to his bedroom knowing that being together was the only way through the rest of the day. I stood at the window and stared at Jess's empty field, the sheep gone, the turnips all eaten.

'Maybe Fox Hill isn't for you,' I said.

'Is fine. It will happen, bruvr. Trust.'

'What shall we do?' I was asking myself the question, but it was Reubs who answered.

He shrugged at first.

'No ideas?' I said.

He threw the question right back at me, 'You?'

'Nope.'

A little smirk crept into the side of his mouth, 'Friday Night Musical,' he said.

He lifted his broken glasses to his head and tapped his temple, showing me how hard he was thinking. 'I got it, bruvr.'

'What would you like to do?'

'Lion King.'

Watching dawn creep from the log store across the pond, wanting to absorb every detail of the morning, I notice a kingfisher tucked into itself on a willow branch. I blink and refocus to make sure it really is there. The bird repositions nearer the water's edge, poised to scoop dragonfly larvae or water beetles. My heart beats in my head as I open the garden doors and quietly lower my body on to the terrace and crawl. I stop a few metres away, hands leaning into my chin, hidden by plant pots and a gangly rose. A technicolour pulse hits the water, and an image of the future flashes into my head. As the bird speeds away, I close my eyes to record the moment. When I open them, whatever I saw has gone.

Before I went to bed last night, I hovered at Reuben's bedroom door and watched the quiet rise and fall of his back as his breath eased him into sleep. How he has navigated the raging emotional storms of these past two years will never cease to amaze me. He has held on for dear life when no one knew how to explain the source of his pain. Sometimes, even if you love someone, it isn't easy giving their feelings a name. And this is why sharing time with him is such a privilege. Through our brotherhood winter, I have learnt to live through him. Yes, we have suffered, individually and together, but those trials have bound us with even more unbreakable bonds. He has taught me how to navigate the backwaters of his mind, and locate the switchbacks and the shortcuts to find our way home. He is my home and always will be.

As I stood in the doorway, casting my eyes around his bedroom, his bed-props laid out neatly by his pillow, I was thankful for these months of silence. In the stillness of dawn, before he woke, I have been able to organise my own humanity. Tidying it from an unruly mess that it was. As he slept, he prepared me to meet each day with purpose and love. He demanded nothing but roused the better parts of me into action. This is why I love him. This is why I couldn't tear myself away from his bedroom door last night, and why I went to bed feeling scared. Soon, he will no longer be by my side and I am already beginning to anticipate the loss. I will return to Jack and we will be together again, but there will only be two of us. The third in our trilogy will be starting his own life in a place he can hardly pronounce. The fact that he is willing to give it a go, is beyond my wildest admiration. If he is willing, then I must try to live without him. If he can do it, so can I.

After breakfast, I feel calm loading the car; most of his things are already there. All the frantic energy has already been spent. There's only his Darth Vader bag, a couple of small boxes of *Lion King* props, his *Joseph* tote and his night bag. Once he's clipped himself into the passenger seat, I pop up to his room to make sure he hasn't left anything behind. By the window, I find a crumpled piece of paper on the floor and flatten it down with my palm to read, *will simon be my friend*. There's also a drawing of a fox on his bedside table, which I take with me downstairs, thinking we ought to have it framed.

We leave as we arrived, quietly, although our neighbours on both sides are sending us away with cake: apple (from Jan) and a lemon drizzle (from Ali) that has only just come out of the oven – Reuben holds it near his tummy, like a hot water bottle, as it fills the car with a warm tang.

He is pensive, so I don't press him for any conversation. I read out Jack's text before we drive away, *Good luck my boys. Let me know when you arrive safely xx*

We head along the coast and I decide to drive through town along South Street rather than go straight to the dual carriageway. A couple of days ago, Reubs and I came to town on a mission to replenish his

Fox

Sleep Well
brother
love you

aftershave stocks. He had appeared in the kitchen holding a bottle of Tommy Hilfiger and lifted it to the light to show me it was empty, taking a good look at the bottle himself to make sure.

'Oh dear,' I said.

'What we do, bruvr?' he asked.

'Disaster,' I replied.

'Do I need more?

'I don't know, Reubs. Your decision. Do you want a full bottle for Fox Hill?'

'Well, yeah.'

The town felt completely different as we walked up South Street together. The surfaces of the street and the shops and market stalls hadn't changed, of course. It was us. Over these past few months, whether we were popping in for food and supplies or on a specific visit to the day centre, whatever we did was overshadowed by the greater purpose of Reuben's recovery. We couldn't just drift through the high street as brothers, aimlessly browsing. Everything had to be part of the master plan. We weren't allowed to just be. For the first time it felt like we were two brothers on holiday. There was no longer any test or chore to fulfil, no checklist to mark off to ensure our trip was successful or constructive in some way. There was no agenda, and I can't remember the last time it felt like that.

On the way back to the cottage, we bumped into Jane and Neill on Annings Lane. They thanked Reubs for his watering skills, and commented that they'd never seen the peace lily looking so healthy.

'It's got so many flowers,' said Jane.

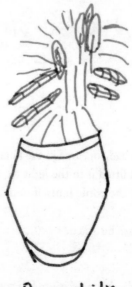

Peace Lily

I winked at Frodo. His face shone with the brilliance of a secret.

When we got back from town, we sat in the garden with our faces in the sun, relaxing, for the rest of the afternoon. The marsh frogs were on the move, crouched in the shallow water behind the reeds. Light filled the valley and we lingered too long because Reuben's face is tinged with patches of cherry-blush burn, his winter skin brushed with spring.

At Stourcastle mill, we stop at the traffic lights and I ask if he realises that he'll be living in one of the most beautiful parts of the world.

'Do I?' he asks.

'You'll have a long line of people wanting to come and see you. You could Airbnb your sofa bed!'

'Shut up, bruvr.'

I turn to look at him.

'Can I come and stay whenever I want, Booba?'

'I wish,' he replies.

I grab his hand until the lights change. We drive off and he counts to ten using both hands, remembering how long we have left together. I wind the windows down and encourage him to wave as we move through the high street.

'Here he is!' I cry. 'Prince Reuben has arrived!'

'Bruvr! Like the Queen.'

He grins, waving to strangers.

I'm so grateful for these last two weeks together, our brothers' holiday. We've had the chance to say goodbye to friends properly, and taken ourselves out for lots of meals. I called Sam and Angie and Anna to thank them properly, and have caught up on emails. I even wrote to the architects of Fox Hill, thanking them for their vision and for giving my brother his own front door and his own key. We've also had online meetings with the care team at Fox Hill, who told me themselves that staggering the tenants' arrivals meant that each team leader and every key worker had time to really understand Reuben's care needs. Nobody was ready for Reuben to move – his carers weren't, he wasn't, and neither was I.

All of the care team are waiting when we arrive: Rosie, Ivy and Meredith, Will, Judy, Stef and Reggie, Meg and Tess. All eyes are on him as he's shown into the staff office, where they've cleared a space for him at one of the desks. He loves the attention, looking up attentively while Rosie runs through the tenancy agreement. She tells him he'll have to sign it before they can give him the keys, and takes out two copies for him to look at.

'Have you ever signed a rental agreement before?' Rosie asks.

'My bruvr,' he says pointing to me with his broken glasses.

She smiles at me. 'Well this time, it's not your brother signing for you. You can sign this one yourself. Are you OK to do that?'

'Yep,' he replies, taking care to look at Rosie, not me. His lips disappear as he takes out one of his felt-tip pens.

The contract is not a block of legal text but twenty-two pages of bubble speech and illustrations. Reuben takes his time, encouraged to look through it all before signing. This is his moment, so I take it as my cue to wait outside the office, and watch from outside as Rosie reads through every page with Reubs. His head bobs up and down whenever she explains something that isn't clear, and once she's confident that he understands, he signs both copies, marking his name, Reuben Coe, in capital letters at the bottom of the last page.

Lauren hands him his new keys and his face lights up. He holds them up for me to see, and I lip-read him say, 'Look, bruvr.'

I make my role very clear: I am a guest, I am sleeping on his sofa bed, I won't have a key. Reubs goes up to spend some time by himself. I sit in the garden and wait for as long as it takes him. This is *his* flat, *his* new home. I don't want him to see everything through me. I don't want to be associated with his memories of walking into Flat 12. We both know that leaving is going to be incredibly difficult for me to do. Any distance will help. It will take a long time to learn to live without each other.

I imagine him standing in his new living room, his right hand still clutching the key to his own front door, looking out over the river valley, the room filled with the soft light of a spring afternoon. What does he notice first? Is it the mugs with foxes that Mum found in the hardware store? Maybe the smart TV that Jack gave him, or the cosy teal-coloured cushions? Does he notice the toaster or the kettle given by friends? What about the plants sent by loved ones? Does he realise that all this is his? *Everything the light touches is yours.*

This is all yours now, Reubs. You no longer have just a room in a house. You have a home. And why shouldn't you? Why shouldn't you have your own front door key? Why should you miss out on all this? How I hope you're happy in your new home. I hope it's the beginning of a new and wonderful chapter in your life. May your green front door be your passage to Narnia, the doorway into your Hobbiton, your Middle Earth, your Pride Rock. I'm sorry no one thought to give you your own home before. And please, whatever you do, leave your fears at the door.

It takes Reuben ages to answer when I knock.

Eventually, I hear him shuffling to open it just a crack.

'Not today, thank you,' he smirks closing the door in my face.

I punch the air and do a little dance in the corridor.

As I pretend to leave, heavy footsteps and lots of grunting, the door opens fully.

'No, bruvr. Joke, bruvr. Look,' he beams, showing me a *Mrs Doubtfire* DVD. Our brilliant friend, Becs (who Reuben calls Rebecca of England), sent a copy through the post and I planted it on the chopping board in the kitchen for him to find.

'Odd!' he exclaims.

I feign surprise, 'Wow.'

'How?' He's genuinely mystified.

'I've no idea. It's a sign, Reubs. Magic.'

I join him inside and he gives me a guided tour as if I've never seen it before. He shows me a small pile of unopened cards on the island in the kitchen.

'Post,' he says proudly. 'Look, bruvr!'

I follow his finger as it curves around the room in a gentle arc.

I spy the Fox lampshade Gracie gave to him, the Fox cushion Rebecca of England sent, the kitchen stocked with pots and pans, the sparkling surfaces, lowered especially for Reuben's height. As the sun creeps further to the south, light streams in through the kitchen window and bathes the space in warmth. Everything in the room is glowing, including Reuben. He clutches the DVD tightly, until his knuckles begin to turn white.

'Shall we watch that tonight, Booba?' I ask him. 'On your sofa, just you and me.'

'We could,' he replies.

I take a deep breath to steady my emotions; I don't want them to get the better of me. I want these moments to be upbeat.

'Look at this place! It's amazing. It's a real home, Reubs.' I draw him closer. 'It's special. You realise? Not like the last place.'

He rolls his eyes and looks at me.

'You did so well,' I say. 'There were good people, but it was still the wrong place for you. I'm sorry.'

'Bruvr!' he tuts, wagging a finger and pretending to tell me off. He should. I want him to. My apology is real, more than he'll ever know. But he's distracted and walks off.

'Look this, bruvr,' he says.

I follow him through to his bedroom and see that he's pointing outside of the window.

'See. Just like Narnia.'

I hadn't noticed it before, but there it is on the drive outside, a lamppost. His portal to another world. We stand together smiling above the roofs of Fox Hill.

'Bruvr?' he asks me.

'What?'

'What evening look like here?'

'I don't know, Reubs. I've never been here in the evening.'

'Not me either.'

'We'll have to wait and see.'

'Well, yeah.'

I head down to get my bags from the car, leaving him to open the cards sent by loved ones. A message pings into my phone. It's from Mum – she's forwarding a message Reuben sent her this afternoon, *will miss brother next week mummy. what I do.*

When I get back to the flat, as I manoeuvre myself towards the sofa bed, my rucksack clips the red heart plate that sits on the hall table. It falls to the floor at my feet and cracks into three pieces and dozens of tiny splinters. The bulk of the heart is still intact – it's really just the lower part that has broken away. I pick up the pieces and hold them in my hand, wondering what to do.

Reuben's face appears in the doorway of his bedroom.

'What that bang, bruvr?'

'Oh dear. Look what happened,' I say, presenting the pieces.

'Bruvr!' he says.

'I'm sorry, Reubs. Silly me!'

'We get new one, bruvr,' he reassures me. 'Charity shop.'

Before it gets dark, we wrap up and head out in search of the sunset. Reubs waves to the care team as he passes the office, and they all wave back. Across the road, we head down a narrow track and come to a gate that opens onto a footpath. The last of the sunlight glistens and the wind ruffles the surface of the river. We edge our way down the steep banks to the water's edge, sharing the field with sheep that hardly lift their gaze as we pass.

We position ourselves at the bend, to take the final crescendo of light before the sun disappears.

'Here you go, Reubs. Brother's Bench.'

'No bench here, bruvr.'

'Just pretend,' I suggest.

He grins as we sit down cross-legged on the grass, facing the river, watching as it flows towards the mill.

*

Back in the flat, Reubs clatters around in a cupboard to reach the mattress topper. I stop preparing supper and watch him puzzle out the pulling mechanism that converts the sofa into a bed. Once he's pulled it down, he starts gently folding the elasticated corners of the bedsheet over the edges. His movements are mesmerising. I've never enjoyed watching somebody make a bed before: the way he places the pillows against the far arm of the sofa, patting them down and then running both hands along the entire length of the duvet to make sure it's perfectly smooth.

After dinner, he clears the table and we load the dishwasher together before settling in the living room. He picks up the blanket sent by a friend of Mum's – it has dozens of foxes on it. He pulls it over his legs, letting out an enormous sigh as he sits to draw.

'Busy day, Reubs?' I ask, but either he doesn't hear or ignores me.

I slide across the sofa bed to read, falling into the silence.

He doesn't need to ask me the time. He knows instinctively that 9 p.m is approaching, so he puts all his felt-tip pens away and closes his sketchpad into his *Joseph* tote bag and heads towards his DVD rack. He slides *Mrs Doubtfire* into one of the slots and I hear him say to himself, 'Watch that tomorrow.'

I want to watch him make his first hot milk and honey in the flat, but as he heads over to the kitchen I decide it would be an intrusion. This is his space, for him to go about it quietly and privately and unobserved. I make do with imagining him instead, smiling as the kettle clips off, grinning as he stirs, seeing him as I want to see him.

Just before he goes through to his bedroom, Reuben walks over to the sofa and kisses me gently on the cheek.

'Night, bruvr. Love you.'

He puts an A4 sheet on my lap, upside down, and I wait until he's in his bedroom before turning the page over.

For brother

3rd

No matter
Where I go
you will always
be my brother
emotinal
For you

am miss you brother
love you

Red name

Brother. Do. you
love. me.

Book Tou

Afterword

In May 2021, after spending ten days sleeping on Reuben's new sofa-bed, I hugged him as tightly as I dared for as long as I could and drove away from Fox Hill. His future hung like an enormous question mark in Dorset's muted skies. Was he strong enough? Will he be lonely? Could I put my trust in the care system for a third time?

brother. do. you. love. me. is a story of change. I changed. Reuben changed. Reuben changed me. Part of us had morphed into the other. We had lived through something that was extraordinary. But on my last day at Fox Hill, Reuben sent mum a text: 'am. miss. my. brother. mummy. what. we. do.' Reading it almost broke me, again. It felt like another abandonment. I wept clutching the steering wheel with white-knuckled determination.

At Fox Hill, there have been many teething problems, mostly due to the lack of continuity – care workers keep moving on, finding a higher wage or an alternative career. This is a universal problem in the care system. Over one particular fortnight, Reubs had seventeen carers on his rota, and I heard reports of hoods and hats and masks being worn by Reuben, along with a stubborn refusal to get up each morning. Alarm bells, all of them.

I emailed the care provider: *Reuben's continued recovery will be based on relationships that forge trust. There is no way he can relate to seventeen people on the level he needs to.* Regular visits help, from Mum and Dad, Jack, Ang, Tommy Boy and me – it meant we were able to keep tabs on Reuben's mental health and remind his core team of carers to read the signs and use the techniques we had suggested to help motivate Reuben. This way, we did at least establish that he was safe and in a familiar, daily routine.

Then, in October 2022, this book was launched.

Someone asked me in an early interview: 'What is your hope for this book?'

'That it gives Reuben his voice back,' I replied.

During our launch, inside the beautiful Normansfield Theatre in Teddington, where we were generously hosted by the Down's Syndrome Association, the tension in Reuben's body and mind began to diminish. Fear seeped out of him. But even with a theatre full of loved ones who had travelled from all over the world, Reuben was struck with stage fright.

'Just you bruv,' he whispered, when it was our turn to step out and say a few words.

Having been so ignored and displaced, we were now asking him to walk into a very public space. The stage was very high, the lights bright. No wonder he was shying away from the spotlight. It was a huge ask. I got down on one knee and told him that I couldn't do it by myself. That I needed him.

'I stay here,' he insisted.

I walked onto the stage alone and welcomed the audience before talking about our long journey. As I read from the book, I noticed Reubs out of the corner of my eye, the shape of him gingerly climbing the five steps to the stage and joining me at in the spotlight. He didn't speak. He didn't need to. All he had to do was take the rapturous applause of 80 people, wrestling with their own intense waves of emotion as they watched us two brothers on stage. As they celebrated his courage, I believe Reubs began to feel validated for the first time in years. A switch was flicked.

In the weeks that followed, we bumbled around England and Wales in a rented VW Campervan that we named 'Red'. Driving from place to place, bookshop to bookshop, festival to festival, Reuben stepped into himself more and more. They were baby steps at first: theatrical facial expressions, raised eyebrows, gestures. He didn't talk in any of the interviews, but he was entirely present. What more could anyone ask? And then, in his own good time, he began to open up: I would hear a whisper or detect the light traces of a spoken word. Before events, I gave him time to draw. Afterwards, I gave him the option to join me for dinner or not. Before bed, I told him that breakfast finished at 9.30am, and he never slept through a single one.

I saw him begin to relate to people, develop crushes for waiters, show them his book and gift them drawings. He pointed to window displays of our book in shops around the country, his inner light ignited. His confidence grew, began to unfurl. We enjoyed a pint in Leeds on a Friday night, a walk by the Mersey in Liverpool. We were both drawn in by the extraordinary beauty of rural Wales. Most importantly, Reuben got used to signing his name in title pages of the book.

On the 8th November, 2022, we were at the Bridport Literary Festival, in the old ballroom of the Bull Hotel, when Reuben took the microphone and spoke. He quoted Mufasa from *The Lion King*, turning to the audience directly and reminding everybody to 'remember who you are.' His faltering voice sucked the air out of the room. We were all stunned and silent. It was the first time I had heard Reuben's voice in years.

As our tour in Red continued, I realised that the whole process of making a book together and then taking it on the road like this, was helping with Reuben's longer-term recovery. Importantly, it was full of personal milestones. In particular, he devised his own entrance for each event, walking in to the theme of Gabriel's Oboe from the film *The Mission*, his trusted paintbrush held aloft as if it were the Olympic torch. Wherever we went, people were moved. Whatever their background and life experiences, the depth of feelings was humbling to observe. And in this communal outpouring of emotions, of empathy and truth, there was an extraordinary human warmth. Reuben's bravery left no room for indifference; we weren't the only ones who changed.

We began to hear from people, sisters and fathers, brothers and mothers, who had been profoundly affected by Reuben's struggles. Our story trickled into a river of shared experiences, and meetings with people like Caroline will never leave me. Her brother Johnny had recently passed, and she didn't think she could be brave enough to read the book, there were just too many parallels with her relationship with Johnny. Caroline wrote to me and we texted for a while, and through this exchange not only did she bring herself to read the book, but she also found the courage to come and hear us at Kendall Mountain Book Festival. We had dinner together after the show, when she said 'You know what. I thought it would be agony to see you and Reubs together. But it has really helped me. He has really helped me. Something in me is healing.'

If the only reason for writing the book was to hear Caroline, that is more than worth it. Caroline has framed a large copy of Reuben's drawing of the lion with the heart. She has hung it on her wall to remind her to #bemorejohnny

Reuben's mission statement had always been 'make everyone and world emotional' and he has certainly kept to his manifesto. His deep-rooted desire to help people was happening right in front of our eyes. At each event, after his final exit to music from *The Color Purple,* he would find me by the book signing table. As we hugged, a long, lingering brotherly hug he would say, 'We did it, bruvr. We did it.'

Back in 2021, when we were living out the final chapters of *brother. do. you. love. me*, we were both scared. I wrote. Reuben drew. I believe he became an artist during those quiet months. He found a new expression; his felt-tips framed my words. One could not be without the other. They are the symmetry of our brotherhood. As we clung to each other, as to a life raft, the tides eventually led us into a safe harbour called Little Toller Books. Adrian and Gracie comforted us and safeguarded our expression. The book was born.

I will never forget the look in Reuben's eyes the first time he held a copy. He became lost in a huge sense of accomplishment, and I was lost watching him. Witnessing the return of his smile has been the greatest privilege of my life. And my greatest lesson is that words and pictures have the power to raise us up, out of trauma, out of pain, out of darkness. If we were not able to express ourselves like this, where might we be?

M. C.

The Corner, Andalusia, 2023

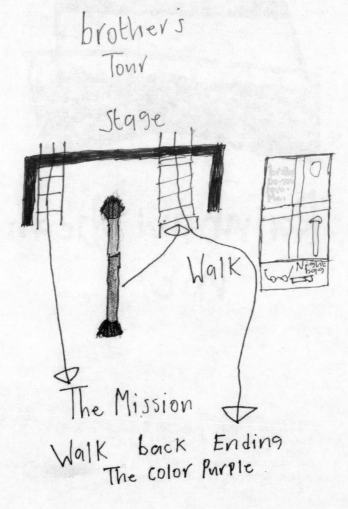

Rainbow beanie
hat

Reuben's Acknowledgements

manni my brother and samwise they after me
angie new friend
anna relaxing music
terry and jan let me stay their shepherds hut
brother nathan loads of texts love him I do and matt I do
jj and corinna love it there make things and games
daddy and mummy love me all the time
cousin ken bbq sausages with coleslaw
geoff and emma appletisers in pub
mary lou she did make me food
my aunty jill
my drama pat – am missing her
tom and maxine
portia luffly cakes
treeman and nik
ali mali
my sister debs
my sister in law
rebecca of england
my cath
aslan keep me safe
my keely
gail like my mum
joel
mark
elaine art
hendog

PumBaa

love you

sleep well

Lion king

Manni's Acknowledgements

For 26 weeks, Reubs and I were held in a cradle of virtual love and for that I will always be grateful. Reubs still has all of your 'Welcome to your New Home' cards displayed on a bookshelf. Almost a year later, he refuses to take them down. Thank you all, near and far, for following our journey and being a part of it. You found a way to communicate love to two brothers as they muddled through. You know who you are. I would like to thank in particular:

Reuben: without you there would be no book, and I doubt I would have ever learnt what it means to truly love.

Andrew: you are the other half of my orange. Thank you for loving and/or accepting each and every segment of me. I love you. Just to let you know. Will you read the book now?

Mum and Dad: for always being there and for bringing Reuben into the world, for without him I may never have known the fullness of life. I love you.

Nathan and Kate: for your creative love and support from across the pond.

Matt: for your skilful insight and encouragement.

Adrian: for being a master sculptor of words. Under your guidance our book emerged.

Gracie: for your passion which is unrelenting and an inspiration to all.

The Little Toller Team – Graham and Jon: thank you for your skill and expertise.

Keely: Reuben would not be where he is today without you.

Angie: for asking twice. Your CARE for Reubs knows no limits.

Ali Mali: truth, honesty and courage and the greatest of these is love.

Terry and Jan: for being constant gardeners throughout wintry gales. You are both exemplary human beings.

Jane and Neill: for lending me your kitchen when the walls of ours were falling in on me. Your sense of living life to the full is an inspiration.

Ali: for your emotional cakes and your hedgerow words of wisdom.

Sophie: for untangling the threads as we walk the lanes of friendship. Your commitment to these words is unfaltering.

Kas Limón: true friendship is our gift to each other: Thank you for always being here when you are nearly always there.

LLL: friendship without fear, laughter without bounds, understanding without judgement.

Debs: for being like a sister to us; then, now and always.

Fer: for holding the fort back in Spain when I disappeared to write.

Clare: the most wonderful writing wizard anyone could hope for.

Babs: you came late to the party but you're staying to the bitter end and that's final.

Sal: for always having our back.

Andy and Pauline: Reuben's Spanish Dad and Mum, such treasured friends.

Diana: Princess Diana, for always treating Reuben like a prince.

Eddy: for your human elegance and for documenting 'that' moment so flawlessly.

Jason and Salud: for being so open and warm during such a closed and cold winter.

Sophy: for trapping my words in the wind and holding them still, until I understood them.

Nikki: for welcoming us and loving us like family.

Phil: for having the vision to identify a need and generously offer a tonic.

Nico: this story begins and finishes with your Amazing Technicoloured Dreamcoat.

Mary-Lou: for asking the question, 'What can I do?' Your kindness knows no bounds.

Tash: for knowing exactly where this story needed to land.

Matt and Anna: walking and talking with you is one of life's great joys.

Becs: for your genius way of loving and for sourcing a DVD of *Mrs Doubtfire*!

Erin: My fellow pilgrim. I love walking through life with you.

Laura: fellow sibling and giggle partner.

Andrew W: for your original insight and continuing support.

Finca Buenvino: and all who dwell within her.

Elaine: for creating a space where I could hear my voice.

Anna G: for cycling in all weather. Thank you for believing me when I told you, 'My brother used to dance in nightclubs.'

Sara and Jen: for your gift of friendship. You are marvellous human beings.

Hendog: a sounding board of creative force.

Annie B: for your cards, phone calls and messages of love and support.

Nadiya: for being wise enough to understand that once Reuben learns, he can lead.

Rebecca: your gifts are now icons.

Ton Ton and Maria: we were few and now we are many. You are both sunshine.

Gene: for your joy, enthusiasm and talent.

Jane: a constant in a shifting world.

Tommy Boy and Maxine: your love for Reubs knows no bounds and keeps him safe.

The Seaside Boarding House: our cravings for your smiles and delicious food kept us going.

MANNI COE grew up in Yorkshire and Berkshire and now lives in Dorset and Andalucia. He works as a walking guide in Spain and around the world.

REUBEN COE grew up in Berkshire. He completed a B-Tech in drama and lived in Spain before moving to north Dorset. His art has been used by St Paul's Cathedral and his range of Christmas cards raised money for the NHS during the pandemic.